THE CHALLENGE OF SUSTAINABILITY

SUSTAINABILITY

Linking politics, education and learning

Edited by Hugh Atkinson and Ros Wade

First published in Great Britain in 2015 by

Policy Press
University of Bristol
1-9 Old Park Hill
Bristol BS2 8BB
UK
t: +44 (0)117 954 5940
pp-info@bristol.ac.uk
www.policypress.co.uk

North America office:
Policy Press
c/o The University of Chicago Press
1427 East 60th Street
Chicago, IL 60637, USA
t: +1 773 702 7700
f: +1 773-702-9756
sales@press.uchicago.edu
www.press.uchicago.edu

© Policy Press 2015

British Library Cataloguing in Publication Data
A catalogue record for this book is available from the British Library

Library of Congress Cataloging-in-Publication Data
A catalog record for this book has been requested

ISBN 978 1 44730 646 7 hardcover

The right of Hugh Atkinson and Ros Wade to be identified as editors of this work has been asserted by them in accordance with the 1988 Copyright, Designs and Patents Act.

Cover design by Policy Press
Front cover image: www.alamy.com
Printed and bound in Great Britain by CPI Group (UK) Ltd,
Croydon, CR0 4YY
Policy Press uses environmentally responsible print partners.

MIX
Paper from
responsible sources
FSC
www.fsc.org   FSC® C013604

Contents

List of tables and figures

Tables

Figures

List of abbreviations and acronyms

ACCU	Asia-Pacific Cultural Centre for UNESCO
BSM	benefit-sharing mechanism
CAP	Common Agricultural Policy
CCS	carbon capture and storage
DCSF	Department for Children, Schools and Families
DCE	Domasi College of Education
DE	development education
DESD	Decade for Education for Sustainable Development
DG	Directorate General
EAP	environment action programmes
EC	European Community
ECJ	European Court of Justice
EDDR	education for disaster risk reduction and redevelopment
EE	environmental education
EFA	education for all
EKC	environmental Kuznet's curve
EIA	environmental impact assessment
EPA	Environmental Protection Agency
EPI	environmental policy integration
ESD	education for sustainable development
ETS	emissions trading scheme
EU	European Union
GATS	General Agreement on Trade in Services
GDP	gross domestic product
GHG	greenhouse gases
GMR	Global Monitoring Report
GW	gigawatt
HE	higher education
HEIs	higher education institutions
ICT	information and communication technology
IEA	International Energy Authority
IK	indigenous knowledge
IPCC	Intergovernmental Panel on Climate Change
LGR	local government representatives
MDG	Millennium Development Goals
MESA	Mainstreaming Environment and Sustainability across African Universities

MFF	Multi-annual Financial Framework
NASA	National Aeronautics and Space Administration
NCADAC	National Climate Assessment and Development Advisory Committee
NCAR	National Centre for Atmospheric Research
NEMA	National Environmental Management Agency
NGO	non-governmental organisation
NOAA	National Oceanic and Atmospheric Administration
NRDC	National Resources Defence Council
NSIDC	National Snow and Ice Data Centre
NYBE	nine-year basic education
ppm	parts per million
OMC	open method of coordination
QMV	qualified majority voting
RCE	regional centre for expertise
RCEGN	Regional Centre for Expertise Greater Nairobi
RE	renewable energy
RSPB	Royal Society for the Protection of Birds
SDG	Sustainable Development Goals
SDS	Sustainable Development Strategy
SEA	Single European Act
SSA	sub-Saharan Africa
STEM	science, technology, engineering and maths
TFEU	Treaty on the Functioning of the European Union
UDP	Uranium Development Partnership
UN	United Nations
UNDP	United Nations Development Programme
UNESCO	United Nations Educational, Scientific and Cultural Organisation
UNFCCC	United Nations Framework Convention on Climate Change
UNRISD	United Nations Research Institute for Social Development
UNU	United Nations University
WEO	World Energy Outlook
WSSD	World Summit on Sustainable Development
WWF	World Wide Fund for Nature

Notes on terminology

While we recognise that a great deal of terminology is open to question and critical examination, terms that may be included in this book include:

- 'majority world' to refer to the majority global population in countries that benefit least from the global economy. Other terms used include 'Southern' (most countries in this position are in the southern hemisphere) and 'developing' countries;
- 'minority world' to refer to the wealthy, industrialised countries. Other terms include 'Northern' countries (most countries in this position are in the northern hemisphere) and 'developed' countries.

All these terms are problematic and contain a mixture of political and cultural implications and are therefore used with caution. While we acknowledge that there are no terms that can fully describe the current complex global political and economic terrain, nonetheless, they can be a useful shorthand. However, we note that they are generalisations that do not fully represent, for example, the emerging economies of the BRIC nations (Brazil, Russia, India and China), nor the emerging economies of post-communist states.

Notes on contributors

Hugh Atkinson is senior lecturer in politics at London South Bank University. He is the author of *Local democracy, civic engagement and community: from New Labour to the big society* (Manchester University Press, 2012). He is a founder member of the Political Studies Association specialist group on environmental politics.

Lyle M. Benko has 40 years' professional experience in formal and non-formal education. He is president of LAMB Environmental and Educational Consulting. In March 2011, he was the recipient of the Saskatchewan Eco-Network Provincial Environment Activist Award.

John Blewitt is director of the MSc in social responsibility and sustainability at Aston University. He is the author of *Understanding sustainable development* (Routledge-Earthscan, 2014).

Tomonori Ichinose is a professor at the Miyagi University of Education whose research interests include diversity education and education for sustainable development.

Takaaki Koganezawa is professor of education at the University of Miyagi, Japan, visiting professor at the United Nations University Institute of Advanced Studies and secretary of the Regional Centre for Expertise Greater Sendai.

John O'Brennan lectures in European politics and society at the National University of Ireland, Maynooth. He is the author of *The European Union and the western Balkans: from stabilisation to normalisation and EU membership* (Routledge, 2014).

Mary Otieno is a lecturer in the School of Education at Kenyatta University, Nairobi, Kenya. Mary is a member of the steering committee of the Regional Centre for Expertise Greater Nairobi. She has wide experience in training, research and publication in education for sustainable development.

Jenneth Parker is research director at the Schumacher Institute for Sustainable Solutions, Bristol, with 20 years' experience in learning for sustainability. Her most recent publication is 'Critiquing sustainability, changing philosophy'. She has provided policy advice for the United

Nations Science and Cultural Organisation and, more recently, the Welsh Assembly Government.

Roger A. Petry is an assistant professor of philosophy at the University of Regina, Canada. His research interests include university innovation for sustainability and strategic dimensions in moving to sustainable production systems. He is co-coordinator of Regional Centre of Expertise Saskatchewan.

Ros Wade is professor of education for sustainable development at London South Bank University and director of the international Education for Sustainability programme. She chairs the London Regional Centre of Expertise in education for sustainable development. Her recent publications include a chapter on 'Promoting sustainable communities locally and globally' in S. Sterling, L. Maxey and H. Luna (eds) *The sustainable university* (Routledge, 2013).

Stuart Wilks-Heeg is senior lecturer in social policy at the University of Liverpool and was the director of the Democratic Audit of the United Kingdom from 2009 to 2012. He has written widely on issues concerning the quality of the democratic process and the challenges to it.

Preface

For some time, we had been exploring the idea of writing a book on the importance of politics, education and learning in building a more sustainable world. But the idea for such a book only really started to take shape as we chatted over hot coffee and delicious American muffins in the beautiful gardens of the Getty Museum in Los Angeles, California in the summer of 2010.

Subsequently, we helped organise academic panels on politics and sustainability at annual conferences of the UK Political Studies Association. Discussions at these panels with academic colleagues helped to sharpen and refine our ideas. This book is a culmination of such various processes.

We would very much like to thank our fellow writers for their thoughtful and critical contributions to this book. It has been a real collaborative effort! Our special thanks go to Emily Watt, commissioning editor at Policy Press. Her support and encouragement have been central in getting this book written and published.

Building a more sustainable world presents us with many challenges but there are good reasons to feel optimistic for the future. This is the essential message of the book.

Hugh Atkinson and Ros Wade

Introduction

Hugh Atkinson and Ros Wade

The authors of this book come from a range of academic disciplines related to political science or education for sustainable development, but they have one central aim: to analyse the challenges we face in making the changes that are needed in order to build an environmentally, socially and economically sustainable world.

The world is facing some very serious social and environmental challenges over the next 50 years. These include climate change, global poverty, inequality, and war and conflict, all set against a backdrop of highly consuming lifestyles and a growing population that is likely to reach 9 billion by the end of the century. Yet, governments have been extremely slow in addressing these issues. One of the obstacles to change has been a reluctance or an inability to integrate social and environmental concerns into policymaking and practice. The concept of sustainable development was devised in order to promote a new way of thinking that incorporates these concerns, and it does provide a new vocabulary of political change. The concept of sustainable development has become increasingly used in mainstream policymaking over the last 10 years, though its meaning and application still remain contested.

There are still many tensions evident within both policy and practice between environmental and development issues. Politicians, concerned about winning elections, seem rather reluctant to promote awareness-raising of the major global and local challenges among the general public in any meaningful way. Equally, the general public, or at least significant sections of it, seem unable (or unwilling) to grasp the challenges ahead for both people and the planet. This raises some key questions about our current education systems and their ability to develop the knowledge, understanding and competences that are need for the world in the 21st century. Despite the Agenda 21 commitments of the world's governments at the 1992 Rio Summit to reorient education systems towards sustainable development, the evidence shows that the process is still very patchy and far from complete.

This book explores the links between politics, pedagogy, learning and sustainability. It seeks to answer a fundamental question: how do we move to a politics in which political leaders are honest with voters about the need to fly less, to use less energy, to use our cars less and to forsake the latest high-tech gadgets? This presents a real challenge for the world's political leaders. Are they capable of making the necessary brave decisions? Such decisions involve spelling out clearly what has to be done if we are to make the world more sustainable and tackle climate change. This will require real sacrifices by consumers in the so-called 'developed' world. How will they respond at the ballot box to such an agenda? Will our political leaders resort to the default position of short-term expediency? There is no magic wand available here but these are issues that need to be seriously addressed. The terms of the debate need to be shifted, so that meeting the challenge of climate change and shaping a more sustainable world is not seen purely in negative terms, but is rather viewed as a real opportunity to build a more sustainable and fulfilling way of life.

The book is divided into four parts. Part One looks at the broad challenges for political action and learning in achieving sustainability. It is broken down into three chapters. Part Two looks at case studies in politics, learning and sustainability, and consists of three chapters. Part Three consists of three chapters, which present a number of case studies on learning for sustainability from a range of global regions, set in both urban and rural communities. It looks at sustainability challenges in relation to power, policy and learning. Part Four brings together some of the key themes that have emerged in the first three parts of the book and looks at the future prospects for sustainability and the planet by contrasting two different scenarios.

Part One: The challenge of sustainability – politics, education and learning

In Chapter One, Hugh Atkinson argues that people and the planet face a number of fundamental challenges in the second decade of the 21st century. These include climate change, increased poverty and rising inequality, deforestation, drought, and rising sea levels. At times, such challenges seem overwhelming. Indeed, there is a real danger of a counsel of despair. It is true that progress on meeting these challenges has appeared painfully slow at times. Politicians and decision-makers have often been guilty of short-term thinking based on the exigencies of the electoral cycle and the demands of our consumerist society when what is needed is long-term strategic thinking.

However, the chapter argues that with strong political leadership backed up by pressure from below, there is a clear opportunity to meet these challenges and move towards a more sustainable world. From the Rio Summit of 1992 to the Kyoto Protocol on climate change in 1998, through to the 2015 Millennium Development Goals (MDGs), there is some evidence of a strengthening global agenda to build a more sustainable and equitable world. True, it is a daunting agenda, but it is one that simply cannot be ignored.

In Chapter Two, Stuart Wilks-Heeg poses the question of whether democracy can deliver sustainability if the achievement of sustainability requires sacrifices that individuals will be required to impose upon themselves via the ballot box. The chapter argues that there may well be a fundamental tension between representative democracy and policy agendas associated with the reduction of carbon emissions, especially when the latter are interpreted as involving significant individual sacrifice and reduced personal consumption.

In the light of this tension, the chapter argues that there are two ways forward for the politics of sustainability. Politicians must either find a means of bringing about a 'smart' redesign of society, in which carbon emissions can be curbed without significant personal sacrifice, or they must seek to secure the 'informed consent' of citizens to fundamental shifts in their behaviour and lifestyles through a significantly more participatory model of democracy.

In Chapter Three, Ros Wade examines the international education commitments of the 1992 United Nations Earth Summit on environment and development in relation to trends in education policy and practice over the last 20 years. Agenda 21 emphasised the imperative to reorient education systems towards sustainable development and laid out a clear programme for governments. The chapter highlights the urgency of this initiative in turning round the oil tanker of over-consumption and unsustainable lifestyles in the wealthier parts of the world and addressing the challenges of poverty, social justice and environmental destruction in the developing world.

However, an overview of current education practice across a range of countries indicates that although policy commitments have increased, practice lags rather far behind. There are clear reasons for this. The last 20 years have seen neoliberal perspectives provide the dominant overarching framework for policymaking. The chapter will argue that marketisation and privatisation trends have frequently skewed educational practice towards unsustainable development. Yet, without a sea change at international and national levels, educational policy will fail to address the huge challenges that the world is facing in the 21st century.

Part Two: What is to be done? Case studies in politics, education and learning

In Chapter Four, Hugh Atkinson analyses the role of the US in respect of the environment and sustainability. Over the last 15 years, there has been an understandable perception of a US with only a limited engagement in the fight against climate change and the broader sustainability agenda. At a federal level, the Bush presidency of 2000 to 2008 certainly lent credence to this view. However, the chapter argues that the actual picture is more nuanced and complex.

Of course, there have been, and there will continue to be, obstacles along the way. Too often, the debate in the US is drowned out by the white noise of a divisive and increasingly hysterical political culture. Yet, despite this, there have been a range of initiatives at federal, state and local level that have sought to engage in a positive way with the sustainability agenda. Furthermore, the election of Barak Obama as president seemed to point to a new activism at the federal level of government. In a speech to the United Nations (UN) in September 2009, Obama spoke of the serious threat of climate change and of the pressing need to take action. The chapter examines whether such rhetoric has been matched by substantive policy action. The analysis in this chapter is set with the context of the constitutional doctrine of the separation of powers and a political culture that eschews active government.

In Chapter Five, John O'Brennan argues that environmental problems are by their very nature potentially existential and traverse international border demarcations. In Europe, the consensus on collective action has grown over the last two decades as problems as diverse as substandard nuclear plants in Bulgaria and Slovakia and the lethal impact of toxic pollutants released into the River Danube have concentrated more and more attention on the need for a European-wide approach to multidimensional problems.

The chapter examines the evolution of European Union (EU) policy in the areas of environment, energy and sustainable development through the lenses of path dependency and historical institutionalism. It argues that environmental policy has developed via a multitude of actors and through a sharing of competences within a multi-level system of governance. Although there remain some very significant challenges for Europe, the cumulative result has been an unprecedented pooling of sovereignty that has enabled the EU to learn and act collectively and forcefully in a vital area of global socio-economic activity.

In Chapter Six, Jenneth Parker explores ways of facilitating effective collaboration between environmental and development organisations (as social movements) to meet the political challenges of global sustainability. The chapter posits a new way of thinking, using the concept of convergence as a means to facilitate the development of global equity within planetary boundaries. Convergence is based on an approach to global eco-justice that was developed during the Kyoto climate change talks by the environmental campaigner Aubrey Meyer. It combines the concept of equal rights for all citizens to use the earth's atmosphere, with a per capita allocation approach. This would mean that rich countries would contract their use of carbon, leaving poorer countries to continue to develop. Convergence would occur when equal levels of development are achieved with sustainable carbon emissions. The chapter looks at the potential of convergence to act as a 'unifying framework' for sustainability practitioners involved in the process of developing the new Sustainable Development Goals, as a successor to the Millennium Development Goals that ran from 2000 to 2015.

Part Three: What is to be done? Case studies in learning for sustainability from across the globe

Chapter Seven presents a number of case studies on education and learning undertaken by postgraduate researchers in education for sustainable development (ESD). The case studies are drawn from Uganda, Rwanda and Malawi. They focus on examples of organisational, local and national change and provide an insight into the interrelationship between local and global issues. Reference is made to the importance of context and appropriacy and to the crucial relevance of local community and indigenous knowledge. The case studies are set within the framework of the politics of knowledge and the challenges that current dominant global knowledge systems pose for ESD.

Chapter Eight presents three case studies of regional centres for expertise (RCEs) in ESD. RCEs were set up to achieve the aspirations of the UN Decade for Sustainable Development (DESD), 2005–14, and to help create a global learning space for sustainable development. An RCE is a network of formal, informal and non-formal organisations mobilised to act as a catalyst for the delivery of ESD. Although sharing common aims, RCEs have a considerable degree of autonomy and are able to determine their own particular priorities based on local circumstances.

The three case studies are: RCE Saskatchewan, Canada; RCE Greater Sendai, Japan; and RCE Greater Nairobi, Kenya. These RCEs have all grown up organically and have been developed by a variety of social actors and stakeholders in their respective regions. They all have different focuses and have responded in different ways to the challenges of sustainability. This is a good example of subsidiarity in terms of ESD policymaking and practice. The case studies are framed within the context of civil society organisations and social movements, with an analysis of the impact and effectiveness of RCEs as agents for change.

In Chapter Nine, John Blewitt makes the important point that over half the world's population lives in cities and that this is increasing exponentially. As a consequence, the 'natural' world is predominantly urban, as is the global economy. The chapter argues that the fate of the planet depends upon the nature of our urban future. If we are to achieve social and environmental justice within the city, there needs to be a transformed and renewed right to urban life. Rights and urban citizenship – and, to a significant degree, social learning for sustainability – entail active engagement in the public realm and genuinely public spaces and places.

Part Four: Emerging themes and future scenarios

Chapter Ten starts with an analysis of some of the key themes that have emerged in the course of writing this book. These include:

- the importance of the link and the interrelationship between politics, education and learning in meeting the challenges of sustainability;
- the need to challenge the current educational paradigm and reshape education systems towards sustainable development;
- the realisation that traditional neoliberal growth models are proving increasingly dysfunctional for people and the planet; yet, despite this, neoliberalism remains robust in influential policy circles;
- the crucial importance of tackling climate change if we are to achieve environmental and social justice; and
- the need for a more honest engagement by politicians with the public about the challenges that creating a more sustainable world presents.

It concludes by setting out two alternative scenarios for the future of people and the planet.

So, what is the central message of this book? It is all too easy to feel overwhelmed by the challenge of building a more sustainable world for both people and the planet. For, as Wilkinson and Pickett (2010, p xi) note, 'We live in a pessimistic period. As well as being worried by the likely consequences of global warming, it is easy to feel that many societies are, despite their material success, increasingly burdened by their social failings'. However, even against such a background, there is still much cause to be positive. For, as Wilkinson and Pickett (2010, p xi) go on to argue, once we acknowledge that we cannot go on as before, that change is necessary, then this realisation itself must give us grounds for optimism: maybe we do, at last, have the chance to make a better world.

The contributors to this book share this optimism. However, we need a fundamental change in the way we do politics, economics and education. The challenges that we face today in combating climate change and building a more sustainable world are complex and multifaceted. As such, they need to be approached in a holistic way by adopting joined-up solutions for joined-up problems. We all have a stake in this. Academics from all disciplines need to break out of their silos and work in a much more interdisciplinary and multidisciplinary manner. To this end, the book will combine both political science and ESD analysis of the challenges of sustainability and climate change.

Political science can facilitate analysis of political motivation, ideological position and political constraints in respect of promoting sustainability and tackling climate change. Political science also offers important insights into how political systems operate and the power relations within them. It helps us to understand the role of pressure groups and social movements in shaping the policy process. At the same time, ESD can help political science become more action-oriented in addressing key global challenges. Congruent to these are the ongoing tensions between the environmental and development agendas and this is where ESD can provide a framework for discussion and strategic action. ESD has a key role in helping to address these tensions and in enabling politicians and decision-makers to move towards a clearer, more fully conceptualised and integrated view of sustainable development. By its very nature, ESD also necessitates the forming of links across subject disciplines, across ministries and departments, and across formal and non-formal actors. Here, political science has a key role in understanding the nature of policy change and implementation.

There is a real need to shift the terms of the debate so that building a more sustainable world is seen as an opportunity to build a more fulfilling way of life, with a focus on well-being and human happiness at the centre of the policy agenda. However, this will require a major psychological adjustment on the part of both the public and political leaders. In any case, we have no option but to try to make things work for the better. Planet earth is the only home we have. There is no escape route to Mars! So, let us give it a go. It might even be fun!

Reference

Wilkinson, R. and Pickett, K. (2010) *The spirit level: why equality is better for everyone*, London: Penguin Books.

Part One

The challenge of sustainability: politics, education and learning

ONE

Planetary challenges: the agenda laid bare

Hugh Atkinson

Introduction

We are now living in what has been described as the anthropocene era. It is an argument that the impact of human behaviour on the planet over a consolidated period of time has been so significant as to constitute a new geological epoch.

This is no more evident than in the challenge of climate change. There is now an overwhelming consensus in the scientific community that climate change is happening and that it is the result of human activity in the shape of the extensive use of fossil fuels such as oil, coal and gas, which we have been devouring since the dawn of the Industrial Revolution. To put it simply, we have taken carbon that has been stored under the earth for thousands of years, burnt it and, in the process, released large amounts of carbon dioxide gas into the earth's atmosphere. Carbon dioxide acts as a 'greenhouse' gas, trapping additional heat from the sun in the earth's atmosphere. As a consequence, the temperature in the earth's atmosphere is rising steadily but inexorably, with untold consequences for both people and the planet. In addition, we have cut down vast acres of the world's forests (which could have acted as a carbon sink by absorbing carbon dioxide in the atmosphere) in a relentless pursuit of economic growth. We simply cannot go on like this. There is no option but to meet the challenge of climate change as part of a broader agenda to develop a more sustainable way of living.

The warning signs are there for all to see. Rising sea levels, the undermining of our ecosystems, biodiversity under threat, desertification and the depletion of water resources present us with a number of significant environmental and public policy challenges. Globally, each year we are using 50% more of the earth's resources than the planet can replenish (WWF, 2012, p 16). Planet earth is being degraded in front of our very eyes. The human impact of all of this becomes clearer each day, with threats to human health, livelihoods and food security that bring in their wake the potential for political, social and economic insecurity and instability. As the German Advisory Council on Global Change argues: 'Rapidly progressing, unabated climate change will constitute a crisis for humankind' (WGBU, 2011, p 33).

Viewed at one level, such challenges seem overwhelming, intractable and nigh on impossible to resolve. Yet, viewed on another level, the challenge we face is really quite simple. We live on a planet whose physical resources are finite. Yet, our increasingly consumerist lifestyles (especially those in the so-called developed world) are eating up these resources at an ever-increasing rate, releasing vast quantities of greenhouse gases into the atmosphere, with huge implications for the climate and the well-being of planet earth. We need a transformative change in the way we do things, with sustainability at the core of our thinking and our actions.

Sustainability and sustainable development

'Sustainability' and 'sustainable development' are relatively new concepts in public policy discourse. As a result, there is an ongoing and contested debate as to both their meaning and their practical applicability. Some commentators ascribe different meanings to the two concepts (Jones and Evans, 2008, p 85). The definitional arguments can be somewhat complicated and even obtuse. For the purposes of this chapter, I will be using 'sustainability' and 'sustainable development' interchangeably.

Since the United Nations (UN) Conference on Sustainable Development in 1992 (the so-called Rio Earth Summit), sustainability has become a key policy paradigm at global, regional, national and local levels. One widely accepted definition of 'sustainability' is that given by the 1987 UN Commission on Environment and Development, which is more commonly known as the Bruntland Report. Bruntland defined sustainable development as 'Development that meets the needs of the present without compromising the ability of future generations to meet their own needs' (UN, 1987). The sustainability agenda looks beyond the economic growth model that has largely dominated public policy since the end of the Second World War. It looks at policy proposals and policy solutions in a more integrated and holistic way. It focuses on issues such as social justice, the protection and enhancement of the natural environment, and sustainable economic growth that involves the prudent use of natural resources.

Building on the work of the Bruntland Report, the 1992 Rio Summit set out three distinctive but interrelated elements of sustainability. They comprised the environmental, the social (which includes social justice and poverty reduction) and the economic. The challenge for sustainability is in achieving the appropriate balance between these three elements. Over time, different weightings have been given to these three elements, depending upon the policy context and the actors involved. Sustainability is a highly politicised (in the broadest sense of the word) policy area. One way to view sustainable development is as a set of three circles; the point where these circles interlock is where sustainable development is taking place (see Figure 1.1).

Figure 1.1: Sustainable development

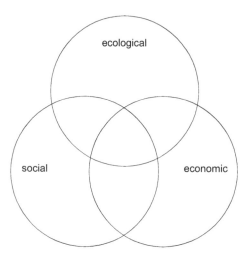

However, such a diagrammatic explanation fails to take into account the fact that we are governed by a set of substantive ecological limits on planet earth. Resources are not infinite. We need to live within planetary boundaries if we are to safeguard our life support system, namely, planet earth. Therefore, a more realistic way to view sustainable development is as three concentric circles, with economic activity and social development taking place within the context of finite ecological limits (see Figure 1.2).

Such a perspective links to the call in the post-2015 Millennium Development Goal (MDG) review process for a redefinition of sustainable development as 'Development that meets the needs of the present while safeguarding the Earth's support system, on which the welfare of current and future generations depends' (Schumacher Institute, 2013).

Figure 1.2: Sustainable development: the ecological limit

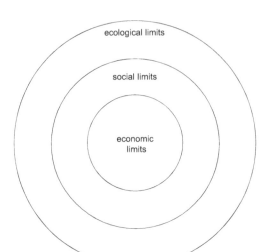

Tackling climate change

Tackling climate change is a central element of the sustainability agenda but it sits alongside a number of other very important elements. These include promoting social and economic justice, eradicating poverty, and supporting human rights. However, in a real sense, tackling climate is effectively key to achieving many of the objectives of the sustainability agenda. To take one example, by virtue of its geographical location, sub-Saharan Africa in particular has been suffering from some of the worst impacts of climate change. Forecasts are for this to continue. Droughts will become more extensive and more prolonged, bringing increased desertification, with major consequences for agriculture and water supplies in a continent that has already been disproportionately affected by poverty. As Ehresman and Stevis (2011, p 88) note: 'the developing world – will likely be hit the worst by climate change'. Yet, the developing world bears the least responsibility for the causes of climate change. In this context, Giddens (2011, p 213) talks of the crucial link between tackling climate change and promoting social justice. There is also the broader issue of the link between social justice and our consumerist culture, which swallows up ever-more of the earth's resources. The resultant 'environmental damage', as Hannigan (2011, p 53) argues, 'falls disproportionately and severely on the poor'.

The evidence of climate change

The UN Intergovernmental Panel on Climate Change (IPCC) is made up of 2000 of the world's leading climate change scientists. Its position is clear: climate change and global warming are a real and present threat and they are caused by the vast amounts of greenhouse gases (principally in the form of carbon dioxide) that we as human beings have been pumping into the earth's atmosphere by our continued burning of fossil fuels (IPCC, 2013). Research published in the journal *Nature Geoscience* in May 2013 shows the probability that warming will reach about four degrees centigrade above pre-industrial levels if the temperature readings of the past decade are taken into account. An increase in temperature of four degrees centigrade could lead to potential catastrophe across large areas of planet earth, causing droughts, floods, storms and heatwaves (as quoted in *The Guardian*, 20 May 2013).

In its 2011 World Energy Outlook (WEO), the International Energy Authority (IEA), which has traditionally adopted a cautious approach to the issue of climate change, argued that the world was locking itself into an unsustainable energy future. Its chief economist, Fatih Birol, has argued that 'As each year passes without clear signals to drive investment in clean energy, the lock in of high carbon infrastructure is making it harder and more expensive to meet our energy security and climate changes' (IEA, 2011). The WEO has set out what it terms a '450 Scenario', which 'traces an energy path consistent with meeting the globally agreed goal of limiting the temperature rise to 2°C' (IEA, 2011). Of energy-related carbon dioxide emissions, 80% are already locked in by existing infrastructure, such as factories and power stations. 'Without further action by 2017', the IEA concludes, 'the energy related infrastructure then in place would generate all the CO_2 [carbon dioxide] emissions allowed in the 450 Scenario up to 2035' (IEA, 2011).

In addition, the UN Framework on Climate Change has concluded that at current levels, within 25 years, the world will have emitted all the greenhouse gases that the atmosphere can cope with for all of the 21st century. The World Wide Fund for Nature (WWF) has calculated that if everyone in the world lived the average lifestyle of those in North America, we would need five planet earths.

Climate change was first identified as a potential threat to the health of the planet in the late 19th century but it was not until the late 1980s that the issue really started to come to prominence. On 23 June 1988, James Hansen, a US scientist with the National Aeronautics and Space Administration (NASA) gave evidence to the US Senate. He told the assembled senators that he was 99% certain that the record temperatures that year in the US were not the result of natural variations, but the result of growing concentrations of carbon dioxide in the earth's atmosphere. 'It is time to stop waffling so much', argued Hansen, 'and say that the evidence is pretty strong that the greenhouse effect is here' (Flavin and Engelman, 2009, p 6). In the 25 years since Hansen gave his testimony, that scientific evidence has grown stronger and stronger.

Atmospheric greenhouse gases, 1900 to 2012

Figure 1.3 shows the amount of greenhouse gases in the atmosphere from 1900 to 2012 as measured in parts per million (ppm). It shows a clear and demonstrable upward trend in such emissions. This upward trend has continued since 2012. In May 2013, the American National Oceanic and Atmosphere Administration (NOAA) observatory in Mauna Loa Hawaii recorded emission levels beyond the milestone of 400 ppm. It is salutary to note that the last time there was such a concentration of greenhouse gases in the atmosphere was several million years ago when the Arctic was ice-free and sea levels were up

Figure 1.3: Atmospheric greenhouse gases, 1900–2012

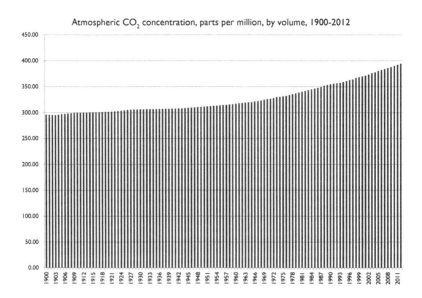

Atmospheric CO_2 concentration, parts per million, by volume, 1900-2012

Source: Base data compiled by Earth Policy Institute from Intergovernmental Panel on Climate Change (IPCC) and National Oceanic and Atmospheric Administration (NOAA)

to 40 metres higher! Responding to these latest findings, Professor Rajendra Pachauri, chair of the IPCC, said:

> At the beginning of industrialisation the concentration of CO_2 was just 280ppm. We must hope that the world crossing this milestone will bring about awareness of the scientific reality of climate change and how human society should deal with the challenge. (*The Guardian*, 11 May 2013).

So, who are the main culprits in terms of greenhouse gas emissions? Historically, the US has been the largest contributor to global greenhouse gas emissions. Table 1.1 shows emissions figures for 2012.

Table 1.1: Percentage greenhouse gas emissions per country, 2012

Country	Total greenhouse gas emissions (%)
China	23.5
USA	23
EU	14
India	6

Source: IPCC (2013).

Percentage of greenhouse gas emissions per country in 2012

In 2012, China (with a population of 1.4 billion) was responsible for 23.5% of all total emissions, just ahead of the US (with a population of 315 million). Ten countries accounted for 67% of all emissions. At the bottom of the list were the Maldives Islands in the Indian Ocean, whose greenhouse gas emissions were negligible. By a twist of irony, the Maldives is one of the first countries to have felt the impact of rising sea levels as a result of climate change. In an attempt to draw attention to the plight of the Maldives, its president actually held a cabinet meeting under the sea in October 2009!

Variations in the earth's temperature, 1900–2012

Figure 1.4 shows us the variations in the temperature of the earth's atmosphere in degrees Fahrenheit from 1900 to 2012. There are variations from year to year but there is a clear upward trajectory. Indeed, 20 of the hottest 21 years since records began in 1860 have occurred in the last 25 years. Official figures released by the American NOAA show that 2012 was the warmest year on record for the US. The principal cause of this upward trajectory, argues the IPCC (2013), is the increasing emissions of greenhouse gases shown in Figure 1.3.

Figure 1.4: Average global surface temperatures, 1900–2012

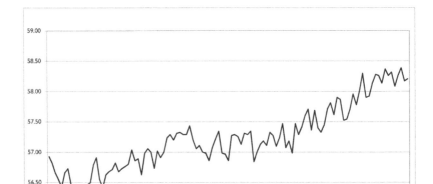

Source: Base data compiled by Earth Policy Institute (2013) from National Aeronautics and Space Administration (NASA) and Goddard Institute for Space Studies (GISS)

There is a growing consensus that this trend of temperature increase is set to continue. The only uncertainty is by how much. The IPCC estimates that global temperatures in the 20th century could increase by anywhere between two and four degrees centigrade (3.6 to 7.2 degrees Fahrenheit). The two degrees centigrade (3.6 degrees Fahrenheit) figure is significant, with many scientists now of the view that any increase beyond this would take us into uncharted territory, with the world experiencing more and more strange and unusual weather events. So, the evidence is clear. Climate change is happening through vast amounts of greenhouse gases being pumped into the atmosphere as a consequence of human activity. True, there is still uncertainty about the precise future impact that this will have on planet earth, but as Gosling et al argue, 'The evidence shows significant changes ahead for many aspects of human and natural system, many of them unprecedented in the course of human existence' (Gosling et al, 2011, p 456). It is to this that I now turn.

The environmental impact of climate change

It has been argued that, 'Like a distant tsunami that is only a few metres high in the deep ocean but rises dramatically as it reaches shallow coastal waters, the great wave of climate change has snuck upon people – and is now beginning to bite' (Flavin and Engelman, 2009, p 6). This is certainly true. The 2006 Stern Report warned of the severe environmental, social and economic consequences of climate change. It warned of how melting glaciers would lead to the increased risk of flooding in the wet season and significantly reduce dry season water supplies to one sixth of the world's population. The Indian subcontinent would be one area particularly hit. Increasing temperatures would lead to declining crop yields, especially in Africa. Ecosystems would come under increasing threat (Stern, 2006, p 56). Urgent action is needed, argued Stern. Eight years later, the situation is even more urgent. The physical impact of climate change is becoming increasingly evident. Rising sea levels threaten the livelihoods of many people, with all that that means for poverty and social and political instability. Delicate ecosystems are being eroded, posing a threat to biodiversity and the balance of nature.

In December 2012, a major weather event wrought havoc on a populous nation, bringing death and destruction in its wake. While the power of Hurricane Sandy was widely reported in the world's media as it pounded the eastern seaboard of the US, the destructive force of Typhoon Bopha went largely unreported as it brought death and destruction to the Philippines. Around 1,500 people are estimated to have died. Now, of course, one should be cautious when drawing conclusions about climate change from specific weather events. But Typhoon Bopha is significant. Normally, typhoons do not travel so far south towards the equator, but such extreme weather events are becoming part of a pattern. Indeed, the number of floods and storms in the archipelago of the Philippines has risen significantly since the 1960s (as quoted in the *Financial Times*, 13 December 2012).

There are many other examples of the impact of climate change and the world's continued dependency on fossil fuels. According to data from the National Snow and Ice Data Centre (NSIDC) in Colorado, sea ice in the Arctic has shrunk to its smallest extent ever recorded. Satellite images from 2012 show that a rapid melt has reduced the area of frozen sea to less than 3.3 million square kilometres, less than half that of 40 years ago. Research published in the journal *Science* in 2012 shows that four trillion tonnes of ice from Greenland and Antarctica has melted in the last 20 years, adding yet further to rising sea levels (quoted in *The Guardian*, 30 November 2012). Research carried out by scientists based on the vessel *Arctic Sunrise* points to the likelihood of the Arctic being ice-free in the summer within 29 years (quoted in *The Guardian*, 15 September 2012). For Nick Toberg, a sea ice researcher at Cambridge University, such evidence is 'staggering'. Toberg argues that:

> It is disturbing, scary, that we have physically changed the face of the planet. We have about four million square metres of sea ice. If that goes in the summer months that's about the same as adding 20 years of CO_2 at current rates into the atmosphere. That's how vital the Arctic sea ice is. (Quoted in *The Guardian*, 15 September 2012).

The delicate ecosystem of the Arctic is under increasing threat as oil corporations see the commercial advantage of oil exploration and drilling in the region. It is estimated that the Arctic holds up to 25% of the world's remaining hydrocarbons. With perverse irony, the rush for oil is a consequence of climate change as global temperatures continue to rise, causing large areas of Arctic ice to melt, thus easing the logistical difficulties for the oil companies as they seek to exploit the vast reserves.

In Africa, climate change now threatens to undermine the whole environmental, social and economic fabric of the continent. There has been comparatively little research into the possible impact of climate change in Africa. But the consensus of the IPCC is that an increase of just two degrees centigrade would bring in its wake more intense droughts, stronger storms, floods, crop losses and rising sea levels. An increase of around four degrees centigrade would have calamitous consequences for much of Africa. In 1906, scientists mapped and named 43 glaciers in the continent of Africa. Today, there remain only five major glaciers, the Rwenzori glaciers in Uganda, but they, too, are under threat. It is likely, writes John Vidal (2011), environment correspondent of *The Guardian* newspaper, that 'the equatorial ice known to the ancient Greeks will almost have certainly disappeared in 20 to 30 years'. The gradual erosion and loss of the African glaciers has multiple effects. Lack of run-off from the glaciers will lead to further clean water shortages, impacting upon food production and increasing human conflict. Conflict and social instability are likely to increase as people battle over declining resources.

—

Tackling climate change is the most important challenge facing the world today. It is a matter of both climate justice and social justice. However, tackling the challenge of climate change and building a more sustainable world cannot be brought about by a few techno fixes. Rather, it presents us with a series of other economic, social and political challenges that must be faced up to. These have huge implications for education and learning and for how we do politics.

Delivering on sustainability: challenges and opportunities

The challenge of tackling climate change and building a more sustainable world is complex, multilayered and hugely problematic. At times, it can seem so daunting that its resolution can appear nigh on impossible. But it is a challenge that we simply cannot afford to duck. As such, it necessitates a multilayered response on the part of civil society, business and the state. It requires action at the local, national, regional and global levels. To analyse both this challenge and the opportunities to meet this challenge, I will now focus on three specific but interrelated themes, namely: economy and society, energy policy, and the politics of it all.

Economy and society

Since the end of the Second World War, the dominant economic paradigm has been one of economic growth (measured by gross domestic product [GDP]) as the key to material happiness and well-being. It came to dominate political discourse and public policymaking. It became the normal way of doing economics. The emergence of neoliberal economics in the 1980s and 1990s strengthened this process even further. There developed a strong belief among many politicians, elites and key decision-makers that markets were 'the primary means for achieving the public good' (Sandel, 2012, p 6).

One might have expected the 2007/08 international financial crisis and credit crunch, a product of reckless banking practices, a consumerism bubble and high levels of personal indebtedness, to have forced a radical rethink of the way we do economics. After all, the crisis did almost bring the global economy to its knees. It was only rescued by a strong dose of good old-fashioned Keynesian social democracy, as governments worldwide pumped huge amounts of money into the banking system. Indeed, commentators such as Michael Sandel (2012, p 6) have argued that 'The era of market triumphalism has come to an end' as the financial crisis 'has cast doubt on the ability of financial markets to allocate risk efficiently'. For Evans et al (2009, p 683), the after-effects of the credit crunch have made it 'possible to challenge dominant political narratives about the supremacy of the market'. Yet, in spite of all that has happened, neoliberal economics has remained remarkably resilient. Its proponents have also remained remarkably thick-skinned, almost shameless one might say. Faith in the market and the pursuit of economic growth may have been dented, but it is far from undermined.

The central question is 'Why?' There is no doubt that contemporary capitalism, with its focus on economic growth and material consumption, has proved itself to be remarkably dynamic, bringing with it many benefits and improving the lives of millions of people. Yet, this is only part of the story. For, as Borghesi and Vercelli (2008, p 33) argue, 'unfettered markets, including deregulation, privatisation and the downgrading of social and environmental standards, are the apotheosis of a more sustainable and equitable world'.

As we survey the global scene in 2014, for millions and millions of people, the relentless drive for greater prosperity has proved illusory. In the developing world, millions remain in poverty. Data from the World Bank, for example, shows that 49% of people in sub-Saharan Africa live in poverty, defined as earning less than US$1.25 a day. In the so-called developed world, we are witnessing ever-increasing concentrations of wealth, rising levels of unemployment and the associated social and health strains that this brings. Government austerity programmes have wreaked havoc on a number of economies, bringing in their wake political and social instability. Unemployment in Spain, for example, stands at 25%, with youth unemployment at 56%. In Greece, 59% of those under 25 are out of work.

Yet, support for the current system has taken on a kind of quasi-religious quality in some quarters, but its environmental, social and economic downsides are clear for all to see. So, what is to be done? A variety of approaches has been either tried or suggested. In the Western world, recycling has taken off apace over the last two decades (for millions in the developing world, such recycling has been commonplace for generations!). There is a growing awareness of how food is grown and the conditions of those that grow that food (witness the growth of Fair Trade). Corporate social responsibility has become part of the lexicon in the commercial sector.

At a public policy level, there have been a number of initiatives. Governments have sought to use directly interventionist measures such as green taxes (eg on oil and petrol) to protect the environment and to mitigate the impact of climate change. On a broader scale, the NASA climate scientist James Hansen has called for a worldwide tax on all greenhouse gas emissions as a means to safeguard global environmental and social justice (quoted in *The Guardian*, 7 April 2012). But the debate about the fairness, effectiveness and political feasibility of such taxes is ongoing (Wilkinson and Pickett, 2010; Casal, 2012).

A less interventionist approach to tackling climate change is to be found in the economics of 'Nudge', associated with the work of Thaler and Sunstein (2008) and Mills (2013), among others. Such an approach eschews such interventionist measures as direct green taxes. Instead, it calls for public policy to be structured so that people have choices over their own actions but are gently nudged (through incentives) to do what is in their own interests (and in the interests of wider society). Thaler and Sunstein (2008, p 16) cite the example of cap and trade schemes to control the emissions of greenhouse gases as an example of the Nudge approach.

One such example is the European Union's (EU's) emissions trading scheme (ETS). It is a market-based system in which companies in areas such as manufacturing and energy production, for example, are able to buy tradable carbon permits. The rationale is that putting a price on carbon will prod such companies to invest more in sustainable energy. However, the ETS has been hit by a number of complex problems in the wake of the 2007 credit crunch. By 2012, the price of carbon had slumped from a peak of US$30 per tonne in 2008 to US$7, and the market had become saturated in permits 'that give companies the right to emit carbon without penalties' (Chaffin, 2012). Of course, the ETS may well be able to respond to such episodic setbacks and make a substantive impact on reducing greenhouse gases. Yet, it is rooted in traditional notions of economic growth and consumption, which, as I have argued earlier, are a major part of the problem. As such, the jury remains firmly out on the ETS.

Technological change

Some would have us believe that technological solutions are the way to solve the problem. Can we, as Rawles (2012, p 233) puts it, 'technofix climate change'? Roberts (2005, p 260) has written of the 'myth of the perfect gadget', whereby it is only a matter of time before the 'right' technology comes along to deal with the challenges that climate change presents. It is a point of view held by a number of energy executives, policymakers and even some environmentalists!

Leach et al (2010, p 1) write of the 'ever more urgent search for big, technically driven, managerial solutions'.

One approach that has come on to the scientific agenda is that of geo-engineering, which is an attempt to engineer the climate (Spectre, 2012). But, as Roy Butterfield, emeritus professor of civil engineering, argues, the global climate is universally acknowledged to be a non-linear, dynamic and chaotic system. In this context, 'Geo engineering is, unfortunately, a totally impractical concept', with the added danger 'that it could be used politically as an excuse for delaying further the drastic measures needed' to tackle climate change and build a more sustainable world (Butterfield, 2012).

For some, the solution to the problems of environmental degradation is to be found in the concept of ecological modernisation. Ecological modernisation is an attempt to square the circle of economic growth and sustainable development by increasing 'the environmental efficiency of the economy through the use of new and clean technologies' (Connelly and Smith, 2003, p 67). Such a process is known as 'decoupling', allowing more economic activity with less environmental damage. For example, there is some evidence, as Jackson (2011, p 69) points out, that there has been an increased efficiency in the use of resources for each unit of economic output, leading to 'declining [carbon] emission densities'. Jackson (2011, p 68) describes such a process as 'relative decoupling'. The problem is that as economic output has increased globally, so has the overall scale of carbon dioxide emissions. Carbon dioxide emissions are 40% higher today than they were in 1990. There is simply no evidence of 'absolute decoupling'. For Jackson (2011, p 76), decoupling as an approach to deal with the 'dilemma of growth' is 'fundamentally flawed'. One example of the ecological modernisation and decoupling approaches is that of the Green Economy.

The Green Economy

The so-called 'Green Economy' is regarded in some circles as the holy grail in terms of moving towards a more sustainable world and tackling climate change. For others, it is akin to the 'myth of the perfect gadget', as described earlier. It was central to discussions and debates at the 2012 UN Conference on Sustainable Development (commonly known as Rio+20).

The Green Economy is predicated on the assumption that green or sustainable growth can be achieved by utilising the latest science and technology. It is part of the mainstream thinking within the UN and international development circles. But the concept of the Green

Economy 'and strategies to promote a green economy are highly contested' (UNRISD, 2012). Jones (2012, p 187) points to the important link between creating green jobs and protecting the environment. But, for Jackson (2012), nobody has yet come up with an honest and clear definition of what is actually meant by sustainable growth. Cable (2012, p 12) goes further, arguing that 'Sustainable growth is nonsensical: growth is not sustainable because resources are not infinite'. Yet, the idea of sustainable growth has gained significant leverage in policy circles.

A 2011 United Nations Educational, Scientific and Cultural Organisation (UNESCO) policy paper, for example, stated that 'Science holds many of the answers to the complex questions we face' (UNESCO, 2011b, p 5). It talks of the need for 'resolute science and technology based solutions' to combat the many social and environmental challenges (UNESCO, 2011b, p 29). No one should deny the important role that science and technology can play in shaping a more sustainable world, but the Green Economy approach is in danger of perpetuating the myth that science and technology are all that is needed. Indeed, as Bowen (2012, p 7) has argued, 'it is not clear whether this new emphasis on green growth represents a paradigm shift or just spin to cover up inconsistencies between economic and environmental objectives of government'.

The challenges that the world faces today are multifaceted and require a variety of social, environmental and economic policy responses, of which science and technology are but a part. Indeed, there is recognition in international circles that 'Green economies on their own are not enough'; there is also a need to build 'green societies', which 'must be fair, equitable and inclusive societies' (UNESCO, 2011b, p 8). The concept of green societies offers us a potentially important way forward. But we must be careful to avoid prioritising the green economy over the green society as the driver for social change.

As mentioned earlier in this chapter, the world's delicate ecosystems are under considerable threat as a result of challenges such as climate change and the over-exploitation of the planet's natural resources. In 2005, the Millennium Eco System Assessment, an international work programme run by 1,300 researchers from 95 countries, published a report based on its research. It is the most comprehensive review of the state of the planet ever conducted. Its findings highlight the real and apparent crisis with regard to the world's ecosystems. The report's broad conclusion is that human activity has changed most ecosystems to such an extent as to threaten the planet's ability to support future generations (Millennium Eco System Assessment, 2005).

One approach put forward to tackle this crisis is that of ecosystem services. This approach seeks to achieve the sustainable use of ecosystem products and services through the adoption of a number of key principles. These include: respecting the biological limits of ecosystem structures; managing ecosystems for long-term benefit as opposed to short-term gain; and involving all relevant stakeholders in decision-making so as to foster equity and inspire active participation in the stewardship of ecosystems (World Resources Institute, 2005).

The ecosystem services approach has been the subject of much academic debate (Godden, 2010; Gonez-Baggethun and Perez, 2011; Connif, 2012). A detailed critique of the ecosystem services approach is beyond the scope of this book; however, some general observations can be made. While the key principles highlighted earlier can be seen to have merit, the reference to services and products in respect of ecosystems could be viewed as having much in common with neoliberal and market-based assumptions of economic growth, as opposed to a distinctive policy agenda based around the principles of sustainability. This is compounded by the fact that the ecosystem services approach seeks to put an economic value on ecosystems, albeit a value that is based on all ecosystems' goods and services, not simply the commodity value of extracted goods. It is an approach that seeks to monetise ecosystems, but nature, ecology and the biosphere have an intrinsic value beyond economics. We cannot lose sight of this.

While the various policy approaches considered in the preceding section may make some contribution to combating climate change and promoting sustainability, they simply do not go far enough. They are still based on the assumption of consuming increasing amounts of stuff (even if some of it is green stuff). The neoliberal economic growth model and its focus on so-called consumer choice, with the acquisition of more and more consumer goods, is eating up the planet's resources at an alarming rate. We need to take action now if we are to avoid what has been described as the 'tragedy of the commons' (Hardin, 1998). The commons are those 'areas and resources that are not under sovereign jurisdiction', but that are open to exploitation for personal profit, with significant environmental costs that impact upon us all (Vogler, 2008, p 358). A good example of the tragedy of the commons is the over-exploitation of the planet's oceans through commercial fishing.

Building a new normal?

In the relentless pursuit of conventional economic growth, we are pumping huge amounts of greenhouse gases into the atmosphere. It is now generally accepted by the scientific community and politicians alike that we need to reduce global greenhouse gas emissions by 80% by the year 2050, using 1990 as a baseline, if we are to avoid the more catastrophic impacts of climate change. This is a daunting challenge and will require a radical reappraisal of how we do economics and, indeed, politics. It also has huge implications for what and how we learn and, therefore, for education policy and practice.

'We need', as Rawles (2012, p 165) has observed, 'a new normal', a new way of looking at our role in the world and our relationship to the planet. In essence, we have become divorced from nature, seeking to constantly shape it to meet our material desires. Yet, we are objectively part of it and we need to recognise this fact (Blewitt, 2008, p ix). We need to examine some of our key assumptions about conventional economics.

Indeed, a debate is opening up about how this might be done, with a growing recognition that we live in a finite world and we need to operate within planetary boundaries. It is a debate that has been going on for 40 years or more. Until the 1960s, environmental issues were, in the main, focused on the protection of wildlife and the countryside. The 1962 book *Silent spring* by Rachel Carson was one of the first accounts to draw attention to the increasingly damaging impact of human actions on the planet, which had intensified significantly with economic growth, as measured by GDP, in the post-Second World War period (Carson, 2003).

The nascent 'green politics' of the 1960s and 1970s sought to challenge traditional notions of material happiness, focusing on quality of life issues, what has been described as 'post-materialism' (Abramson and Inglehart, 1995). The 1987 Brundtland Report and the 1992 Rio Summit drew an explicit link between environmental protection, social development and economic growth through the concept of sustainable development, which is now part of the mainstream policy agenda (although debates over its substantive meaning and impact rage on!). Over recent years, there has developed a growing body of literature and thinking on broader notions of happiness and well-being that go beyond traditional notions of material satisfaction.

The negative impact on personal health of consumerism has been described by various psychologists as *affluenza*, which is like a 'painful, contagious, socially transmitted condition of overload, debt, anxiety and waste resulting from the dogged pursuit of more' (Graaf et al, 2001, p 122). Developing the concept of *affluenza*, Oliver James (2007, p 142) has linked rising consumption and the influence of advertising with high levels of anxiety and depression. Wilkinson and Pickett (2010, p 217) note how available evidence shows 'that further economic growth in the developed world no longer improves health, happiness or measures of well being'. Indeed, as Jackson (2011, p 85) argues, there is 'yet no credible, socially just, ecologically sustainable scenario of continually growing incomes for a world of 9 billion people'.

A 2010 report coordinated by the world-renowned economist Joseph Stiglitz argued that there was a real need to 'Identify the limits of GDP as an indicator of economic performance and social progress' and to consider 'what information might be required for the production of relevant indicators of social progress' (Stiglitz et al, 2009, p 2). Helliwell, Layard and Sachs (2013, p 5) have also written of the importance of the role of happiness in shaping public policy.

Developing this theme, Reich (2011, p 75) has argued that we need to view economic growth not as 'an end in itself', but as a means to improve the quality of our lives. This, of course, will include personal material well-being, but it is clear that we need to go beyond the narrow neoliberal view of economics. Reich (2011, p 76) talks of the need to make room for what he calls 'the consumption of public improvements that benefit all'. He gives as examples an atmosphere less polluted by carbon, better schools and better health care. There is real validity in what Reich has to say. Linked to this is the overwhelming case for greater equality. Greater equality is not just a matter of social justice, but makes economic sense. Research shows that concentrations of wealth not only lead to greater poverty and social exclusion, but also have a negative impact on the functioning of the economy (Reich, 2011). Furthermore, recent worldwide statistics suggest that more equal societies are more sustainable and manage to provide public goods such as health and education at a reduced environmental cost (Wilkinson and Pickett, 2010).

One such approach is that of New Economics (Simms and Boyle, 2009). For the UK-based New Economics Foundation, 'The UK and many of the world's economies are increasingly unsustainable, unfair and unstable'; what is needed, it argues, is a 'Great Transition – to transform the economy so that it works for people and planet' (New Economics Foundation, 2014). In a similar vein, the US-based New Economy Coalition talks of 'an economy that is restorative to people, place and planet', and that operates according to the principles of 'democracy, justice and appropriate scale' (New Economy Coalition, 2014).

In essence, New Economics challenges neoliberal assumptions about the value of traditional measures of economic growth, such as GDP. It aims to place the well-being of people and the planet at the heart of the economic policy agenda.

At a broader policy level, we have seen the development of new systemic approaches in an attempt to meet the twin challenges of climate change and sustainability. There are many good examples of the kind of radical thinking and policy ideas that we need if we are to shape a more sustainable world. One such example is the idea of contraction and convergence. Developed by Aubrey Meyer, a musician and environmental activist, it looks at the issues of climate change and sustainability from the perspective of global eco-justice (Meyer, 2001). It argues for the notion of the equal right of all citizens to use the earth's atmosphere, with an equal per capita allocation. This would mean that more developed countries would contract their use of carbon while poorer countries continue to develop. Convergence would happen when equal levels of development are achieved within sustainable carbon emissions. This is an important policy goal, but it faces any number of barriers and constraints, not the least of which is political will.

One important achievement on the global political agenda, it could be argued, was the establishment of the Millennium Development Goals (MDGs) under the auspices of the UN. There are eight such goals, including commitments to: reduce global poverty; achieve universal primary education; tackle global health problems (including child mortality); promote the empowerment of women; and deliver on environmental sustainability (UNDP, 2013). All 189 member states of the UN have signed up to these goals. The year 2015 has been set as the year for achieving the MDGs. There has been undoubted progress in achieving some of these goals, but the picture is complex. The MDG to achieve universal primary education is on track, as is the MDG to promote greater gender equality and support women's empowerment. There has also been real success in attempts to tackle HIV/Aids and malaria. However, the target to halve extreme poverty by 50% will not be met, nor will attempts to eradicate hunger (UNDP, 2013). Climate change has had an impact here. For, as the United Nations Development Programme (UNDP, 2013) points out, climate-related shocks such as extreme weather have led to increased food insecurity and widespread hunger.

A UN High Level Panel, appointed in July 2012, is currently working on a set of proposals for development goals for the period beyond 2015. These goals need to have sustainability at their core. What is needed is a set of explicit Sustainable Development Goals (SDGs). The developed world needs to put its money where its mouth is and to give financial support to poorer countries in their attempts to tackle climate change. Any future set of SDGs must also tackle the issue of armed conflicts and the global arms trade that fuels such conflicts. This has to be a central element in efforts to create a more socially just and sustainable world. The 2011 Global Monitoring Report notes that in the decade to 2008, 35 countries experienced armed conflict, of which 30 were either low-income or lower-middle-income countries (UNESCO, 2011a, p 6). The social consequences of this are immense. For example, in conflict-affected poor countries, 28 million children of primary school age are not in school. As the report cogently argues: 'The hidden crisis in education in conflict affected states is a global challenge that demands an international response' (UNESCO, 2011a, p 6).

Energy policy

Central to any transformative change in the way we do economics is energy; not just the type of energy we use, but how efficient we are in its usage. As Abramsky (2010, p 78) has noted: 'the world stands at what is likely to be its last window of opportunity to shift toward a sustainable energy system and avoid the full impact of the crises being fuelled by conventional energy industries'. We simply have to move away from our addiction to fuels such as coal, oil and gas. We have to stop being fossil fuel junkies. We need to make a step change in our use of sustainable and renewable energy sources if we are to hit the globally agreed target of an 80% reduction in greenhouse gases by 2050. We need to recalibrate our thinking. Renewable energy sources such as solar, tidal and wind power have to become central elements in a new sustainable energy mix. We have no choice but to embrace these low carbon technologies if we are to avoid the further degradation of planet earth. Politicians seem to get this, at least in their public utterances. But, and it is a big but, they are still prone to short-term expediency and quick policy fixes, in part dictated by the exigencies of electoral politics. I will return to this shortly.

Renewable energy

For those seeking to combat climate change and to shape a more environmentally sustainable world, a key part of the answer lies in the development of renewable energy. The whole area of renewable energy is complex and contested and definitions vary, but in broad terms, one can define it as energy that is produced from resources that do not deplete when their energy is harnessed, such as sunlight, wind and wave power. This is in contrast to fossil fuel resources such as oil, which are finite. Such energy sources have an important role to play in tackling climate change as they have a low carbon impact.

It is important to note, however, that despite the clear benefits of renewable energy sources with regard to climate change, they do also have some environmental impact. For example, tidal barrages can produce clean energy but may also have a negative impact on delicate local ecosystems. For some campaigners, wind farms are a visual blight on the landscape. The increasing use of biofuels, using food crops such as corn to produce ethanol as a non-fossil fuel substitute to power motor vehicles, has been widely criticised in development circles. The last three years has seen a series of food riots in developing countries as a result of food shortages resulting from the production of ethanol. This led the UN special rapporteur on the right to food, Jean Ziegler, to argue that biofuels 'were a crime against humanity' (as quoted in *The Guardian*, 26 November 2013).

The environmental non-governmental organisation, Worldwatch Institute (2013), reports that renewable energy technologies are quickly cementing themselves as a key pillar of energy sector development. The year 2011, for example, saw total investment in renewable energy and fuel increase by 17% on 2010, itself a previous record year for investment, with some US$257 billion being invested in the renewable sector. At present, Germany produces some 25% of its energy from renewable sources. The US is currently some way short of Germany, with 14% of its electricity coming from renewable sources, though this is still a significant figure. China is spending US$294 billion in the five years from 2010 to 2015 on investment in renewables. In the summer of 2013, the Chinese company Trina Sola won a contract to supply just over 1 million photovoltaic (solar) panels for a 250 megawatt power facility to be built in the Nevada desert in the US. It is one of the world's largest projects of its type.

For the IPPC, renewable energy offers the opportunity to contribute to a number of sustainability goals. These include: climate change mitigation; improved health and environmental outcomes; and social and economic development. These are valid arguments. Indeed, as Barbier (2010, p 43) argues, moving to a low carbon economy is 'imperative for improving the human development prospects of the world's poor'.

However, renewable energy should not be seen as a magic bullet, for, as noted earlier, all energy sources have some environmental impact. It would be wrong to suggest that renewable energy offers a perfect public policy solution to the challenges of sustainability and climate change. However, renewable energy, used in a judicious and efficient way and in the context of a clear recognition of the ecological limits of the planet, is the best available policy option we have. Simply using renewable energy to go on as we have been doing, pursuing traditional notions of economic growth and consumerism, is not the approach we need. Renewable energy should be a central element of a new paradigm. It should not be used to breathe life into an old and discredited one. But renewable energy is central to renewing the way we do economics!

Fracking and all that gas

Fracking, or, as it is sometimes called, hydraulic fracturing, is a technology that involves pumping water at high pressure into shale beds to release trapped natural gas, and increasingly in the US, oil as well. It is a highly controversial technology. For its supporters, it is a crucial element in filling the energy gap. To its opponents, it is an environmental disaster.

Fracking is allowing access to oil reserves that were previously too expensive or difficult to exploit. The analysts, IHS Global Insight, estimate that by 2015 the US will be producing more oil from techniques such as fracking than from conventional means. In 2008, the country produced 5 million barrels of oil a day. By 2013, this figure had risen to over 7 million barrels a day. The British Geological Survey estimates that Britain is sitting on shale deposits that could satisfy the UK's gas needs for the next 40 years.

A wide range of criticisms have been levelled at the use of fracking. These include pollution of the water supply, earth tremors brought on by the process and the physical degradation of the environment. The natural gas produced from shale produces half the carbon dioxide per unit of energy as coal. This would seem to present some advantages in terms of combating climate change. However, research conducted by the NOAA in conjunction with the University of Colorado estimates that natural gas producers in an area known as the Denver Julesburg basin in Colorado are losing 4% of gas (in the form of methane) to the atmosphere. This is worrying as methane is some 25 times more efficient than carbon dioxide at trapping heat in the atmosphere (Tollefson, 2012). A 2012 study by Tom Wigley from the National Centre for Atmospheric Research (NCAR) concluded that unless methane leakage rates can be kept below 2%, substituting gas for coal is not an effective means of combating climate change (NCAR, 2011).

Carbon capture and storage

Carbon capture and storage (CCS) is a technology that attempts to capture carbon dioxide from the industrial production process (eg factories and energy power plants) and store it underground in saline aquifers or old oil wells, thus preventing its release into the atmosphere. However, as Lynas (2008, p 273) observes, it is an unproven technology with the danger of carbon dioxide leaking from faulty underground reservoirs. For Robert Engelman (2012), president of the Worldwatch Institute, 'CCS is worth exploring as one of a large array of potential strategies for slowing the build up of CO_2 in the atmosphere'. But there is a need for high levels of investment if such potential is to be realised. For Engelman (2012), there is little evidence that that is going to happen. Chivers is even more sanguine about the prospects for CCS. For him, even the most optimistic industry experts expect CCS to be operational only by 2030, far too late to avoid 'run away climate change' (Chivers, 2010, p 111).

The chimera of nuclear power

Reactions to the issue of nuclear power are mixed and varied. In France, it has long been a key component of its energy mix, supplying some 75% of its electricity supply. Although it has attracted opposition in some quarters, it has been rather muted. In the US, nuclear power makes up 19% of electricity supply. At times, environmental groups have raised concerns about the safety of nuclear power, most notably, after the major incident at the Three Mile Island nuclear reactor in Pennsylvania, where on 20 March 1979, there was a partial nuclear meltdown. However, such concerns have limited resonance in the broader population.

In Germany, by contrast, there has been significant concern about the safety of nuclear power, voiced by the German Greens in particular. As a consequence, the German Chancellor Angela Merkel announced the phasing out of the country's nuclear programme by 2022. In Britain, there have been long-standing concerns about the safety and environmental impact of nuclear power since the first nuclear power station was built in the 1950s. Nuclear power has never produced more that 20% of Britain's electricity needs and that figure has been reducing as old plants have closed. By the mid-1990s, the future of nuclear power looked very uncertain.

Yet, two decades later, the picture seems to have changed. In 2013, the Conservative–Liberal Democrat Coalition government announced a new programme of nuclear reactors, stating that 'nuclear power will continue to be a key part of our low carbon energy mix' (HM Government, 2013). The reasons for this policy shift are complex, but, among other factors, the government argues that nuclear power is an important component in the battle against climate change. Nuclear power is a carbon-free technology. As such, it does not produce greenhouse gases. It is an argument that is being heard more widely in policy circles internationally.

It is also an argument that has also been taken up by a number of high-profile environmental campaigners. James Lovelock, environmental guru and author of the Gaia Hypothesis, argues that climate change is such a major challenge to the planet that we need to embrace nuclear power. He accuses those in the environment movement who oppose nuclear power of being 'wrong-headed'. For Lovelock, now is not the time to experiment with 'visionary energy solutions' (Lovelock, 2004). Another leading environmentalism and author of 'Six degrees: our future on a hotter planet', Mark Lynas, advocates the wider use of nuclear power 'in order to avoid more carbon emissions' (Lynas, 2012). In the US, Stewart Brand, a key figure in shaping the modern environmental movement and editor of the *Whole Earth Catalogue*, has argued that 'nuclear is green' (Brand, 2012).

Despite this, many others in the environmental lobby remain deeply sceptical of the role of nuclear energy as a sustainable energy source, citing, for example, the problems of the waste produced by nuclear and how to store it. It has been estimated that the cost of dealing with the waste produced by the UK nuclear industry will be in the region of £70 billion.

Mark Lynas has acknowledged the downsides of nuclear power. In addition to what he described as the 'unsolved question of what to do with highly radioactive wastes' (Lynas, 2008, p 273), he also refers to the danger of major accidents at nuclear power plants. Recent events in Japan underscore this concern. In March 2011, the after-effects of a tsunami caused major damage to the Fukushima nuclear power plant, resulting in a major radiation leak. In September 2013, a surge was reported in the radiation levels leaking out of the plant, with levels twice that considered safe by the Japanese authorities. In addition, although nuclear power as a non-fossil fuel does not appear to directly produce greenhouse gases, to build a nuclear power plant is a huge capital project, involving a large amount of embedded energy in terms of materials, transport and the use of fuel, which, by their very nature, emit greenhouse gases.

The politics of it all

There is no doubt that climate change presents us with a considerable challenge. But it is not an insurmountable challenge. There are grounds for optimism. We should not underestimate the human capacity for making the necessary changes towards a more sustainable way of life. We have the skills and the knowledge to deal with climate change. There is, for example, a potentially abundant supply of renewable energy sources such as solar, wind and tidal, which could shift us away from our dependence upon fossil fuels. The missing ingredient in all of this is political will.

To be fair, politicians and decision-makers at the global, national and local levels do seem to recognise that there is a problem. Indeed, there has been no lack of summits, conferences and gatherings, from the Rio Earth Summit of 1992 to the 1997 Kyoto Protocol on climate change, and right through to the 2012 UN Climate Change Conference in Doha. There have been some important achievements along the way. The Kyoto Protocol, for example, was an important global agreement that set out agreed targets for reductions in greenhouse gas emissions. It was far from perfect – indeed, Lemos and Agrawal (2009, p 91) talk of its 'lacklustre accomplishments' – but it was an important achievement nonetheless. However, the overall record of political action to tackle climate change is mixed to say the least. The Doha UN Climate Change Conference in 2012 was, in the eyes of most observers, a major disappointment, with world leaders in effect putting off key decisions to another day. The 2013 gathering in Warsaw fared little better. As Farley and Smith (2014, p 79) observe: 'there is an evident gap between talk and action'. There are various reasons for this.

First, there is the nature of the problem itself. Tackling climate change is of a different order to previous environmental challenges. As Sedlacko and Martinuzzi (2012, p 3) observe, climate change is an example of what has been termed a 'wicked problem'. It is, as Jordan et al (2011, p 122) argue, 'Complex, unprecedented and its worst impacts will be felt by people we won't meet, decades into the future'. Tackling climate change presents us with a broad and multilayered challenge, encompassing a wide variety of issues. These range from combating poverty in the developing world to energy security in the developed world. Conventional models of political decision-making struggle to cope with such challenges. This can, in part, explain the slow process of political agreement at the international level.

Second, by its very nature, tackling climate change necessitates long-term strategies and commitments. Yet, politicians invariably think in the short to medium term, governed by the exigencies of the electoral cycle. In short, they want to get elected. And there can be no getting away from the fact that effective action on climate change will require real sacrifices by voters, in particular, in the developed world. How do we move to a new kind of politics in which politicians are honest with their electorates about the need to use less energy, to fly less frequently and to make less use of their cars? A major shift is needed in the psychology of politicians and voters alike. Are politicians capable of making the necessary 'brave decisions', spelling out the sacrifices that need to be made? How will voters respond at the ballot box?

This brings us, third, to the issue of public policy and democracy. Meadowcroft (2012, p 283) writes of the 'difficulties which democratic political systems experience in managing environmental problems'. Arias-Maldonado (2012, p 97) goes even further, asking whether 'Sustainability is compatible with democracy'. The answer to this must surely be 'yes'. By its very nature, building a more sustainable world necessitates a broad base of public support and public action. A top-down political approach will not work. Political will may seem to be in short supply at the moment, but, as Flavin and Engelman (2009, p 8) have cogently argued, it is 'a renewable resource'.

It is true that in seeking to combat climate change, politicians face a real dilemma. Telling voters (especially in the developed world) that tacking climate change will require fundamental changes to traditional notions of economic growth and individual prosperity hardly seems like a recipe for success at the ballot box. Yet, the fact remains that for millions of the world's poor and unemployed, the current system is simply not delivering what it is supposed to deliver. We need to move to what Jackson has described as 'prosperity without growth' (Jackson, 2011). Politicians need to shift the terms of the debate, so that meeting the challenge of climate change is not seen in negative terms, but instead viewed as a real opportunity to build a more sustainable and fulfilling way of life. However, this will require a qualitative psychological adjustment on the part of both politicians and voters alike, especially those in the developed world, who for more than five decades since the end of the Second World War have operated within a paradigm whose modus operandi was the pursuit of ever-increasing economic growth, supporting a seemingly unstoppable tidal wave of consumerism. Therefore, there is also a really important role here for education for sustainable development.

Conclusion

Tackling climate change and creating a more sustainable way of living is the greatest challenge facing us in the 21st century. The speed and degree of environmental change that we are witnessing is unprecedented (Lord, 2011, p 5). It is all too easy to feel overwhelmed by this challenge and to fall into a counsel of despair. As Berners-Lee and Clark (2013, p 3) observe, 'some of the facts about climate change are uncomfortable'. Yet, not taking action is simply not an option. Planet earth is the only home we have. Its resources are limited. We need to have a different kind of politics and a different kind of economics if we are to work within the carrying capacity of the earth. Politicians need to be honest with voters and citizens, but voters and citizens need to be honest with themselves. Awareness of the issues is not enough – this needs to translate into action.

We need a radical reconfiguration of the way we do politics and economics at local, national and global levels if we are to move towards a more sustainable way of living and protect the planet on which we all depend. This is not to suggest that we need to start again and change everything. Not only would this be nigh on impossible, but it would ignore the real latent potential that already exists to build a more sustainable world. As a recent report by the WWF (2012, p 6) notes, 'we have more than 50 years of experience and scientific know how. We have the passion and the determination to build a future where people and nature thrive'.

At the local, national, regional and global levels, there are a myriad of actions – some seemingly small, some large – which, taken together, are having a significant impact upon tackling climate change and building a more sustainable world. So, we do not want to throw the baby out with the bath water, but we need to recognise the reality of planetary boundaries and adopt new ways of thinking. It is a challenge that cannot be avoided, but it is also a challenge that can be met.

References

Abramsky, K. (2010) *Sparking a worldwide energy revolution: social struggles in the transition to a post-petrol world*, Oakland, CA: AK Press.

Abramson, P. and Ingelhart, R. (1995) *Value change in global perspective*, Michigan, MI: University of Michigan Press.

Arias-Maldonado, M. (2012) *Real green: sustainability after the end of nature*, Surrey: Ashgate.

Barbier, E. (2010) *Rethinking the economic recovery: a global green deal*, Cambridge: Cambridge University Press.

Berners-Lee, M. and Clark, D. (2013) *The burning question*, London: Profile Books.

Blewitt, J. (2008) *Understanding sustainable development*, London: Earthscan.

Borghesi, S. and Vercelli, A. (2008) *Global sustainability: social and environmental condition*, Basingstoke: Palgrave Macmillan.

Bowen, A. (2012) 'Green growth, what does it mean?', *Environmental Scientist*, December.

Brand, S. (2012) 'Some environmentalists back nuclear power', *San Francisco Chronicle*, 13 June.

Butterfield, R. (2012) 'The Guardian letters page', *The Guardian*, 13 September.

Cable, S. (2012) *Sustainable failures: environmental policy and democracy in a petro dependent world*, Philadelphia, PA: Temple University Press.

Carson, R. (2003) *The silent spring*, New York, NY: Mariner Books.

Casal, P. (2012) 'Progressive environmental taxes: a defence', *Political Studies*, vol 60, no 2, pp 419–33.

Chaffin, J. (2012) 'Cheap and dirty', *Financial Times*, 14 February.

Chivers, D (2010) *The no-nonsense guide to climate change: the science, the solutions, the way forward*, Oxford: New Internationalist.

Connelly, J. and Smith, G. (2003) *Politics and the environment: from theory to practice*, London: Routledge.

Connif, R. (2012) 'What's wrong with putting a price on nature?', *Enviro 360*, 18 October, Yale School of forestry and Environmental Studies, New Haven, CT.

Engelman, R. (2012) 'Growth of carbon capture stalled in 2011'. Available at: www.worldwatch.org/growth-carbon-capture-and-storage-stalled-2011

Evans, J., Jones, P. and Krueger, R. (2009) 'Organic regeneration and sustainability or can the credit crunch save our cities', *Local Environment*, vol 14, no 7, pp 683–98.

Farley, F.M. and Smith, Z.A. (2014) *Sustainability: if it's everything is it nothing?*, London: Routledge.

Flavin, C. and Engelman, R. (2009) 'The perfect storm', in Worldwatch Institute (ed) *State of the world 2009: confronting climate change*, London: Earthscan.

Giddens, A. (2011) *The politics of climate change*, Cambridge: Polity Press.

Godden, D. (2010) 'Valuing eco system services: a critical review', 54th Annual Conference, Australian Agricultural and Resource Economics Society, 10–12 February, Adelaide, Australia.

Gonez-Baggethun, E. and Perez, M. (2011) 'Economic valuation and the commodification of eco system services', *Progress in Physical Geography*, vol 35, no 5, pp 613–28.

Gosling, S., Warren, R., Arnell, N., Good, P., Caesar, J., Bernie, D., Lowe, J., Van der Linden, P., O'Hanley, J. and Smith, S. (2011) 'A review of developments in climate change science. Part II: the global-scale impacts of climate change', *Progress in Physical Geography*, vol 35, no 4, pp 443–64.

Graaf, J., Wann, D. and Naylor, T. (2001) *Affluenza: the all consuming epidemic*, San Francisco, CA: Berret-Koehler Publishers.

Hannigan, J. (2011) 'Social challenge: causes, explanations and solutions', in T. Fitzpatrick (ed) *Understanding the environment and social policy*, Bristol: The Policy Press.

Hardin, G. (1998) 'The tragedy of the commons', in J. Baden and D. Noonan (eds) *Managing the commons*, Indiana, IN: Indiana University Press.

Helliwell, W., Layard, R. and Sachs, J. (2013) *World happiness report*, New York, NY: Columbia University, Earth Institute.

HM Government (2013) *The UK's nuclear future*, London: HMSO.

IEA (International Energy Authority) (2011) 'The world is locking itself into an unstoppable energy future which would have far reaching consequences, IEA warns in its latest World Energy Outlook', press release, 9 November. Available at: www.iea.org/newsroomandevents/pressreleases/2011/November/name,20318,en.html

IPCC (2013) *Climate change 2013, synthesis report: contribution of working groups I, II and III to the fifth assessment report*, Cambridge: Cambridge University Press.

Jackson, T. (2011) *Prosperity without growth: economics for a finite planet*, London: Earthscan.

Jackson, T. (2012) *Leuphana Sustainability Summit*, 29 February, Luneburg, Germany: University of Leuphana.

James, O. (2007) *Affluenza*, London: Random House.

Jones, P. and Evans, J. (2008) *Urban regeneration in the UK*, London: Sage.

Jones, V. (2012) *Rebuild the dream*, New York, NY: Nation Books.

Jordan, A., Huitema, D. and Van Asselt, H. (2011) 'Climate change policy in the European Union', in A. Jordan, D. Huitema, H. Van Asselt, T. Ray and F. Berkhout (eds) *Climate change policy in the European Union: confronting the dilemmas of mitigation and adaptation*, Cambridge: Cambridge University Press.

Leach, M., Scoones, I. and Stirling, A. (2010) *Dynamic sustainability: technology, environment and social justice*, London: Earthscan.

Lemos, M. and Agrawal, A. (2009) 'Environmental governance and political science', in A. Agrawal, M. Delmas, M. Lemos and O. Young (eds) *Governance for the environment: new perspectives*, Cambridge: Cambridge University Press.

Lord, N. (2011) *Early warming: crisis and response in the climate-changed north*, Berkeley, CA: Counterpoint.

Lovelock, J. (2004) 'Nuclear power is the only green solution', *The Independent*, 24 May.

Lynas, M. (2008) *Six degrees: our future on a hotter planet*, London: Harper Perennial.

Lynas, M. (2012) 'In defence of nuclear power'. Available at: www.marklynas.org/2012/in-defence-of-nuclear-power/

Meadowcroft, J. (2012) 'Pushing the boundaries: governance for sustainable development and politics of limits', in J. Meadowcroft, O. Langhelle and A. Ruud (eds) *Governance, democracy and sustainable development: moving beyond the impasse*, Cheltenham: Edward Elgar.

Meyer, A. (2001) *Contraction and convergence: the global solution to climate change*, Cambridge: Green Books.

Millennium Eco System Assessment (2005) *Eco system and human well being: general synthesis*, Washington DC: Island Press.

Mills, C. (2013) 'Why nudges matter: a reply to Goodwin', *Politics*, vol 33, no 1, pp 28–36.

NCAR (National Centre for Atmospheric Research) (2011) 'Switching from coal to natural gas would do little for global climate, study indicates'. Available at: www2.ucar.edu/atmosnews/news/5292/switching-coal-natural-gas-would-do-little-global-climate-study-indicates

New Economics Foundation (2014) 'Homepage'. Available at: www.neweconomics.org

New Economy Coalition (2014) 'Homepage'. Available at: www.neweconomy.net

Rawles, K. (2012) *The carbon cycle: crossing the great divide*, Isle of Lewis: Two Ravens Press.

Reich, R. (2011) *Aftershock: the next economy and America's future*, New York, NY: Vantage Books.

Roberts, P. (2005) *The end of oil: on the edge of a perilous world*, New York, NY: First Mariner Books.

Sandel, M. (2012) *What money can't buy: the moral limits of markets*, London: Allen Lane.

Schumacher Institute (2013) *The Bristol declaration: a city's contribution to the post-2015 global development conversation*, Bristol: Schumacher Institute for Sustainable Systems.

Sedlacko, M. and Martinuzzi, A. (2012) 'Governance for sustainable development, evaluation and learning: an introduction', in M. Sedlacko and A. Martinuzzi (eds) *Governance by evaluation for sustainable development: institutional capacities and learning*, Cheltenham: Edward Elgar.

Simms, A. and Boyle, D. (2009) *The new economics: a bigger picture*, London: Earthscan.

Spectre, M. (2012) 'The climate fixer: is there a technological solution to global warming?', *The New Yorker*, 14 May.

Stern, N. (2006) *Stern review on economics of climate change*, London: HMSO.

Stiglitz, J., Sen, A. and Fitooussi, J.P. (2009) *Report of the Commission on the Measurement of Economic Performance and Social Progress*. Available at www.stiglitz-sen-fitoussi.fr/en/index/

Thaler, R.H. and Sunstein, C.R. (2008) *Nudge: improving decisions about health, wealth and happiness*, London and New Haven, CT: Yale University Press.

Tollefson, J. (2012) 'Air sampling reveals high emissions from gas field: methane leaks during production may offset climate benefits of natural gas', *Nature*, 7 February.

UN (United Nations) (1987) *UN Commission on Environment and Development*, New York, NY: UN.

UNDP (United Nations Development Programme) (2013) *Assessing progress in Africa towards the millennium development goals*, New York, NY: UNDP.

UNESCO (United Nations Science and Cultural Organisation) (2011a) *EFA global monitoring report – the hidden crisis: armed conflict and education*, Paris: UNESCO.

UNESCO (2011b) *From green economies to green societies*, Paris: UNESCO.

UNRISD (United Nations Research Institute for Social Development) (2012) *Social dimensions of green economy*, Research and Policy Brief 12, Geneva, Switzerland: UNRISD.

Vidal, J. (2011) 'Glaciers melt into history as Africa faces climate disaster', *The Guardian*, 2 December.

Vogler, J. (2008) 'Environmental issues', in J. Baylis, S. Smith and P. Owen (eds) *The globalisation of world politics*, Oxford: Oxford University Press.

WGBU (German Advisory Council on Global Change) (2011) *World transition: a social contract for sustainability*, Berlin: WGBU.

Wilkinson, R. and Pickett, K. (2010) *The spirit level: why equality is better for everyone?*, London: Penguin Books.

World Resources Institute (2005) *The world resources 2005*, Washington, DC: World Resources Institute.

Worldwatch Institute (2013) 'Developing renewable energy indicator'. Available at: www.worldwatch.org/developing-renewable-energy-indicators

WWF (World Wide Fund for Nature) (2012) *Annual review 2012 – a thriving future for the natural world: how we're making progress*, Godalming, Surrey: WWF UK.

TWO

The politics of sustainability: democracy and the limits of policy action

Stuart Wilks-Heeg

Introduction

This chapter examines the vexed issue of whether democracy represents part of the problem or part of the solution for efforts to forge an ecologically sustainable future. This is a debate that first emerged in the 1970s and that has recently been rekindled by the failure of national governments to reach international agreements with respect to reductions in carbon emissions and climate change mitigation. In response to this debate, the chapter offers two central arguments. First, it advances the view that Churchill's famous maxim 'Democracy is the worst form of government, except for all the others which have been tried from time to time' clearly applies to sustainability issues. Second, it proposes that governing for sustainability will require an active, urgent process of policy learning to ensure that the advantages of democratic approaches can be harnessed. These lessons will need to inform the framing of environmental policy at all levels of decision-making.

This first half of the chapter reviews the debate about authoritarian versus democratic approaches to environmental problems. It notes that many of the same shortcomings of existing representative democracy with respect to sustainability are identified by both schools of thought. The central point of disagreement relates to whether further ecological degradation is best achieved by limiting democracy or by deepening and extending it. The second half of the chapter then turns to examine the relative merits of democracy and non-democracy from both a theoretical and empirical perspective. The weight of evidence points clearly to the conclusion that democratic decision-making provides the preferred route to a sustainable future, if only as the 'least worst' option. Having concluded that democracy offers relative advantages over authoritarian approaches, the remainder of the chapter addresses the question of how democracies can better adapt to the challenges of sustainability.

Democracy and sustainability: two schools of thought

> Even the best democracies agree that when a major war approaches, democracy must be put on hold for the time being. I have a feeling that climate change may be an issue as severe as a war. It may be necessary to put democracy on hold for a while. (James Lovelock, cited in Hickman, 2010)

> The vision I see is not only a movement of direct democracy, of self- and co-determination and of non-violence, but a movement in which politics means the power to love and the power to feel united on the spaceship Earth. (Kelly, 1982)

There is a long-standing debate about whether environmental problems are most likely to be tackled successfully under democratic or authoritarian models of governance. Indeed, there are substantial bodies of both theoretical and empirical work that seek to assess the relative merits of democracy and non-democracy in tackling a wide range of ecological challenges. At the slight risk of simplification, two rival schools of thought may be identified, which I have chosen to label, respectively, as the 'green authoritarianism' and 'green democracy' perspectives. Despite significant shifts in environmental policy debates over time, these two contrasting positions can be traced back to the period in which a growing awareness of ecological issues first emerged in the late 1960s and 1970s.

Perhaps unusually for such diametrically opposed perspectives, there are enormous overlaps in the analyses of the problem offered by proponents of both 'green authoritarianism' and 'green democracy' solutions. The 'green authoritarianism' school argues that democracy will always be deficient in addressing environmental problems, since it will be virtually impossible to secure popular consent for almost universally unpopular policy measures. Consequently, and generally reluctantly, it is argued that only authoritarian regimes will be able to impose changes that will involve reduced levels of consumption, falling material standards of living, the placing of restrictions on the personal and corporate use of fossil fuels, and so on. The 'green democracy' perspective offers much the same by way of diagnosis of the problem, identifying particular institutional flaws in the operation of representative democracy with respect to environmental policymaking.

However, advocates of this perspective argue that the problem is that there is too little, rather than too much, democracy. The shortcomings of representative democracy in handling environmental problems are therefore best overcome by deepening and extending democracy in a variety of ways.

It is important to note that the 'green authoritarian' and 'green democracy' viewpoints do not cover the full range of perspectives on democracy and the environment. Sitting in-between these two contrasting schools of thought are a range of positions that see existing political arrangements as perfectly adequate for the task of addressing environmental issues. However, rather than making a robust case for how existing forms of representative democracy deal with environmental issues, these *status quo* positions generally downplay either the scale or urgency of ecological concerns. These perspectives may be grouped under three main headings: 'deny', 'defer' and 'displace'. The first position ('deny') takes issue with scientific evidence about issues like climate change and suggests that environmental questions have become a Trojan Horse for those who wish to impose extreme left-wing political agendas (for examples, see Monbiot, 2010). The second stance ('defer') urges against taking drastic short-term measures in response to environmental concerns on the grounds that other issues are more pressing (Lomborg, 2001, 2007). Central to this perspective is the view that human societies are inherently adaptable and processes of technological innovation will provide solutions to environmental problems over time. The third position ('displace') accepts that environmental problems exist but does not see them primarily as a political issue. The market mechanism, rather than the state, is seen as the most effective means of reducing environmental harm (Anderson and Leal, 2001).

While all three of these perspectives have achieved some prominence, I do not propose to discuss them in any further detail here. Along with the other authors who have contributed to this volume, I accept the scientific consensus that urgent action is needed to tackle environmental problems, particularly climate change. In addition, while technological innovation and market adaptation will be necessary to achieve a sustainable future, experience to date suggests that these processes alone will be far from sufficient (Robbins et al, 2010). Only a few fringe accounts suggest that environmental problems can be tackled without concerted government action or that governments are already doing enough to prevent profound and irreversible ecological damage. Achieving sustainability, therefore, requires political will to be mobilised to introduce significant policy change. The question is, how?

Green authoritarianism

While early environmental movements tended to be highly democratic in character, and have generally remained so ever since, a handful of early writers on the subject saw political liberties and democratic decision-making as a major obstacle to saving the planet (Heilbroner, 1974; Ophuls, 1977; Gurr, 1985). Much of this work took its cue from Hardin's (1968) evocative metaphor of 'the tragedy of the commons'. Hardin used this notion, which refers to the overgrazing of livestock on commonly owned pastures, as a metaphor to illustrate how apparently rational behaviour on the part of individuals leads to collective ruin arising from environmental pollution and resource depletion. As such, Hardin (1968, p 1245) argued that 'we are locked into a system of "fouling our own nest", so long as we behave only as independent, rational free-enterprisers'. While he did not advocate the curtailing of democratic freedoms, Hardin did suggest that it was necessary to restrict specific liberties, including the 'freedom to breed', and argued that this should be achieved through coercion, albeit 'mutual coercion, mutually agreed upon by the majority of the people affected' (Hardin, 1968, p 1247).

It was the subsequent work of Heilbroner (1974), Ophuls (1977) and later Gurr (1985) that made the direct case that democracy would be rendered unviable by ecological problems and resource scarcity. It is important to underline that their case rested not on a desire to see authoritarian rule, but on an argument that democracy would collapse under conditions of extreme environmental stress arising from 'the limits to growth' (Meadows et al, 1972). The common thread in these accounts was that democracy requires the existence of levels of prosperity and equity that would become unattainable under conditions of resource scarcity. The ecological limits to wealth creation and distribution would thus reveal democratic institutions to be fragile. As a consequence, authoritarian regimes or a 'sovereign power' would have to emerge to maintain social order and impose shared economic sacrifices on the population.

As is well known, the 'tragedy of the commons' and 'limits to growth' arguments that underpinned the conclusions reached by these authors were subject to robust challenge and ultimately gave way during the 1980s to the notion of sustainable development. Nonetheless, the question of whether democracies were fundamentally ill-suited to addressing environmental problems remained. The emergence of a scientific consensus on the urgent need to tackle climate change, and the failure of national governments to take sufficient action to cut carbon emissions to the levels recommended, have brought the question back into sharp focus. Shearman and Smith (2007, p 2) argue that democracy has failed with respect to climate change and that 'a form of authoritarianism based upon the rule of scientific experts' is likely to be the only alternative. Wells (2007, p 208) suggests that failure to find solutions to global environmental problems may come to necessitate the emergence of a 'Green Junta' capable of delivering 'strong government for a crowded planet'. Beeson (2010, p 276) proposes that in the specific context of South-East Asia, authoritarian regimes may well be better placed to tackle environmental problems than democracies. As the opening quotes to this section of the chapter illustrate, even James Lovelock, originator of Gaia theory, has come to the view that it may be necessary to put democracy 'on hold'.

Green democracy

While there is a superficial logic to the case for green authoritarianism, the flaws in the argument are legion, as I will explain in a moment. Yet, while ideas about Green Juntas or dictatorships of experts are likely to be well wide of the mark, the same cannot be said about the diagnosis that democracies are struggling to deal with environmental problems. Indeed, it is vital to recognise, following Holden (2002), that a variety of compelling reasons have been offered as to why democracy, in its current form, is 'totally unsuitable' for the task of addressing environmental problems. However, the 'green democracy' perspective sees these shortcomings as evidence that new forms of democracy must be developed rather than as a case for non-democratic alternatives. Before considering the options that have been put forward for reforming democracy, it is therefore important to consider the specific problems that these accounts identify with how democracies currently approach environmental problems. Four primary problems are referred to in the literature.

First, there is the problem of *short-termism*. It is widely argued that the electoral cycle, typically, three to five years in a representative democracy, renders it extremely difficult to tackle environmental problems. The causes and consequences of environmental damage are long-term dynamics. Climate change is a key example. It is widely recognised that a series of short-term measures must be taken by national governments to reduce carbon emissions in order to minimise the long-term risks associated with rising average global temperatures. However, in a democracy, short-term economic performance and public perceptions of material living standards remain crucial factors in determining a government's prospects of re-election. Politicians will generally be reluctant, therefore, to advocate policies that can only achieve long-term goals as a result of considerable short-term sacrifice (Johnston, 2007). Consider, for example, the challenge of convincing electors of the need to reduce energy consumption now in order to reduce the impact of climate change 30, 50 or even 100 years hence. As Held and Hervey (2009, p 5) note: 'it is extremely difficult for governments to impose large-scale changes on an electorate whose votes they depend on, in order to tackle a problem whose impact will only be felt by future generations'.

Second, we have the question of *geographical mismatch*: the temporal constraints on how democracies approach environmental issues are compounded by a set of spatial limitations. Democracy evolved as a system for governing nation-states (albeit with varying degrees of sub-national autonomy for regions and localities). However, the organisation of democracy around nation-states restricts the possibilities of addressing environmental problems as cross-border and planetary concerns. It has frequently been noted that pollution does not respect national borders and it is therefore well-established that problems such as ozone depletion and climate change cannot be addressed by nations acting unilaterally. Yet, multilateral arrangements for environmental policymaking are accepted to be too weak. A key problem for almost all attempts to secure international cooperation in environmental matters is that such efforts are consistently undermined by governments who avoid compliance because their ultimate accountability is to national electorates (Held and Hervey, 2009).

Third, there is the issue of *knowledge deficits*. While environmental policy debates must be informed by expert scientific knowledge, the task of communicating technically complex issues to lay audiences, ranging from cabinet ministers to the general public, presents a significant democratic challenge (Lafferty and Meadowcroft, 1996; Holden, 2002). Patterns of causality tend to be complex in environmental science and, as with any academic discipline, there are inevitably gaps in the knowledge base, as well as evidence that is either partial or contested. Where research appears to reach ambiguous conclusions about the causes of particular problems, their likely consequences or the need for, and likely effectiveness of, policies intended to tackle them, it will inevitably compound the constraints on policy action. Indeed, in a democracy, any apparent contradictions are likely to be seized upon, and misrepresented, by media outlets, pressure groups and interest organisations to dissuade politicians from taking action.

Fourth, there is the debate about *power imbalances*. All of the preceding constraints are likely to be further compounded by the resource inequalities in pressure group politics. In recent decades, established democracies have witnessed a surge in the membership of environmental organisations. However, while these organisations often have many more members than political parties, their influence is modest compared to the peak organisation of business, or even individual corporations. The power of corporate interests to skew policy outcomes in a democracy is well established. These dynamics are nowhere more evident than in environmental policy, where large corporations often have most to lose from enhanced environmental regulations.

In recognising these problems, however, the 'green democracy' perspective makes the case for more democracy rather than less. It is flawed democracy, rather than democracy per se, that is the barrier to moving to a stronger version of sustainability (O'Riordan, 1996). Starting from this principle, a range of suggestions have been made for ways in which further democratisation would enhance environmental policy responses. While highly diverse in character, these proposals are linked by a common thread, namely, to overcome one or more of the constraints outlined earlier.

A common theme is the need for far greater use of deliberative democracy, through which citizens would be actively engaged in the process of debating evidence of environmental problems, considering policy scenarios and alternatives, and advising on, or making, decisions about policy choices (Gunderson, 1995). The central characteristic of deliberative decision-making is that it is an iterative process of debate, though which participants' views are shaped by exposure to evidence and debate. Deliberative approaches range from the convening of focus groups to provide feedback to policymakers through to the delegation of decision-making to citizens' juries or, in Germany, 'planning cells' (Coenen, 2009). It is argued that, in contrast to representative democracy, deliberative mechanisms promote far greater understanding of the issues at stake and bind participants much more strongly to environmental commitments (Gunderson, 1995). While the use of deliberative decision-making in general remains limited, there is evidence to support its effectiveness in environmental policy. Niemeyer (2012, pp 4–5) finds that where the engagement of citizens is 'authentic', 'there is already a good deal of theoretical and empirical support for the argument that deliberation produces improved environmental outcomes'. Principles of deliberative democracy have also been applied to the international level to make the argument for 'stakeholder democracy' in global environmental governance (Bäckstrand, 2006).

Others have proposed alternative ways of overcoming the temporal and spatial problems outlined earlier. For instance, Dobson (1996, p 125) advocates reforms to representative democracy that would take account of three new constituencies of interest: future generations, other species and citizens elsewhere. He proposes that representatives of each of these constituencies would be returned to parliament by proxy electorates, thereby ensuring that these interests are taken into account in the policy process. Reforms to improve transparency and flows of information and to tackle imbalances of power among interest groups have also been proposed. As part of a wider package of measures, O'Riordan (1996, p 150) advocates 'an ecological right to know' as a means of ensuring maximum public knowledge about environmental conditions. He also proposes the development of 'ecological corporatism', through which environmental and welfare organisations would secure representation in round-table deliberations with government, business and unions (O'Riordan, 1996, p 150).

The political limits of sustainability

> If we were to put forward a solution to climate change, something that would involve drastic cuts in economic growth or standards of living, it would not matter how justified it was, it would simply not be agreed to. (Blair, 2005)

> I have therefore come to believe that an essential prerequisite for saving the environment is the spread of democratic government to more nations of the world. (Al Gore, 1992, cited in Neumayer, 2002, p 139)

At this stage, it may be wise to pause for a reality check. The claims made earlier for the benefits and viability of deliberative democracy might risk appearing overly optimistic. Meanwhile, proposals to establish democratic rights for future generations or for non-humans may sound utopian, at best. There is certainly no shortage of proposals for how democratic environmental governance could be improved, but is there any realistic hope that they would overcome the well-documented shortcomings of democracy outlined earlier? Can there be any grounds for believing that democracy, reformed or otherwise, is capable of responding to the challenge of environmental harm? When it comes to saving the planet, is democracy better than authoritarianism, in theory or in practice?

Why democracy is better in theory

In fact, the theoretical advantages of democracy over authoritarianism are substantial with respect to environmentalism. A key source in this respect is Payne (1995), who argues that a number of core features of democratic politics mean that environmental issues are more likely to be taken up than under non-democratic regimes. The freedom of the press ensures that information about environmental problems is available. Because citizens are better informed about the issues, moreover, they will be able to take advantage of both the freedom of speech they enjoy in a democracy to express their concerns and also the freedom of association to form interest groups making the case for policy action. Since governments are more accountable in a democratic system and must respond in some way to such pressures from civil society: they will be forced to respond to concerns about environmental issues and, indeed, broader sustainability issues such as equality, access to education and human rights. Competitive elections and party systems may also bring environmental issues on to the electoral agenda, either through existing parties or the formation of green or ecology parties. Finally, Payne argues that democracies are also more likely to cooperate internationally on a variety of matters, including efforts to tackle cross-border environmental problems.

Since non-democracies are characterised by an absence of such political freedoms and competitive political pressures, they lack the mechanisms through which environmental issues can come on to the agenda. Authoritarian leaders are not held to account, place restrictions on the availability and dissemination of information, and limit the scope for groups to mobilise and campaign (Winslow, 2005). Moreover, as Congleton (1992) suggests, authoritarian rulers tend to operate with even shorter time frames than democratic governments because of their continual concern to suppress dissent and opposition of any kind. As Ward (2008, p 387) explains, 'authoritarian rulers do not have incentives to adopt, or to stick with, sustainable policies. They prioritise rapid economic development to gain legitimacy and to bolster external security'. Finally, authoritarian leaders have potentially more to gain from economic activities that result in environmental harm. The profits from ecological damage may result in personal material gain for an authoritarian leader, who will be able to insulate him/herself from the harmful effects of such enterprises (Winslow, 2005).

Likewise, permitting economically profitable but environmentally damaging activity may serve as a means of securing continued political support from a narrow elite of wealthy individuals who are its primary beneficiaries (Ward, 2008). Even accepting the power imbalances that characterise interest group politics in democracies, there are 'many examples where business interests have been overwhelmed by environmental interests' (Bättig and Bernauer, 2009, p 289). It is extremely difficult, if not impossible, to identify equivalent scenarios under authoritarian regimes.

Democracy is also better in practice

Political theory is one thing. But do democracies ever live up to the ideal-type put forward by Payne? Evidence on the benefits of democracy for environmental outcomes is mixed (Winslow, 2005; Li and Reuveny, 2006; Ward, 2008), but is certainly strong enough to confirm that democracies generally outperform non-democracies in environmental protection. An array of quantitative studies have identified that democracy has a positive effect with respect to a range of environmental policy commitments and outcomes. Neumayer (2002, p 155) finds that democracy is positively associated with making environmental data available and with ensuring that a higher percentage of land is subject to special environmental protection. Both Torras and Boyce (1998) and Barrett and Graddy (2000) find that higher levels of political and civil rights lead to lower levels of air and water pollution. Harbaugh et al (2002) and Gleditsch and Sverdrup (2002) produce similar findings with regard to the positive effect of democracy on, respectively, sulphur dioxide and carbon dioxide emissions. Li and Reuveny (2006) reaffirm these findings with respect to sulphur dioxide and carbon dioxide, as well as finding that democracy is associated with lower levels of organic water pollution, deforestation and land degradation.

There is also evidence to suggest that democracies play a more constructive role in attempts to forge international cooperation to tackle cross-border environmental problems. Gleditsch and Sverdrup (2002) find a positive correlation between democracy and the ratification of environmental treaties. Similarly, Neumayer (2002) finds that, among both developed and less-developed countries, there is strong evidence that democracies are more likely to sign and ratify environmental agreements and take part in multilateral environmental organisations. With regard to international cooperation generally, it has also been demonstrated that democracies rarely, if ever, go to war with one another (Dorussen and Ward, 2008; Inglehart and Welzel, 2009).

Presented in this way, the relative benefits of democracy for sustainability are evident. However, a number of important cautions and caveats must be added. First, the relative advantage of democracy as a regime type across different types of environmental harm is highly uneven (Li and Reuveny, 2006). On some variables, notably, deforestation rates, the benefits of democracy are inconsistent and contested (for a discussion, see Winslow, 2005). Second, although democracies are more likely than non-democracies to sign up to international environmental agreements, there is no evidence that they perform better in delivering against these commitments. Bättig and Bernauer (2009) find that there is a 'words–deeds' gap in how democracies have responded to climate change. They examine 185 countries from 1990 to 2004 with respect to the extent of their cooperation in efforts to tackle climate change. While democracy is found to have a positive effect in securing commitment to climate change mitigation, there is no clear independent effect in relation to subsequent changes in emission levels.

This 'words–deeds gap' may partly be explained by substantial time lags in democracies bringing about improvements in environmental quality (Li and Reuveny, 2006; Gallagher and Thacker, 2008). While there is fairly consistent overall evidence that democracy is better for the environment than authoritarianism, it would be stretching this conclusion to breaking point to suggest that democracy provides a definitive route to sustainability. There is no democracy in the world that surpasses the United Nations Human Development Index threshold for high human development and that is within the World Wide Fund for Nature's measure of available world bio-capacity per capita. Indeed, the only country that does succeed on both these criteria is the clearly exceptional, and non-democratic, case of Cuba (Wilkinson and Pickett, 2009).

Nonetheless, if the choice is narrowed down to one of democracy versus authoritarianism, there are strong theoretical and empirical grounds to suggest that democracy is, by some margin, the lesser of two evils. Winston Churchill's maxim that 'Democracy is the worst form of government, except for all the others which have been tried from time to time' applies particularly well to environmental sustainability issues. While democracy produces a very weak version of sustainability, stable autocracies clearly produce the worst environmental outcomes (Ward, 2008). This conclusion is reinforced by case studies of environmental policy in authoritarian regimes, which clearly demonstrate that they have worse records than liberal democracies (Jancar-Webster, 1993; Desai, 1998). As Ward (2008, p 406) puts it: 'liberal democracy can be given the more positive report, although green theorists will no doubt remark on the numerous ways in which it could do better'.

Can democracy do better?

Quite aside from evidence that democracies perform better on most environmental policy outcomes, there are other good reasons to suppose that democracy is 'the only game in town' when it comes to sustainable development. There were perhaps understandable reasons in the 1970s for authors such as Heilbroner (1974) and Ophuls (1977) to see democracy as fragile or under threat. However, the direction of travel in political systems globally since the late 1980s has been very much towards democracy. There were only 25 countries classified as democracies in 1950. By 1990, following the collapse of communism in Eastern Europe, this number had grown to 65 (Dahl, 1998, p 8). Freedom House (2012) counted 117 electoral democracies in 2011 based on its widely used definition, with democracies amounting for 60% of all countries in the world. Admittedly, the recent growth in the number of democracies globally arises in part from the rise in the number of independent countries. Nonetheless, it is virtually unthinkable that this long-run process of democratisation could be reversed, or that any serious attempt would be made to do so. The question that is therefore raised is whether environmentalists should 'just try to make the best of available political structures' or whether a more radical democratic transformation is required (Dryzek, 1996, p 110).

The 'green democracy' perspective discussed earlier in this chapter offered a variety of proposals for ways in which democratic governance could be reconfigured, in some cases, quite radically, to ensure stronger environmental outcomes. While there is sound evidence to support the claims made for the advantages of deliberative democracy, adopting it on a large scale would require a radical shift from current norms of representative democracy. It is far from clear where the impetus for such changes would come from, particularly in established democracies, where there are few pressures from either elites or the public for such changes. Certainly, the importing of deliberative elements into existing environmental decision-making has been shown to be both viable and promising. Building on this experience, while also rendering environmental decision-making more open and transparent, should help to move democratic approaches to environmental issues closer to the theoretical model offered by Payne (1995). However, as yet, there are few, if any, genuine examples of a generalised shift from representative to deliberative democracy. As such, a 'realist' viewpoint would almost certainly have to start from the premise that existing systems of representative democracy will remain dominant for some time to come.

Given this context, the viability of achieving a more sustainable future within existing institutional frameworks hinges crucially on the relationship between economic development, liberal democracy and environmental harm. There is a long-standing recognition of the historical relationship between (capitalist) economic growth and democracy. The original hypothesis put forward by the 'modernisation school' (Lipset, 1959) was that development both induces and sustains democracy. The notion of development as a more or less automatic trigger for democracy has been increasingly challenged. Hadenius and Teorell (2005, p 102) find that while development has a casual effect in moving semi-democracies towards democracy, it has little impact on authoritarian regimes. In a similar vein, Przeworski et al (2000, p 78) offer compelling evidence that development is far less important in generating democracy than in sustaining it. Setting aside disagreements about causality for a moment, it is undeniable that the rise of liberal democracy has been underpinned by continual improvements in material living standards facilitated by economic growth (and the widespread availability of cheap fossil fuels). Conversely, historical experience clearly suggests that long periods of economic stagnation or decline have a destabilising effect on democratic institutions. It was for this reason that some of those who assumed that there were ecological 'limits to growth' in the 1970s felt that democracy would be rendered unworkable by environmental crises. The one solution to this conundrum that would prevent the slide into authoritarianism would be if development were not a zero-sum game between economic growth and environmental damage.

It is well known that energy use, pollution, deforestation and other environmental harms initially increase sharply with economic development. Indeed, measures of energy use were once used as a standard indicator of development, based on the assumption that more developed economies would automatically use ever-higher levels of energy per capita. However, since the 1970s, some evidence has emerged that beyond a particular level of national income, environmental harm tends to be reduced. Much attention has been paid to testing the hypothesis of the 'environmental Kuznets curve' (EKC). In essence, the EKC suggests that although resource use and emissions per capita increase sharply as gross domestic product (GDP) per capita rises, once a specific level of development is achieved, per capita resource use and pollution will decline rapidly as per capita income increases. The EKC has often been cited as evidence that environmental quality is effectively a 'luxury good' that requires a specific level of development to be achieved (Yandle et al, 2002). It also offers the optimistic scenario that most contemporary environmental problems will fade over time as development proceeds based on principles of 'ecological modernisation'.

In truth, however, there is no consistent evidence to support the existence of an EKC (Stern, 2004). While the hypothesis holds for certain pollutants, it clearly cannot be generalised for all forms of environmental degradation. Moreover, cross-national comparisons reveal huge variations in the relationship between economic growth and environmental outcomes. Unsurprisingly, where environmental variables such as per capita emissions do show improvements over time, policy choices are the determining factor, rather than income levels (Martin, 2002). Similarly, Jahn (1998) finds a strong negative association between (neo)liberal policy regimes, in which environmental regulation tends to be weakest, and measures of environmental quality. These observations are significant in light of two other pieces of evidence: first, the advantages of democracy for sustainability may only emerge over time; and, second, some models of representative democracy are likely to boast better track records than others.

In their analysis of the relationship between democracy and environmental policy outcomes, Gallagher and Thacker (2004) examine this time-lag effect. They develop the notion of 'democracy stock', which refers to the 'accumulation and evolution of democratic institutions over time'. Gallagher and Thacker then apply this measure to time-series data on changes in sulphur and carbon dioxide emissions. Their findings suggest that countries with longer histories of strong democracy have seen higher reductions in pollution over time. Or, put another way, their findings offer evidence that while democracy does bring environmental benefits, it only does so in the long run. The delayed effect of democracy on environmental policy may help explain the contradictory results obtained from attempts to model how levels of environmental damage change at different stages of development.

Finally, it is important to note that there is evidence to suggest that some models of democracy appear to be more effective in tackling environmental problems than others. In particular, the cluster of countries in Northern Europe with stronger environmental outcomes, notably, the Nordic states, the Benelux countries, Austria and Germany, appears to be associated strongly with neo-corporatist interest group arrangements (Scruggs, 1999; Jahn, 1998). Neo-corporatism is characterised by forms of functional representation through which key economic decisions are negotiated between governments and key interest groups, notably, business organisations and trade unions. A defining feature of what Lijphart (1999) describes as 'consensual democracy', neo-corporatism is especially evident in smaller North European states with proportional electoral systems and a high degree of openness to the global economy. There is much evidence that these arrangements help to reduce socio-economic inequality and provide for a longer-term focus in economic management and related public policy decisions. There are plenty of examples of how such thinking can productively shape environmental policy in consensual-corporatist democracies. Carter (2007) cites Norway and Sweden as cases where environmental interests have become integrated into different aspects of the neo-corporatist policy process. Similarly, the growth of the green technology sector in Germany from the 1990s onwards was supported by neo-corporatist-style arrangements. While underlining that these countries can by no means be considered 'paragons of ecological virtue', Carter (2007, p 234) underlines that they provide a clear contrast to Anglo-American societies, 'where environmental groups generally remain outsiders in the policy process and market liberal ideologies have exercised most influence'.

Conclusion

This chapter has shown that there is much agreement that the current structures and process of representative democracy present a problem for the achievement of sustainability. Both the 'green democracy' and 'green authoritarianism' perspectives point to similar ecological flaws in representative democracy. The tendency for democratic politics to focus on the short-term interests of electors within a nation-state framework is clearly at odds with the development of long-term solutions for global ecological problems. Similarly, the priority given to political and economic considerations ahead of scientific evidence reflects the difficulty in achieving a broad societal consensus in a democracy about the need to take tough policy choices.

Nonetheless, there is scant evidence to suggest that non-democratic approaches provide any kinds of alternative. There are very strong theoretical, pragmatic and empirical reasons to support the view that democratic decision-making constitutes 'the only game in town' when it comes to adapting to the challenges of sustainability. When it comes to a straight comparison between regime types, democracy outperforms autocracy. However, while the relative advantages of democratic decision-making on national environmental policy outcomes are demonstrable, the evidence base does not live up to the persuasive theoretical assumptions that democratic institutions will reduce environmental harm as part of a process of ecological modernisation. Despite its clear theoretical superiority over authoritarianism, democracy offers neither an ecological panacea nor a 'quick fix' with respect to what are generally regarded as problems requiring urgent action. Additional questions arise as to whether national governments, democratically elected or not, are able to work together to tackle environmental problems requiring international cooperation.

There are a few, small grounds for optimism. Democracy does appear to deliver very clear ecological benefits over the longer term. Meanwhile, models of consensual-corporatist decision-making, as well as experiments in deliberative democracy, provide some pointers as to how a democratic route to sustainability could be forged. Crucially, the process of learning from the more successful examples of national policy frameworks for sustainability must be combined with more effective mechanisms of global governance in environmental policy. If these objectives are to be achieved, the task of harnessing, and strengthening, the relative advantages of democratic approaches to environmental challenges must become a central focus for research, policy transfer and political reform strategies at both the national and the international levels.

References

Anderson, T.L. and Leal, D.R. (2001) *Free market environmentalism* (rev edn), New York, NY: Palgrave.

Bäckstrand, K. (2006) 'Democratizing global environmental governance? Stakeholder democracy after the World Summit on Sustainable Development', *European Journal of International Relations*, vol 12, no 4, pp 467–98.

Barrett, S. and Graddy, K. (2000) 'Freedom, growth and the environment', *Environment and Development Economics*, vol 5, no 4, pp 433–56.

Bättig, M.B. and Bernauer, T. (2009) 'National institutions and global public goods: are democracies more cooperative in climate change policy?', *International Organization*, vol 63, no 2, pp 281–308.

Beeson, M. (2010) 'The coming of environmental authoritarianism', *Environmental Politics*, vol 19, no 2, pp 276–94.

Blair, T. (2005) Speech at the World Economic Forum, Davos, 26 January.

Carter, N. (2007) *The politics of the environment: ideas, activism, policy*, Cambridge: Cambridge University Press.

Coenen, F. (ed) (2009) *Public participation and better environmental decisions*, New York, NY: Springer.

Congleton, R.D. (1992) 'Political institutions and pollution control', *The Review of Economics and Statistics*, vol 74, no 3, pp 412–21.

Dahl, R. (1998) *On democracy*, New Haven, CT: Yale University Press.

Desai, U. (ed) (1998) *Ecological policy and politics in developing countries: economic growth, democracy, and environment*, Albany, NY: State University of New York Press.

Dobson, A. (1996) 'Representative democracy and the environment', in W.M. Lafferty and J. Meadowcroft (eds) *Democracy and the environment*, London: Edward Elgar, pp 124–39.

Dorussen, H. and Ward, H. (2008) 'Inter governmental organizations and the Kantian peace: a network perspective', *Journal of Conflict Resolution*, vol 52, no 2, pp 189–212.

Dryzek, J.S. (1996) 'Strategies of ecological democratization', in W.M. Lafferty and J. Meadowcroft (eds) *Democracy and the environment*, London: Edward Elgar, pp 86–107.

Freedom House (2012) *Freedom in the world 2012*, Washington, DC: Freedom House.

Gallagher, K.P and Thacker, S.C. (2008) 'Democracy, income and environmental quality', Working Paper 164, PERI, University of Massachusetts Amherst.

Gleditsch, N.P. and Sverdrup, B.O. (2002) 'Democracy and the environment', in E.A. Page and M. Redclift (eds) *Human society and the environment: international comparisons*, Cheltenham: Edward Elgar, pp 45–70.

Gore, A. (1992) *Earth in the balance*, San Diego, CA: Harcourt Brace Jovanovich.

Gunderson, A.G. (1995) *Environmental promise of democratic deliberation*, Madison, WI: University of Wisconsin Press.

Gurr, T.R. (1985) 'On the political consequences of scarcity and economic decline', *International Studies Quarterly*, vol 29, no 1, pp 51–75.

Hadenius, A. and Teorell, J. (2005) 'Cultural and economic prerequisites of democracy: reassessing recent evidence', *Studies in Comparative International Development*, vol 39, no 4, pp 87–106.

Harbaugh, W.T., Levinson, A. and Wilson, D.M. (2002) 'Reexamining the empirical evidence for an environmental Kuznets curve', *Review of Economics and Statistics*, vol 84, no 3, pp 541–51.

Hardin, G. (1968) 'The tragedy of the commons', *Science, New Series*, vol 162, no 3859, pp 1243–8.

Heilbroner, R. (1974) *An inquiry into the human prospect*, New York, NY: W.W. Norton.

Held, D. and Hervey, A.F. (2009) *Democracy, climate change and global governance: democratic agency and the policy menu ahead*, London: Policy Network.

Hickman, J. (2010) 'James Lovelock: humans are too stupid to prevent climate change', *The Guardian*, 29 March.

Holden, B. (2002) *Democracy and global warming*, London: Continuum.

Inglehardt, R. and Welzel, C. (2009) 'How development leads to democracy: what we know about modernization', *Foreign Affairs*, vol 88, no 2, pp 33–48.

Jahn, D. (1998) 'Environmental performance and policy regimes: explaining variations in 18 OECD-countries', *Policy Sciences*, vol 31, no 2, pp 107–31.

Jancar-Webster, B. (1993) *Environmental action in Eastern Europe: responses to the crisis*, Armonk: ME Sharpe.

Johnston, R. (2007) 'Representative democracy and environmental problem solution', in J. Pretty et al (eds) *Sage handbook of environment and society*, London: Sage, pp 281–98.

Kelly, P. (1982) Acceptance speech for the Right Livelihood Award, Stockholm, 9 December.

Lafferty, W.M. and Meadowcroft, J. (1996) *Democracy and the environment: problems and perspectives*, London: Edward Elgar.

Li, Q. and Reuveny, R. (2006) 'Democracy and environmental degradation', *International Studies Quarterly*, vol 50, no 4, pp 935–56.

Lijphart, A. (1999) *Patterns of democracy: government forms and performance in thirty-six countries*, New Haven, CT: Yale University Press.

Lipset, S.M. (1959) 'Some social requisites of democracy: economic development and political legitimacy', *The American Political Science Review*, vol 53, no 1, pp 69–105.

Lomborg, B. (2001) *The skeptical environmentalist*, Cambridge: Cambridge University Press.

Lomborg, B. (2007) *Cool it: the skeptical environmentalist's guide to global warming*, New York, NY: Knopf Doubleday.

Martin, C.M. (2002) 'The environmental Kuznets curve: a survey of the empirical evidence of possible causes', Discussion Paper Series No 391, Interdisciplinary Institute for Environmental Economics, University of Heidelberg.

Meadows, D.H., Meadows, D.I., Randers, J. and Behrens, W.W. (1972) *The limits to growth: a report to the Club of Rome*, New York, NY: Universe Books.

Monbiot, G. (2010) 'For deniers, politics beats the science. Handouts beat both', *The Guardian*, 23 August.

Neumayer, E. (2002) 'Do democracies exhibit stronger international environmental commitment? A cross-country analysis', *Journal of Peace Research*, vol 39, no 2, pp 139–64.

Niemayer, S. (2012) 'Building the foundations of deliberative democracy: the deliberative person and climate change', Working Paper 2012/1, Centre for Deliberative Democracy & Global Governance, Australian National University.

Ophuls, W. (1977) *Ecology and the politics of scarcity*, San Francisco, CA: W.H. Freeman.

O'Riordan, T. (1996) 'Democracy and the sustainability transition', in W.M. Lafferty and J. Meadowcroft (eds) *Democracy and the environment*, London: Edward Elgar, pp 140–56.

Payne, R. (1995) 'Freedom and the environment', *Journal of Democracy*, vol 6, no 3, pp 41–55.

Przeworski, A., Alvares, M., Cheibub, J.A. and Limongi, F. (2000) *Democracy and development: political institutions and material well-being in the world, 1950–1990*, Cambridge: Cambridge University Press.

Robbins, P., Hintz, J. and Moore, S.A. (2010) *Environment and society*, Chichester: Wiley Blackwell.

Scruggs, L. (1999) 'Institutions and environmental performance in seventeen Western democracies', *British Journal of Political Science*, vol 29, no 1, pp 1–31.

Shearman, D. and Smith, J.W. (2007) *The climate change challenge and the failure of democracy*, Westport, CT: Praeger.

Stern, D.I. (2004) 'The rise and fall of the environmental Kuznets curve', *World Development*, vol 32, no 8, pp 1419–39.

Torras, M. and Boyce, J.K. (1998) 'Income, inequality, and pollution: a reassessment of the environmental Kuznets curve', *Ecological Economics*, vol 25, no 2, pp 147–60.

Ward, H. (2008) 'Liberal democracy and sustainability', *Environmental Politics*, vol 17, no 3, pp 386–409.

Wells, J. (2007) 'The Green Junta: or, is democracy sustainable?', *International Journal of Environment and Sustainable Development*, vol 6, no 2, pp 208–20.

Wilkinson, R. and Pickett, K. (2009) *The spirit level: why more equal societies almost always do better*, London: Allen Lane.

Winslow, M. (2005) 'Is democracy good for the environment?', *Journal of Environmental Planning and Management*, vol 48, no 5, pp 771–83.

Yandle, B., Vijayaraghavan, M. and Bhattarai, M. (2002) *The environmental Kuznets curve: a primer*, Bozeman, MT: Property and Environment Research Centre.

THREE

Learning, pedagogy and sustainability: the challenges for education policy and practice

Ros Wade

Introduction

This chapter will examine the international educational commitments of the 1992 United Nations (UN) Rio Earth Summit on Environment and Development in relation to trends in educational policy and practice over the last 20 years. The Rio Summit commitments were contained in the text of Agenda 21, which emphasised the imperative to reorient education systems towards sustainable development and laid out a clear programme for governments. Many organisations and commentators (for example the United Nations Educational, Scientific and Cultural Organisation [UNESCO], United Nations Environment Programme [UNEP] and the Stakeholder Forum) have highlighted the urgency of putting these commitments into practice to turn round the oil tanker of over-consumption and unsustainable lifestyles in the wealthier parts of the world and to address the poverty and environmental devastation in other parts. Education for sustainable development (ESD) was seen as one of the key driving forces for this.

The notion of sustainable development and that of *education* for sustainable development are closely interlinked, and ESD can be viewed as the learning (both formal, non-formal and informal) that is necessary to achieve sustainable development (UNESCO, 2007a). However, it is important to remember that the concepts of 'ESD' and, indeed, 'sustainable development' have relatively recent origins and are both seen as 'emerging' and contested. How they are interpreted will depend very much on the ideological, philosophical, cultural and ethical perspectives of those using them. Nonetheless, commitments to ESD are rooted in international policy and endorsed at the highest level by UN agencies and by the member states that have signed up to them. There is broad agreement among policymakers and practitioners that ESD covers a very broad spectrum, from formal sector education to community activism, social learning, organisational learning and awareness raising. For the purposes of this chapter, I will focus primarily on the formal education sector.

Evidence indicates that governments were initially very slow to address their commitments to ESD and so other policy actors, in particular, environmental and development non-governmental organisations (NGOs), started to take the lead. This chapter will look at the influence of the NGO sector in relation to UK policy on ESD. It will also set out to look at some of the blocks and constraints on, as well as the opportunities for, change, locally and globally.

The UNESCO overview in 2012 of ESD policy and practice across a range of countries (UNESCO, 2012) indicates that national policy commitments have increased in the last 20 years and ESD practice has developed considerably, though this is obviously very variable from nation to nation. Concerns about climate change and related threats have clearly helped to put this on the political agenda. The global fiscal crisis has also presented an opportunity for global leaders to review current unsustainable economic and social practices, but there is little evidence so far of this in actual policy or practice. To many working in ESD, this illustrates the urgent need for ESD for politicians and policymakers! However, at a global policy level, there has at least been more agreement about integrating ESD within the Education for All (EFA) targets of the Millennium Development Goals (MDGs).

Since the 1980s, we have seen neoliberal perspectives form the overarching framework for policymaking, and this chapter will give consideration as to how this has shaped educational policy trends. It will argue that marketisation and privatisation trends have frequently skewed educational practice towards unsustainable development rather than helping to address the huge challenges that the world is facing in the 21st century. Other issues, such as a lack of joined-up policymaking and departmental turf wars, have further slowed the process of reorienting education systems.

The chapter will argue that these have still not been addressed and that without a sea change at international and national levels, educational policy will fall far short of enabling current and future generations to live sustainably. What is still needed is the *political* will to promote ESD pedagogy and practice to enable change for a sustainable planet.

Setting the context for education for sustainable development

Concerns about sustainability started to surface internationally throughout the latter half of the 20th century, culminating in the first Earth Summit of 1992 in Rio de Janeiro, which drew up an extensive blueprint for sustainable development in the text of Agenda 21 (Quarrie, 1992). This process was an attempt to broker agreements on the environment and on development with all the member states of the UN and to pull together vastly different issues of concern from the minority wealthy, industrialised world and from the majority world, which had been largely excluded from the benefits of economic globalisation. The Rio Earth Summit of 1992 represented the first time that the world's governments had come together to acknowledge the huge challenges of future planetary sustainability.

In Agenda 21, the commitments of this summit recognised the imperative of integrating development and environmental issues in order to address poverty and the aspirations of a 'developing' world while also tackling the environmental degradation and depletion caused by the unsustainable development of the past decades. It recognised that 'development' takes place within the finite limits of the earth's resources and that we all have a responsibility to respect these both for current and for future generations. It was a huge achievement for the world's governments to sign up to such commitments to achieving sustainable development for all and the summit recognised the key role of a number of major groups, including trades unions, indigenous people, NGOs, local authorities and the business sector.

In particular, Agenda 21 recognised the central role of education and learning, and committed governments to reorienting education systems towards sustainable development. However, it was notable that educators were not identified in Agenda 21 as one of the major groups. Commitments to education proliferated in the text; indeed, the only word to receive more mentions was 'government'. Unfortunately, these commitments were very slow to have any impact and as early as 1996, UNESCO was reporting that 'education [is] the forgotten priority' and 'is often overlooked or forgotten in developing or funding action plans at all levels, from local government to international conventions' (UNESCO, 1996). The weakness of the ESD lobby may in part be seen as contributing to this lack of progress. In trying to address this, the international NGO ESD group lobbied unsuccessfully to try to get educators added as a major group for the delivery of Agenda 21.

Agenda 21 called for environmental education (EE) and development education (DE) to be cross-cutting themes in all education policies and practice (Quarrie, 1992, p 221) The implication was that from this synergy, the concept of ESD would somehow emerge. Agenda 21 was, of course, a compromise of compromises, as it was the result of many months (if not years) of negotiation between more than 178 different countries and related power blocs; in its own way, it was a remarkable achievement as it provided a basis for educators and policymakers to start to develop a more coherent understanding and practice of ESD. However, ESD is a very new, complex and contested concept, which is still emerging, so this was no easy matter (Huckle and Sterling, 1996; Sterling, 2001, 2013).

As presently constructed, education can be broadly divided into three orientations: the vocational/neo-classical; the liberal progressive; and the socially critical. Practitioners of ESD tend to position themselves mainly within 'socially critical' education, where 'the teacher is a co-ordinator with emancipatory aims; involves students in negotiation about common tasks and projects; emphasises commonality of concerns and works through conflicts of interest in terms of social justice and ecological sustainability' (Fien, 1993, p 20). However, this orientation tends to portray knowledge as mainly socially constructed, and some say that it fails to give enough weight to the learning needed to live within the set biophysical boundaries of our world. This is a big challenge in an era when it seems that economic ways of knowing dominate all other narratives; hence, it is not surprising that ESD is a contested concept.

Nonetheless, as the lead UN agency for ESD, UNESCO has succeeded in achieving a broad consensus that ESD is facilitated through participatory and reflective approaches and is characterised by the following:

- it is based on the principles of intergenerational equity, social justice, fair distribution of resources and community participation, which underlie sustainable development;
- it promotes a shift in mental models that inform our environmental, social and economic decisions;
- it is locally relevant and culturally appropriate;
- it is based on local needs, perceptions and conditions, but acknowledges that fulfilling local needs often has international effects and consequences;
- it engages formal, non-formal and informal education;
- it accommodates the evolving nature of the concept of sustainability;
- it promotes lifelong learning;

- it addresses content, taking into account context, global issues and local priorities;
- it builds civil capacity for community-based decision-making, social tolerance, environmental stewardship, an adaptable workforce and the quality of life;
- it is cross-disciplinary – no one discipline can claim ESD as its own, but all disciplines can contribute to ESD; and
- it uses a variety of pedagogical techniques that promote participatory learning and critical reflective skills.

UNESCO further describes ESD-related processes as involving:

- Future thinking: actively involving stakeholders in creating and enacting an alternative future.
- Critical thinking: helping individuals to assess the appropriateness and assumptions of current decisions and actions.
- Systems thinking: understanding and promoting holistic change.
- Participation: engaging all in sustainability issues and actions (UNESCO, 2007a).

This agenda is a challenging one for governments and policymakers as it cuts across traditional policy areas and implementation involves a number of different government agencies at both national and local levels. In relation to formal sector education, there is a clear need for collaboration between education and environment ministries and there can be many blocks and obstacles to this, not least the turf wars over resources and influence that shape much policymaking.

Above all, ESD is concerned with change – in ways of thinking, being and acting – on all levels, from the personal to the political, from the local to the global. This is a radical agenda that does not sit easily with many policymakers and politicians.

The role of non-governmental organisations in education for sustainable development – the limits of political action?

Because governments were initially so slow to take the initiative on education after the first Earth Summit, this role was mainly taken up by NGOs and committed activists (Wade and Parker, 2008). Their work tended to have two strands: one of support, training and awareness raising for educational practitioners; and the other of advocacy and lobbying for policy change. Since 1992, therefore, many NGOs have actively sought to influence the national political landscape strategically with regard to ESD. Alliances were formed in order to navigate the difficult terrain of government policy and practice. In the UK, for example, the Development Education Association (DEA), the Council for Environmental Education (CEE) and the World Wide Fund for Nature (WWF UK) had some success in influencing the government, for example, through the Commission for Sustainable Development. Specific approaches have also had results, such as the work of Oxfam, the Royal Society for the Protection of Birds (RSPB) and the WWF in Wales to incorporate ESD into educational requirements[1] within the school curriculum and within teacher training. The master's course in ESD at London South Bank University[2] was also an example of the work of the environmental and development NGO sector, which funded and set up the course to build a constituency for change.

However, the work of NGOs would always be limited by scarce resources and capacity and could never compensate for the involvement of governments in driving things forward. Their key role and skill was in advocacy and lobbying for change with the power brokers and the influential, while, at the same time, offering some support to educational practitioners and champions of ESD. NGOs and activists alone could not bring about radical change in educational policy and practice as this is a domain that, over the last 20 years, has been increasingly taken under the control of central government, as is the case in England since the introduction of the national curriculum.

It should be noted that the education chapter (Chapter 36) of Agenda 21, 'Promoting education, public awareness and training', attempted to bring the two existing constituencies of EE and DE into a relationship by brokering a new inclusive concept of ESD. However, these constituencies have different histories and different roots, so this was no easy matter. In Western, high-consuming countries, DE was very much linked to the human rights and social justice agenda, while EE developed out of a concern for protection and conservation of the natural environment, which was being threatened by the actions of human beings.

This was not the case in all parts of the world, however. In many Southern and emerging countries, EE and DE issues are very obviously interconnected and linked, and there has not been a long history of separate constituencies. In South Africa, for example, Lotz-Sisitka (2004, p 67) points out that 'environmental education is strongly focused on the social, political, economic and biophysical dimensions'. Therefore, she sees no perceived dichotomy between social justice and environmental protection. However, this viewpoint is not necessarily always translated into practice, as shown in a review of progress towards Agenda 21 in Kenya, where Dorcas Otieno (2005) reported that 'the environment has been looked at in great detail from the biophysical view but with less emphasis on economic and social perspectives'. Balancing social and ecological needs and rights, however, is no easy matter. The process of achieving sustainable development will not be straightforward as there are many conflicting views on how to do this, depending on ideological frames and political allegiance. There are also many vested interests and power is unevenly distributed between and within countries. There is obviously no quick fix to integrate environmental and development concerns into educational policy and practice but it is clear that educators have a key role to play in helping to take this forward. This is illustrated by the ongoing discourse on ESD competences, which is 'based partly on the presumed lack of relevance of current educational provision and the need to produce "change agents"' (Mochizuki and Fadeeva, 2010, p 392).

The dynamics of change are, of course, very complex and changes in educational policy and practice are set within broader social change and are part of a much bigger policy agenda. I will return to this later.

The role of the United Nations Educational, Scientific and Cultural Organisation

At the international level, as the key lead UN organisation responsible for education agendas, the role of UNESCO in promoting and supporting change also needs to be recognised. UNESCO was responsible for taking a lead on the education commitments (Chapter 36) of Agenda 21. This focused on education, training and public awareness, with four overarching goals:

1. Promote and improve the quality of education: The aim is to refocus lifelong education on knowledge, skills and values citizens need to improve their quality of life;
2. Reorient the existing education programmes: From pre-school to university, education must be rethought and reformed to be a vehicle of knowledge, thought patterns and values needed to build a sustainable world;
3. Raise public awareness and understanding of the concept of sustainable development: This will make it possible to develop enlightened, active and responsible citizenship locally, nationally and internationally;

4. Train the workforce: Continuing technical and vocational education of directors and workers, particularly those in trade and industry, will be enriched to enable them to adopt sustainable modes of production and consumption. This includes a social component (e.g. equity, human rights). (UNESCO, 2012, p 11)

However, UNESCO is, of course, dependent on funding and resources from member-state governments, and the response of governments to this challenge reflected their response to ESD generally. In other words, it was very limited and meagre, with the exception of a few countries, such as Japan. Despite the very limited funding available for ESD, UNESCO has, nonetheless, managed to mobilise groups of ESD educators across the globe and has provided various forums and networks of mutual support. One example of this is the UNESCO International Teacher Education network (IN), which meets biannually under the leadership of Professor Charles Hopkins, UNESCO chair, at York University, Toronto. The IN is comprised of teacher education institutions from about 60 nations around the world and the member institutions work to incorporate sustainability into their programmes, practices and policies: 'Each member institution addresses environmental, social, and economic contexts to create locally relevant and culturally appropriate teacher education programmes for both pre-service and in-service teachers' (UNESCO, 2013).

Another example is that of the regional centre of expertise (RCE) initiative, set up by the United Nations University Institute of Advanced Studies (see Chapter Eight of this book). In 2013, this involved over 100 RCEs in ESD operating in a wide range of countries and global regions, including Europe, Asia, Africa and the Americas.

Policy and practice in ESD have certainly developed over the last 10 years, and in many countries, there is now government policy in place in all areas of the formal education sector, from schools to higher education (UNESCO, 2013). In addition, national legal requirements on sustainable development in relation to other sectors, such as the built environment, have created space and demand for training at a range of levels. At the international level, education was further endorsed at the second World Summit on Sustainable Development (WSSD), which took place in Johannesburg in 2002. This also attempted to make links between ESD and EFA (basic education as a requirement for the achievement of the MDGs on poverty reduction). Since UNESCO had been given the task of taking the lead internationally in both areas, it made very good sense to bring them together.

In 2005, the UN acknowledged the Decade of ESD (DESD) from 2005 to 2014 and an implementation plan was produced and agreed. In this plan, education was viewed as a prime lever for social change, described by UNESCO in the implementation plan for the DESD in the following way: 'It means education that enables people to foresee, face up to and solve the problems that threaten life on our planet' (UNESCO, 2005).

Understanding the causes of change in policy and practice is, of course, a complex area of study and is like trying to unravel a complicated, interconnected and tangled web of relationships and conflicts with a vast array of actors and influences. It is an iterative, not linear, process, where policies are 'the operational statements of values, statements of "prescriptive intent", which are then contested in and between the arenas of formation and implementation' (Bowe et al, 1992, p 20).

Educational change cannot, of course, be separated out from social change, as the relationship is strongly interconnected. All educational (and social) change is a site of struggle because, as Ginsburg et al (1991, p 7) point out:

> The timing and focus of educational reform cannot be adequately understood by conceiving of society as a homeostatic system, characterised by consensual relations transacted by persuasion and led by those who possess a 'moral force'. Instead we start with the assumption that at the world system and national levels the social formation is inherently conflict laden and characterised by fundamental contradictions.

There is a challenge here for educators to get involved in these conflicts and actively influence policy and practice change, whether through their professional bodies or trades unions or through their engagement with wider political processes. Yet, ESD as currently constructed pays only limited attention to issues of ideology and power. ESD educators would benefit from more engagement with political science in order:

> to develop skill sets and routes to change with its understanding of the nature of barriers to change, of how political systems work and of how the levers of power operate. ESD is limited in its understanding of power relations while having such an understanding is a strength of Political Science. (Atkinson and Wade, 2013, p 48)

Rio plus 20 – where are we now?

Twenty years on, at the Rio plus 20 Conference in 2012, UNESCO presented a report on progress with ESD so far. According to this report:

> in 2008, the proportion of countries evoking ESD or related fields in their development education programs is about 50%. In some cases, ESD is evoked or included as a theoretical frame without the evidence of inclusion on the curricula or project development. Education by itself is sometimes described as a tool for sustainable development, without really including ESD. From a 50 country sample 26 countries reported no evidence of ESD in 2008, but by 2012 after the boost of the Bonn Conference in 2009, 16 of them fall no longer in that category. We can perceive an estimated increase of 34% from 2008 to 2012. This allows us to have an approximation of the rate of adoption of ESD. (Wals, 2012, p 12)

Although it is clear that the picture is very uneven, and in some cases rather limited, policy and practice in ESD have at least moved on and developed since 1992 and since the start of the UN DESD in 2005. For example, the Gothenburg Recommendations on ESD, adopted on 12 November 2008 as part of the UN DESD, called on ESD to be embedded in all curricula and learning materials (UNESCO, 2008). In a number of countries, there is now a developing government policy in place in areas of the formal education sector, from schools to higher education. In Denmark, for example, ESD has been introduced into key aspects of the curricula with a focus on children, young people and adult learners (Danish Ministry of Education and Children, 2009). In the Netherlands, ESD has become an important element of the formal curriculum, from primary school to higher education (Dutch Ministry of Education, 2008). In Wales, ESD has been embedded in the curricula, with a focus on schools, youth, further education, work-based learning, higher education and adult and continuing education (Welsh Assembly, 2006).

At the international level, ESD was again strongly endorsed at the Rio plus 20 WSSD in 2012. This also highlighted the importance of links between ESD and EFA. With the deadline for the achievement of the MDGs in 2015, the concept of Sustainable Development Goals (SDGs) is also being discussed at international policy level, and, if adopted, this could give further impetus to the ESD agenda (Sachs, 2012).

During the last five years, many NGOs in the UK have stepped back from the policy agenda with regard to ESD, though many are still involved in practice. WWF UK and Oxfam, for example, who have led the way in the UK to a large extent, have reorganised their education teams and also cut their staff numbers dramatically. WWF's education team was influential in shaping government policy in England, for example, through the *Sustainable schools programme* (DCSF, 2008). A member of the WWF's education team was actually seconded to the Department for Education and Science (DfES) for over a year to develop and work on this. However, since restructuring in 2013, the WWF's education team is much less focused on the wider agendas of ESD. This could be attributed in part to the success of NGOs in helping to achieve some policy change and in getting this agenda taken up within mainstream debates. However, the lack of alternative voices will undoubtedly affect the shape of future ESD developments and discourse. There is also an obvious danger of capture of ESD by mainstream agendas and, hence, the dilution of its transformational and radical role. Indeed, Selby and Kagawa (2011, p 47) ask whether ESD has been 'striking a Faustian bargain' with neoliberal, economic growth perspectives that they feel run counter to achieving sustainable development. Selby and Kagawa remind us that central to all ESD debates about change is the issue of power.

Education for sustainable development – the political landscape

Education represents one of the largest resource commitments of the public sector, so it is not surprising that governments take a close interest in it and that it reflects certain ideological perspectives. In the last two decades, many would argue that it has reflected the rise of neoliberal ideas (Selby and Kagawa, 2011; Blewitt, 2013), both in terms of the purpose and the delivery of education.

This has led to two complex and seemingly contradictory trends, which are frequently taking place at the same time:

- the centralisation of government control over curricula, structures and delivery; and
- the marketisation of formal education.

Centralisation has led to what is often called a 'compliance culture' within education, with a focus on targets, tests and tick boxes, something that leaves little space for the critical thinking and questioning required by ESD. In the UK, in terms of curricula, the focus has increasingly been on literacy, numeracy and the science, technology, engineering and maths (STEM) subjects, rather than the broader issue-based approaches and interdisciplinarity required by ESD.

At the same time, education is increasingly seen as a commodity rather than a process, and this is illustrated, for example, within the international General Agreement on Trade in Services (GATS). GATS aimed to deregulate international markets in services (Robertson et al, 2006), including education, and opened the door for private corporations to take over the running of education systems, with all the possible implications for democracy and accountability that this might bring. The dangers of such deregulation have already been highlighted, for example, by disastrous water privatisations in countries such as Tanzania (Rice, 2007). In UK education terms, this marketisation trend can be identified in the academy school and so-called 'free school' programmes, where the running of schools is being opened up to charitable foundations like the Harris Foundation or to large private sector education providers. This trend is prevalent and growing in line with the strength of neoliberal hegemony across the globe and is increasingly embracing the higher education sector. In Kenya and Uganda, for example, there are a growing number of private universities. However, this is not to say that this trend has merely negative results for education. On the contrary, it can facilitate the opening up of a more creative space for innovative educational initiatives, such as the human scale school movement, which is committed to promoting the whole school as a sustainable community (Walker, 2008). However, the outcomes of marketisation will clearly depend upon the dominant global ideological and ethical frameworks, as well as the ideological and ethical perspectives of each educational provider. History shows us that neoliberal capitalism usually leads to increasing accumulation of capital and power in the hands of a few organisations and, hence, to monopolies in the market. There is already evidence that this may be starting to happen with educational provision, with big, multinational US providers offering degree courses in law, for example.

However, increasingly, the business sector is making it clear that they need graduates who are sustainability-literate, and recent student surveys indicate that this is keenly reflected in the student body also. So, there are reasons to be hopeful that these requirements may start to be incorporated into future curricula. A survey in 2011 of over 5,000 first-year UK students also found that:

overwhelmingly, skills in sustainable development are viewed as significant for employability and over 80% of respondents believe these skills are going to be important to their future employers; – respondents placed high value on many of the aspects of sustainable development for use in HE in relation to increasing their ability to perform well in their course; – sustainability concerns are significant in students' university choices; – the vast majority felt that sustainable development is something universities should actively incorporate and promote. (Bone and Agombar, 2011, p 6)

Nonetheless, a note of caution should be sounded here, as the clear emphasis is on a rather narrow view of sustainability skills rather than the broader notion of ESD. As Bone and Agombar (2011, p 12) go on to say: 'the EfS agenda advocates the need for a broader range of skills that can challenge societal norms, and transform educational practice'. Nonetheless, 'HEIs [higher education institutions] therefore are in a unique position to be critical of wider society, and challenge reforms and policies that shape the sustainability agenda' (Bone and Agombar, 2011, p 12).

The tension between a technocratic, instrumental approach focused on a narrow range of skills and targets and the broader goals of ESD is evident at the international level also. The MDG target for EFA focuses on the numbers of children attending primary school, and, indeed, much progress has been made on this in many countries. However, as we know from experience, funding and resources usually follow targets and, hence, also affect how targets are delivered. Quantity does not necessarily mean quality, as the UN EFA (UNESCO, 2007b, p 2) report underlined: 'Being in school or in an adult learning programme will not have positive impact unless it is of high quality and leads to usable knowledge and competencies'. The slow progress in integrating ESD with the EFA goals has been a concern of UNESCO for some time (Wade and Parker, 2008). As the lead agency for education, UNESCO's ESD work has been greatly hampered by the lack of commitment and support from member states for ESD. It has had to rely on the mobilisation of educators and activists, and while this has had some quite impressive results, it can be no replacement for government support and funding.

ESD has sometimes been seen as more urgently needed in wealthier countries as their citizens have a disproportionate impact upon global sustainability, and they can thus be regarded as more important agents of change. However, ESD is also vitally important for poor communities, especially those that depend directly upon ecosystem goods and services. These distinctions, however, may be rather simplistic in today's rapidly changing world, where income divisions within countries as well as between countries are growing wider. Although the scale of poverty is very different, poverty reduction and regeneration strategies are now increasingly part of the landscape in wealthy countries also, with large numbers of people facing fuel poverty and relying on food banks.

A focus on the education of powerful political elites in developing countries is also clearly integral for ESD. Elites need to understand the impact of high-consumption lifestyles upon global ecosystems and on the life chances of the poor. Politicians have been slow to take up the challenges of sustainability, both from a lack of understanding and a piecemeal approach to policy, and also from a lack of political will. Discussions in one of the high-level groups during the UNESCO ESD mid-Decade Bonn Conference underlined this issue when delegates identified politicians and policymakers as a key target for ESD (Wade, 2009).

According to UNESCO's (2012) report, *Shaping the education of tomorrow*, much progress has been made with regard to ESD. However, this report also highlights the importance of politicians and policy-makers:

> As the DESD approaches 2014, its final year, continued support for ESD is crucial. Governments and stakeholders must further ESD's development as a catalyst for innovation and transformation. A range of interactive, integrative and critical forms of learning are emerging. They seem essential for reorienting education, as well as everyday routines in schools, communities and workplaces, towards sustainability. (UNESCO, 2012, p 67)

In order to ensure support for ESD, one top priority to guide the way ahead is capacity-building for ministries of education and key change agents.

Education for sustainable development – where are we going?

The UNESCO (2012) report identifies a wide range of responses to ESD across countries. It seems clear that there are two main strategies for ESD: one is the add-on and integration strategy; the other is the whole-system redesign strategy. The first seeks to widen the space within existing, often national, curricula for ESD; the second challenges the entire system by reorienting it towards sustainable development.

The UNESCO (2012) report collated responses received from key informants in all member states (except for Myanmar, Thailand and Benin, who did not send a response), and these showed that there is a wide range of activity and progress in ESD. For example, in Finland, it was reported that:

> All schools were required to draw up a SD [sustainable development] plan by the end of 2010. This plan must contain the following: implementation of ESD, account on how the school will change its operations and everyday activities so that these correspond to the targets set in the plan as well as who is responsible for the implementation. The promotion of sustainable development has been incorporated into the national curricula in basic education and in general and vocational upper secondary education. (UNESCO, 2012, p 33)

And in the Asia-Pacific region:

> there has been great progress in both implementation of programmes at the school level and in the reforms needed to include sustainability into education. China has designated 1,000 schools as experimental schools for Education for Sustainable Development (ESD) and has included ESD in the National Outline for Medium and Long-term Education Reform and Development (2010–2020). These changes have allowed (exploring) school reform and the inclusion of sustainability practices in the educational system. (UNESCO, 2012, p 38)

Of course, while there is room for some optimism that commitments to ESD are at last starting to be taken seriously in policy terms, this does not necessarily translate into practice at all levels. The relationship between policy and practice is a complex one and a site of struggle over understanding and interpretation (Bowe et al, 1992). In addition, as yet, there is little evidence in the report of the integration of ESD into teacher education. It is also clearly beyond the remit of UNESCO to explore the depth and understanding of ESD in practice. Therefore, there is no room for complacency.

In particular, while some progress in the UK was acknowledged in the report, this has been somewhat taken over by events resulting from a change in government. Despite all the international agreements and the general consensus that ESD is essential if we are to address the huge challenges ahead, the Coalition government under Secretary of State for Education Michael Gove has chosen to downgrade and water down ESD commitments within the English school curriculum. It has abandoned the sustainable schools programme, closed down the Sustainable Development Commission, downgraded the role of the UNESCO National Commission and even considered removing the teaching of climate change from the geography curriculum in England; all this despite rising concerns about the effects of climate change locally and globally, as outlined in Chapter One of this book, and the election pledge to be a 'green government'. By contrast, in a number of other countries, there has been a growing focus on climate change education and disaster management. According to UNESCO (2012, p 19): 'The biggest growth field in ESD is ESD related to climate change. Many governments are developing educational responses to climate change and natural disasters, especially in countries most at risk.'

It is interesting to note that the attempt to remove the study of climate change from the English geography curriculum was met with a groundswell of protest from educators, environmentalists and universities, which led to the retention of the theme of climate change in the curriculum for 11–14 year olds (Wintour, 2013). This is one example of how educators can make a difference to policy, with over 65,000 people signing a petition protesting against Gove's proposal. The devolved administrations in the UK have followed different paths and it is to be hoped that their differing political agendas will enable ESD to be strengthened rather than watered down in their curricula.

Non-formal and informal education

While the main focus of this chapter has been on statutory formal education, this is not to discount the importance of the non-formal and informal sectors. Indeed, some might say that they are even more important, as this is where ESD can be applied directly and more immediately to sustainability issues and problems. Outside the statutory formal sector, many of the professional bodies (eg for civil engineering) in the UK have now produced guidelines for ESD, and these, in turn, are influencing curricula at degree level and in vocational courses. However, there are certain professions, such as the civil service (Robertson, 2009), that have proved more intransigent

---

to ESD, though politicians and policymakers are clearly a key target group for ESD (Wade, 2009). Nonetheless, trades unions and civil society organisations like Commonwork and the Botanic Gardens Conservation International (BGCI) have been developing educational programmes for their own constituencies and stakeholders in the UK outside the formal sector. In some cases, this has led to collaborations with formal sector organisations and accreditation of courses through local colleges or universities.

Adult basic education and literacy classes have also provided fruitful areas for ESD, as exemplified in the collection of case studies from the Asia-Pacific region in *Tales of HOPE* (ACCU, 2012). Building on the legacy of Paulo Freire, in Latin America, there are also many examples of popular ESD. Freire worked with marginalised and oppressed groups in Brazil to build what he called 'transforming consciousness' to enable them to take action to change their lives. He felt that formal education processes could perpetuate oppression unless they encouraged autonomy and critical thinking about how society operates (Freire, 1972). As always, it is the poorest and most vulnerable who have to contend with the most immediate challenges of sustainability and the dangerous consequences of climate change.

Grass-roots educators have a long history of developing learning programmes that engage stakeholders in problem solving or in action to change their situations. For example, in the Philippines, 'functional literacy programmes have focussed on community empowerment and sustainable development. Sustainable agriculture education was initiated in 2003 to develop capabilities of vegetable farmers to transform their conventional farming practice to a more sustainable farming system' (D'Souza, 2012, p 45). Chapters Seven and Eight of this book also provide further examples of the importance of non-formal and informal education.

It is evident that NGOs continue to play a crucial role in community education (ACCU, 2012), which is still very under-researched (Flowers et al, 2009) despite its prominence in UN commitments and within the DESD implementation plan. Non-formal education has long been the poor relation and usually the first to have government funding withdrawn in times of economic austerity. There are many reasons for this that we do not have time to examine here, but the desire of governments for centralised control of curricula is likely to be one of them. Non-formal education does not lend itself to this, of course. I would argue that it is actually a false dichotomy to distinguish between formal and non-formal education as they both form part of a whole picture of education and learning, and one can (and, many would say, *should*) feed into the other. Formal education has not yet proven very fertile ground for ESD to take root, as highlighted in the UNESCO (2012) report.

The potential for more synergy between formal and non-formal education is illustrated by an ACCU case study from Bansankong, Thailand on ESD and cultural diversity, where they have developed a strong and 'integrated agricultural programme that is mainstreamed as part of the school's curricular and extra curricular activities' (ACCU, 2012, p 109). The resulting food produce is sold to the school's own canteen and profits are invested back or used for the students' scholarship fund. The case study concludes that school–community interaction has been intensified due to the fact that the learning contributed to the betterment of their community (ACCU, 2012, p 109).

Joined-up policy-making: the need for synergy between Education for All and education for sustainable development

As the lead body responsible for education at the global level, UNESCO has been responsible for all UN educational agendas, including Early Childhood Education, Technical and Vocational Education and Training (TVET), EFA and ESD. The UNESCO mid-DESD review in 2009, nonetheless, highlighted that 'at the mid-point of the Decade, however, it is too early to speak of "one concerted UN response" to ESD and there remains much work to be done' (UNESCO, 2009, p 39). UNESCO has long recognised that this has been a problem and commissioned a paper in 2007 to help to promote a dialogue between the various stakeholders of these different educational agendas, especially those of EFA and ESD. The paper (*EFA–ESD dialogue: educating for a sustainable world* [Wade and Parker, 2008]) highlighted some of the key challenges and provided a framework for developing synergy between the various educational agendas. The need for this synergy was endorsed by a number of conferences and fora (eg Bonn in 2009 and Tokyo in 2009) and by EFA and ESD educators at the UK Forum for International Education and Training (UKFIET) conference in September 2013. This synergy would enable a more holistic and joined-up approach to educational policymaking and practice that could serve to energise and mobilise global, national and regional educational communities.

However, this educational synergy is not very evident in two key international reports of 2013, for example, the report of the High Level Panel of Eminent Persons on the Post-2015 Development

Agenda (2013). Nonetheless, it was encouraging to note that these reports acknowledged the need for a more holistic approach to global policymaking, which put sustainable development at the core and recognised that the MDGs had failed to develop clear linkages between development and the environment. However, as Robbie Guevara (2013, p 109) has pointed out, there is, nonetheless, a conspicuous 'silence' with regard to ESD, which is not mentioned at all in either report. ESD is crucial if the commitments to sustainable development are to be taken seriously. As Guevara (2013, p 109) points out, ESD provides an essential learning framework for 'simultaneously understanding the local and the global, together with taking a holistic and integrated approach to the social, economic, environmental, and governance dimensions of society'.

Once again, it seems that policymakers may have downgraded the educational agenda or else they see it merely as an instrumental tool for implementation. A look at past experience or at any body of research on educational policymaking will demonstrate that such an approach will be doomed to failure. The challenges of sustainability that we face demand wide popular engagement and a global, national and local response by all key stakeholders. Education and learning are part of the iterative dynamic of social change: in order to change society, we need to change the way we learn and educate; and in order to change the way we learn and educate, we need to change society.

It is not yet clear what kind of global policy framework will follow on from the MDGs, which come to a conclusion in 2015, but broad discussions are taking place about *sustainable* development goals, which may serve at last to integrate the development and environmental agendas. The role of education in this is still unclear, however.

Conclusion

To effect change, it is necessary to understand the nature of political institutions and political leadership at the global, regional, national and local levels. Political leaders and political institutions tend to operate in the short to medium term. The kind of change inherent in ESD – for example, radically changing our lifestyles to combat climate change – is, in many ways, outside the normal framework of political discourse. What we are talking about here is ongoing and long-term change. Politicians do not tend to think in the long term. Their actions are often shaped by the exigencies of the electoral cycle. The demands of ESD might appear to be at odds with this view. While political science can offer no magic cure to such a set of circumstances, it can at least help to set out the problems and offer some possible solutions.

At the same time, we cannot afford to wait for politicians and policymakers to take up this agenda. As educators and as citizens, we need to become more politically astute and aware and to engage in and influence the key policy debates and discussions. We need to take part in fora and coalitions active in this at local and global levels, such as trades unions, professional organisations, NGOs and RCEs.

The world is facing some very serious social and environmental challenges over the next 50 years. These include climate change, global poverty and inequality, war and conflict, and peak oil, all set against a backdrop of highly consuming lifestyles and a growing world population, which is likely to reach nine billion by the middle of the century. In order to address these immense future challenges, new forms of learning are needed that break through the current hegemony and navigate the barriers between disciplines, between sectors and between cultures. More of the same sort of education, which has led us to this unsustainable impasse, is not appropriate if we seriously want to develop sustainable communities, locally and globally. Some gains have been made with regard to education policy and practice but there is a long way to go, and what is needed are politicians and policymakers who are prepared to lead the debate and fulfil their Agenda 21 commitments to reorient education systems towards sustainable development. As engaged educators, academics and citizens, let us help them to do this.

Notes

[1] Under the heading of 'global citizenship' and 'education for sustainability'.

[2] See: www.lsbu.ac.uk/efs

References

ACCU (Asia-Pacific Cultural Centre for UNESCO) (ed) (2012) *Tales of HOPE 111: EFA–ESD linkages and synergies*, Japan: ACCU.

Atkinson, H. and Wade, R. (2013) 'Education for sustainable development and political science: making change happen', in S. McCloskey (ed) *Policy & practice; a development education review. Development education without borders*, issue 17, autumn, Belfast: Centre for Global Education. Available at: www.developmenteducationreview.com/issue17

Blewitt, J. (2013) 'EfS: contesting the market model of higher education', in S. Sterling, L. Maxey and H. Luna (eds) *The sustainable university*, Abingdon, Oxon: Routledge.

Bone, E. and Agombar, J. (2011) *First-year attitudes towards, and skills in, sustainable development*, York: Higher Education Academy.

Bowe, R., Ball, S. and Gold, A. (1992) 'The policy process and the processes of policy', in R. Bowe, S. Ball and A. Gold (eds) *Reforming education and changing schools*, London: Routledge.

Danish Ministry of Education and Children (2009) *Education for Sustainable Development: a strategy for the UN Decade 2005-2014*, Copenhagen, Denmark.

DCSF (Department for Children, Schools and Families) (2008) *Sustainable schools programme. Planning a sustainable school: driving school improvement through sustainable development*, London: HMSO. Available at: http://webarchive.nationalarchives.gov.uk/20130401151715/https://www.education.gov.uk/publications/eOrderingDownload/planning_a_sustainable_school.pdf

D'Souza, D. (2012) 'The power of partnerships to achieve EFA–ESD synergy', in ACCU (ed) *Tales of HOPE 111: EFA–ESD linkages and synergies*, Japan: ACCU.

Dutch Ministry of Education (2008) *Learning for sustainable development, 2008–2011: from strategy to general practice*, The Hague, Netherlands: Dutch Ministry of Education.

Fien, J. (1993) *Education for the environment: critical curriculum theorising and Environmental Education*, Geelong: Deakin University Press. Available at: http://www.multilingual-matters.net/irgee/008/0140/irgee0080140.pdf (accessed 6 January 2007).

Flowers, R., Guevara, J.R. and Whelan, J. (2009) 'Popular and informal environmental education: the need for more research in an "emerging" field of practice', in *Report 2/2009 popular education*, Keitschrify fur Weiterbildungsforschung 32, Jahrgang, Bonn: Deutsches institute fur Erwachsenenbildung. Available at: www.die-bonn.de/doks/report/2009-umweltbildung-01.pdf

Freire, P. (1972) *The pedagogy of the oppressed*, London: Penguin.

Ginsburg, M., Cooper, S., Raghu, R. and Zegarra, H. (1991) 'Educational reform: social struggle, the state and the world economic system', in M. Ginsburg (ed) *Understanding educational reform in a global context: economy, ideology and the state*, New York, NY, and London: Garland Publishing.

Guevara, J.R. (2013) 'The silence around education for sustainable development must be broken', in J. Larjanko (ed) *2013 adult education and development year book – post 2015*, Institut for Internationale Zusammen arbeit das Deutsches Volkshochschul Verbandes. Available at: http://dvv-international.de/index.php?article_id=1460&clang=1

High Level Panel of Eminent Persons on the Post-2015 Development Agenda (2013) 'A new global partnership: eradicate poverty and transform economies through sustainable development', 30 May. Available at: www.un.org/sg/management/hlppost2015.shtml

Huckle, J. and Sterling, S. (eds) (1996) *Education for sustainability*, London: Earthscan.

Lotz-Sisitka, H. (2004) *Positioning South African environmental education in a changing context*, Howick, SA: SADC Regional Education Programme/Share-Net.

Mochizuki, Y. and Fadeeva, Z. (2010) 'Competences for sustainable development and sustainability: significances and challenges for ESD', *International Journal of Sustainability in Higher Education*, vol 11, no 4, pp 391–403.

Otieno, D. (2005) 'Towards developing an ESD strategy for Kenya: experiences and perspectives', Kenya Organisation for Environmental Education. Available at: www.ceeindia.org/esf/download/paper44. pdf (Also presented at UNESCO Conference on ESD, Ahmedabad, India, 2005. See: www.ceeindia.org/esf)

Quarrie, J. (ed) (1992) *Earth Summit 1992*, London: The Regency Press.

Rice, X. (2007) 'The water margin', *The Guardian*. Available at: www.theguardian.com/business/2007/aug/16/imf. internationalaidanddevelopment

Robertson, A. (2009) 'Education for Sustainability and civil service training', Unpublished masters' dissertation, LSBU.

Robertson, S.J., Bonal, X. and Dale, R. (2006) 'GATS and the education service industry: the politics of scale and global reterritorialisation', in H. Lauder, P. Brown, J. Dillabough and A.H. Halsey (eds) *Education, globalisation and social change*, Oxford: Oxford University Press.

Sachs, J. (2012) 'Rio+20: Jeffrey Sachs on how business destroyed democracy and virtuous life', *The Guardian*. Available at: www. guardian.co.uk/sustainable-business/rio-20-jeffrey-sachs-business-democracy

Selby, D. and Kagawa, F. (2011) 'Development education and education for sustainable development: are they striking a Faustian bargain?', *Policy and Practice: A Development Education Review*, no 12 (spring), pp 15–31. Available at: www.developmenteducationreview.com/ issue12-focus3

Sterling, S. (2001) *Sustainable education: revisioning learning and change*, Schumacher Briefings 6, Totnes: Green Books.

Sterling, S. (2013) 'The sustainable university: challenge and response', in S. Sterling, L. Maxey and H. Luna (eds) *The sustainable university*, Abingdon, Oxon: Taylor and Francis.

UNESCO (2008), http://www.desd.org/Gothenburgl%20 Recommendations.pdf. Accessed 14 September 2014.

UNESCO (United Nations Educational, Scientific and Cultural Organisation) (1996) *Promoting education, public awareness and training.* Report of the Secretary General to the 4th session UN Commission on Sustainable Development. Paris, UNESCO.

UNESCO (2005) 'UN decade for sustainable development 2005–2014'. Available at: http://unesdoc.unesco.org/ images/0014/001403/140372e.pdf

UNESCO (2007a) 'Introductory note on ESD – DESD', in *Monitoring & evaluation framework*, Paris: UNESCO.

UNESCO (2007b) *Education for All Global Action plan 2007*, UNESCO, Paris.

UNESCO (2009) 'Review of contexts and structures for education for sustainable development'. Available at: http://unesdoc.unesco.org/ images/0018/001849/184944e.pdf

UNESCO (2012) *Shaping the education of tomorrow. 2012 report on the UN decade of education for sustainable development*, Paris: UNESCO.

UNESCO (2013) 'UNESCO chair on reorienting teacher education to address sustainability: international network'. Available at: http://www. unesco.org/new/en/education/themes/leading-the-international-agenda/education-for-sustainable-development/partners/educators/ teacher-education/

Wade, R. (2009) 'Report on high level workshop on ESD–EFA synergy', unpublished UNESCO Mid Decade Bonn Conference Report.

Wade, R. and Parker, J. (2008) *ESD policy dialogue no 1: EFA–ESD dialogue: educating for a sustainable world*, Paris: UNESCO.

Walker, C. (2008) 'As if size mattered: the evolution of the human scale approach towards education for sustainability', in J. Parker and R. Wade (eds) *Journeys around education for sustainability*, London: London South Bank University.

Wals, A. (2012) *Shaping the education of tomorrow: 2012 report on the UN decade of education for sustainable development*, Wageningen University, The Netherlands: UNESCO (abridged, condensed, adapted and edited version of Wals, A. [2012] *Shaping the education of tomorrow: 2012 full-length report on the UN decade for education for sustainable development*, Wageningen University, The Netherlands: UNESCO).

Welsh Assembly (2006) *Education for sustainable development and global citizenship: a strategy for action*, Cardiff: Welsh Assembly.

Wintour, P (2013) 'Energy secretary urges Michael Gove to re instate climate change in the curriculum', *The Guardian*, 2 May. Available at: http://www.theguardian.com/politics/2013/may/02/michael-gove-climate-change-curriculum

Part Two

What is to be done? Case studies in politics, education and learning

FOUR

Climate change and environmental policy in the US: lessons in political action

Hugh Atkinson

Introduction

The chapter focuses on political responses in the US to the policy challenges of mitigating climate change and promoting the broader environmental and sustainability agenda. Over the last two decades, there has been an understandable perception of a US with only a limited engagement in the fight against climate change and the broader sustainability agenda. Indeed, as Reich (2008, p 5) argues: 'As a nation the United States seems incapable of doing what is required to reduce climate change'. The failure of the US Congress to ratify the 1997 Kyoto Protocol on the reduction of greenhouse gases and the record of the George W. Bush presidency certainly lend some credence to this viewpoint. However, this chapter will argue that the actual picture is much more complex and nuanced.

The last two decades have seen an ever-growing partisan divide within the US political system. The political debate between the two main protagonists – the Democrat and Republican Parties – has become ever-more rancorous, reaching new heights of bitterness and political venom. If anything, this process has intensified since the election of Barack Obama in 2008. Too often, the debate about sustainability and tackling climate change in the US has been drowned out by the white noise of an increasingly partisan and hysterical political culture that militates against reasoned debate and argument at the federal level of government. Mix this in with the constitutional doctrine of the 'separation of powers' and the result has been policy gridlock across a number of issues, ranging from the economy to immigration. Action on tackling climate change and promoting sustainability has not been immune to this. Leading politicians, specifically conservative Republicans and 'Tea Party' supporters, pour scorn on the very existence of a climate change problem, ignore or subvert the science, and argue that the whole thing is a put-up job designed to increase big government and undermine US values. Action on climate change and on the broader environmental and sustainability agenda has become mired in the machinations of the political beltway in Washington DC.

But it was not always like this. In the period from 1964 to 1980 – what has been described as the 'golden age' of US environmental policy – a whole raft of legislation was passed and initiatives were pursued. These included the protection of wildlife, support for the ecosystem and measures to ensure air and water quality. There was a broad consensus across the political spectrum that these were desirable policy outcomes and that the government had a key role to play in delivering them. Nothing better illustrates this consensus than the setting up of the US Environmental Protection Agency (EPA). It was supported by a Democratic Congress and signed into law by Republican President Richard Nixon. How times have changed. There is a real paradox in the fact that just as the global agenda on sustainability and the environment was starting to take off, for example, with the 1987 Brundtland Report and the 1992 Rio Summit, it was in the process of stalling in the US.

The chapter is divided into five sections. First, the policy challenge of climate change and sustainability is set in its broader context. Second, there will be an analysis of the 'golden age' of environmental policy. Third, there is a broad survey of the climate change and sustainability agenda in the US over the last two decades. Fourth, the legacy of George W. Bush will be analysed. Fifth, there will be a focus on the record so far of Barack Obama. Finally, there will be a round-up of some policy initiatives at the sub-federal level in the US.

The challenge of climate change and sustainability: evidence and debate

Chapter One set out the clear evidence of the human impact on the environment and the world's climate. It demonstrated how the fight against climate change, as part of a broader strategy to build a more sustainable world, is one of the most significant policy challenges of the 21st century. The evidence on the damaging impact on the global environment of the increasing levels of greenhouse gases being pumped into our atmosphere has been there for all to see for some time. As far back as 1988, the US scientist James Hansen presented evidence to the US Congress on the link between climate change and the increase in greenhouse gases in the atmosphere (Flavin and Engelman, 2009, p 6).

The 2006 Stern Report (Stern, 2006) spelt out in stark terms the environmental, social and economic challenges that will occur if politicians, citizens and communities at large do not make the right choices now and in the years ahead. The latest published report from the United Nations (UN) Intergovernmental Panel on Climate Change (IPCC) shows that greenhouse gas emissions continue to rise, with the possibility of global temperature increases above two degrees centigrade within the next 20 to 30 years (IPCC, 2013).

In the specific context of the US, evidence suggests that climate change will lead to rising sea levels, which will threaten many coastal cities. Data also point to a loss of between 30% and 70% of the snow pack in the Rocky Mountains, which is significant as it provides much of the water for the American West (Gertner, 2007). It is forecast that that rainfall in the Western US will decrease by 20% between 2040 and 2060 (Revkin, 2008). The US National Climate Assessment Report published in 2013 showed the impact of increasing storm surges, floods and droughts on the lives of Americans (NCADAC, 2013). Research published by the California EPA shows that lakes are warming, sea levels are rising and wildfires are spreading as the impact of climate change takes hold throughout the state.

A recent report by the National Oceanic and Atmospheric Administration (NOAA) shows that 2012 was the warmest year on record for the contiguous US. The average temperature for the year was 55.3 degrees Fahrenheit, a full degree warmer than the previous record year (1998) and 3.3 degrees above the entire average of the 20th century (NOAA, 2012). In May 2013, the NOAA observatory in Mauna Loa Hawai recorded greenhouse gas emission levels beyond the milestone of 400 parts per million (ppm). Christina Figueres, the lead official on climate change at the UN, has argued that 'rapid climate change must be countered with accelerated action' (*The Guardian*, 9 March 2013). But the prospects of this are problematic to say the least. Indeed, Pieter Tans, who has the lead responsibility for measuring greenhouse gas emissions at the NOAA, has stated that the prospects for keeping global temperatures below a two-degree centigrade increase are fading fast (quoted in *The Guardian*, 9 March 2013).

The outcome of the 1992 Rio Summit, the UN Convention on Climate Change and the subsequent 1997 Kyoto Protocol, which set out clear targets for the reduction of greenhouse gases in the developed world, seemed to signal that tackling climate change was firmly on the global policy agenda. But the reality since has been much more mixed. The Kyoto Protocol was an important milestone but the US failed to engage with the process. The US Senate failed to ratify it and the subsequent George W. Bush administration sought to undermine the principles that underlay Kyoto at every turn.

The election of President Obama in 2008 seemed to presage a more constructive engagement by the US with the climate change challenge, both on a domestic and global level. Obama appeared committed to the principles of Rio and Kyoto. In addition, the election of President Obama in 2008 seemed to point to a new activism at the federal level in respect of climate change and sustainability. In a speech to the UN in September 2009, Obama spoke of the serious threat that climate change presented to the future of the planet and why decisive and immediate action was necessary.

Despite high hopes in the sustainability and environmental lobby, the record of his first term was mixed to say the least. Buffeted by domestic economic and political pressures, the Obama administration was accused by many of being a major obstacle to further international agreements. Rio +20 and the 2012 UN Doha gathering promised much but delivered little of substance. Since his re-election in November 2012, he has again stated his commitment to combat climate change. The substantive nature (or otherwise) of this commitment will be analysed later on in this chapter.

The golden age

It is no exaggeration to say that the current political debate in the US about climate change, the environment and sustainability is highly conflicted, being marked by rancour and open hostility. But this has not always been the case. In the period from 1964 to 1980, environmental policy (as it was then called) was an important part of the policy agenda, attracting considerable support across party lines. This period has often been referred to as the 'golden age' of environmental policy (Klyza and Sousa, 2008, p 1; Bailey, 2010, p 168). The US Congress enacted 22 major laws in this period. One of the principle achievements was the creation of the EPA; today, the *bête noire* of large swathes of the Republican Party and the Tea Party movement. The EPA was set up by Congress and the White House in response 'to the growing public demand for cleaner water, air and land' (Storey, 2010, p 342). Born in the wake of increasing concerns about environmental pollution, the EPA was established on 2 December 1970 to consolidate in one agency a variety of federal government environmental protection activities. Its stated mission is to 'protect human health and the environment' (EPA, 2008). The EPA is responsible for enforcing national environmental standards, backed up by statute.

Other notable pieces of legislation passed during the 'golden age' included the Clean Air Act 1970, the Federal Water Pollution Control

Act 1972, the Resource Conservation and Recovery Act 1976 and the Comprehensive Environmental Response, Compensation and Liability Act 1980, in addition to a number of other laws concerning wildlife protection, waste management, mining activities and energy policy. These have made an important contribution to the quality of the US environment (Rosenbaum, 2007; EPA, 2008).

What was remarkable about this legislative programme was the high degree of political consensus and strong bipartisan support among Democrats and Republicans in the US Congress. A very good illustration of this was the Endangered Species Act 1973, whose genesis lay in concerns about the threat to the US bald eagle and bison populations. It was passed unanimously in the Senate and by 345 votes to four in the House of Representatives. It was then signed into law by Republican President Richard Nixon. In 1977, the Tennessee Valley Authority had to abandon a large-scale dam project due to concerns about the threat it posed to the endangered snail darter! The 1970s also saw a concomitant rise in the number of campaigning environmental groups, such as the Sierra Club, Friends of the Earth and Greenpeace. This reflected a growing awareness among sections of the electorate about the need to take the environmental agenda seriously.

In the words of Klyza and Sousa (2008, p 1), the strong bipartisan support for the environmental agenda 'triggered a profound expansion of government power'. Such an extension of federal government power was like a red rag to a bull to those public and political forces (principally in the Republican Party and sections of the business community) for whom the US tradition was firmly rooted in small government and individual freedom. The 'golden era' began to lose its shine as environmental policy became increasingly presented as unwarranted government intervention. It 'became a focal point for political struggle' (Klyza and Sousa, 2008, p 1). Political conflict has reached new heights over the last 20 years, as partisanship within the party system has intensified. This has resulted in an intensely divided and conflicted polity. I will develop this theme in the following section.

Climate change and sustainability over two decades: a broad survey

The policy landscape in the US has changed significantly since the 'golden age'. As Klyza and Sousa (2008, p 1) note: 'Environmental policy making looks very different'. We now have what can be described as a policy gridlock, which is a product of both political and institutional forces.

The last 20 years has seen an increasingly bitter party-political divide between the Democrat and Republican Parties about the general policy approach that the US should adopt in seeking to meet the challenges of the 21st century. More specifically, the challenges of climate change, energy use and the sustainability of the natural and social environment have laid bare deep fissures in the US body politic and the scope and role of government.

Compounding this problem is the very nature of the US constitution itself. The US is governed by the principle of the 'separation of powers', with each of the three branches of the federal government (in Washington), the presidency, the Congress and the Supreme Court, having their own defined powers and areas of competence. Such a system was originally conceived as an attempt to diffuse political power and avert autocracy (memories of past monarchical rule from Britain still being fresh in the mind). But, taken together with increasing political partisanship and conflict, it has often resulted in institutional fragmentation and policy stasis.

Constraints on the policy agenda

On a general level, policy challenges such as combating climate change and promoting environmental sustainability are complex, multifaceted and difficult to deal with. They require joined-up and holistic thinking and a great deal of inter-agency working. Governments, not just those in the US, are not generally very good at this. Indeed, as Bailey (2010, p 168) notes: 'The challenge of engineering significant and coherent change in environmental policy is considerable'. This has been clearly illustrated over the last two decades. Indeed, only two significant pieces of legislation have been enacted since the Clean Air Act 1990.

This general governance problem has been compounded in the US context over the last two decades by a number of key factors. First, the growing partisan divide that has characterised US politics for the last two decades has had a major impact on the environmental policy process. Within Congress, and especially the House of Representatives, many conservative and Tea Party-leaning Republicans regard the whole environmental and sustainability agenda, and, in particular, policies to tackle climate change, as nothing but a naked ruse to further strengthen the power of the federal government. In this febrile political atmosphere, attempts to deal with problems in the natural atmosphere face significant obstacles. Viewed through such a lens, international agreements on, for example, the reduction of greenhouse gases are no more than an attempt to undermine US political and economic sovereignty.

Second, business interests and conservative politicians have long been critical of the overweening power of the federal government and its agencies in respect of environmental laws and regulations and the financial burden that this has imposed upon the private sector (Klyza and Sousa, 2008, p 3). This has had a major impact on the policy debate. Third, in order to explain the environmental row-back from the 'golden age', it is important to understand the nature of laws passed during this period. Many of them were broad in scope and the devil was often in the detail of implementation. Fleshing out the details of these policies involved an array of government agencies, congressional committees, environmental groups, lobbyists and the courts. The result was legislative conflict and policy gridlock.

Fourth, the development of environmental laws from the 'golden era' has created what Bailey (2010, p 170) has described as a 'green state', made up of lobby groups and vested interests 'that constrain change'. This reflects a possible reluctance by established green interests to adapt to new challenges and a desire to protect their own established turf. One might argue that they have become part of a conservative environmental establishment stuck in a mindset of the past, when what is needed is a new mindset to both articulate and respond to the very different challenges that climate change presents.

Fourth, with regard to the environment and strategies to tackle climate change in the US, the policymaking arena is crowded with vested interests on various sides of the argument, each pushing their own agenda. This can often result in suboptimal solutions that fail to deal with the problem. This is further compounded by the constitutional doctrine of the separation of powers, which can often lead to fragmentation in decision-making. Turf warfare between federal government agencies, ideological battles within Congress, presidential edicts, initiatives at the level of individual states and court rulings have produced a patchwork quilt of policies that lack coherence.

Fifth, it is also important to understand the public mood in relation to the environmental agenda. During the 'golden age', there was a broad consensus among the public about the need to tackle environmental problems. This seems to have continued, with opinion surveys apparently showing that 'the proportion of Americans who identified themselves as active participants in the environmental movement, or sympathetic towards its goals, stayed around the 70% mark throughout the 2000s' (Bailey, 2010, p 170). This has led some scholars to speculate that concern for the environment has become a 'core American value'

(Guber, 2003). But a word of caution is needed here, for, as Bailey (2010, p 172) argues, 'Less certain are the depth, intensity, and even meaning of the public's concern for the environment'. Survey data for the 2000s show that public concern for the environment lacks the saliency of other issues, such as defending the US against terrorism or improving the economy (Bailey, 2010, p 173). As Klyza and Sousa (2008, p 2) argue, public support for strong environmental protection continues to be 'relatively fragile'. This is reflected in public attitudes to action on climate change. For example, a May 2012 Stanford University/ Ipsos Public Affairs poll showed that 62% of Americans supported government action on climate change. In 2010, the figure stood at 72%. Furthermore, as Cohen and Millar (2012, p 40) note, climate change in the US has become an ideological issue, with voters tending to divide along party lines. Research by the Brookings Institute showed that, in 2010, only 52% of Americans believed there to be solid scientific evidence that global warming was taking place. Drilling down into the figures, we find that 69% of Democrat voters believed there to be evidence, compared with only 40% of Republican voters (Borick et al, 2011, p 4).

Finally, one of the key constraints to the further development of the environmental and sustainability agenda over the last two decades has been the nature of climate change itself. The challenge it presents is of a different order to what one might term traditional environmental problems, such as air and water pollution. That is not to suggest that the solutions to such problems have been easy or that the policy agenda has not been contested. They have involved financial costs and some adjustments to the way people live their lives. But the challenge of climate change requires real and significant sacrifices on the part of the citizens of the US (as, indeed, in the rest of the developed world) and an almost certain reduction in lifestyles. For a people brought up in a culture of consumerism, this is a significant psychological challenge. The real deprivations that many Americans have suffered in the aftermath of the credit crunch only add to this challenge. It is also a difficult sell for politicians. Telling voters that they should expect less is not a good way to get elected. It requires a set of brave political decisions and actions!

The George W. Bush legacy

Elected in November 2000 in the most controversial of circumstances, George W. Bush attracted the opprobrium of the environmental lobby from the outset of his administration. Farley and Smith (2014, p 97) talk of the overtly negative attitude during the Bush presidency towards policies on the environment. If US environmentalists had their own court, then George W. Bush would have been one of the first in the dock. Let us consider the charge sheet.

Crucially, less than three months into the Bush presidency, the White House signalled a major retreat on the climate change policies of the previous Clinton presidency when it declared that the Bush administration had 'no interest in implementing the Kyoto Protocol' (Bailey, 2010, p 176). In 2001, Bush announced the withdrawal from the Kyoto Protocol, arguing that it would cost the US around 5 million jobs if implemented. As McKay (2009, p 405) notes, this led to accusations that the US had become 'an environmental rogue state'.

A central element of the Bush agenda was to actively undermine the science behind climate change. According to former Democratic Vice President Al Gore (2008, p 200), a long-time campaigner on climate change and environmental matters, Bush 'publicly demeaned scientists in his own administration' who wrote official reports that emphasised the dangers facing the US in respect of climate change. More generally, as Mazmanian and Kraft (2009, p 20) argue, under the Bush presidency, there was 'a range of legislative, administrative and judicial assaults on environmental policy'. Evidence suggests that the Bush administration interfered in the terminology that was used in official government scientific reports. Equally alarming is the claim that several sections of EPA reports were censored after interventions by the White House (Mooney, 2006).

Furthermore, as Bailey (2010, p 175) notes, President Bush used his executive powers to undermine 'decades if not a century of progress on the environment', weakening environmental protection legislation in order to favour and benefit mining and other industries. In addition, as Storey (2010, p 195) observes, Bush 'eased environmental controls on coal fired power plants, and expanded logging and oil developments on federal government land'. In the dying days of his second term, President Bush, using his executive powers, pushed through a number of potentially environmentally damaging measures. For example, he rescinded a requirement for federal agencies to seek advice from government wildlife experts before opening up new areas for logging or road construction. He also stopped the EPA from carrying out an investigation into the impact of climate change on endangered and protected species (Bailey, 2010, p 177). In 2004, the National Aeronautics and Space Administration (NASA) scientist James Hansen went on record to accuse the Bush administration of trying to block the release of data that showed an acceleration in global warming. Commenting on the Bush record, the National Resources Defense

Council (NRDC, 2005) has argued that his administration led the most thorough and destructive campaign against US environmental safeguards in the last 40 years.

The Obama era

The election of the Democratic Party candidate, Barak Obama, as president in November 2008 seemed to point to a new activism at the federal level with regard to climate change and sustainability. He received the backing of all the major environmental lobby groups, with opinion polls consistently showing that voters thought he had better policies on the environment and energy. Indeed, his vice president, Al Gore, had put the issue of climate change firmly on the political agenda in 2006 with the release of the documentary film *An inconvenient truth*.

Obama took over the reins of office in January 2009. He had been elected in the most difficult of circumstances, with the financial crisis and credit crunch rocking the very foundations of both the US and global economies. As Bailey (2010, p 167) notes, Obama 'signalled his intention to break decisively with the policies of his predecessor and give environmental issues, particularly energy reform and climate change, a high priority in his administration'. In his inaugural address on 20 January 2009, he talked of the environmental threats that excessive US energy use posed to the planet. He made reference to the 'spectre of a warming planet'. He also spoke of his ambition to 'harness the sun and the winds and the soil to fuel our cars and run our factories'. Obama also made a number of high-profile appointments to drive the agenda forward. These included the Noble laureate Steven Chu as Energy Secretary and Lisa Jackson as the new head of the EPA. In addition, Carol Browner was given the task of coordinating action on climate change across various government agencies.

Addressing the UN General Assembly in September 2009, Obama spoke of the necessity of those wealthy nations, including the US, who had 'done so much damage to the world in the 20th century' to take the lead in the fight on climate change. He also spoke of the need 'to help the poorest nations both to adapt to the problems that climate change has already wrought and help travel on a path of clean development'. Obama acknowledged the major challenge this presented, not least in 'the midst of a global recession', and that it would 'be tempting to sit back and wait for others to move first'. 'But', he argued, 'we cannot make this journey unless we all move forward together'.

But, to what extent has this fine rhetoric been matched by substantive policies in the first term of the Obama presidency? Obama issued a number of presidential orders shortly after taking office that reversed a number of the policy initiatives of the Bush era. On 26 January 2009, the Obama administration published its 'New energy for America' plan. The policy document set a target of an 80% reduction in US greenhouse gas emissions by 2050. It outlined plans to invest US$150 billion in the green economy, generating 5 million jobs over 10 years (White House, 2009). Its stated aim was to make the US a world leader in tackling climate change. In 2011, the White House issued the policy document *Blueprint for a secure energy future*. It argued that 'Leading the world in clean energy is critical to strengthening the American economy and winning the future' (White House, 2011, p 4).

Despite such initiatives, the reality of partisan politics cast a shadow on the climate change and sustainability agenda during Obama's first term. Indeed, the US Congress had reached a virtual impasse on environmental and related legislation (Cohen and Millar, 2012, p 42).

In November 2012, the president was re-elected to serve a second term. During the preceding election campaign, Obama took part in three televised debates with his Republican rival, Mitt Romney. The issue of climate change did not feature in any of the debates. Despite this inauspicious start, there have been some indicators that tackling climate change and promoting sustainability are beginning to move up the Obama policy agenda once more. In his State of the Union address to Congress on 12 February 2013, Obama made a detailed case for addressing climate change, arguing that:

> We can choose to believe that super storm Sandy and the most severe drought in decades, and the worst wildfires some states have ever seen were all just a freak coincidence. Or we can choose to believe in the overwhelming judgement of science ... and act before it is too late.

Obama called on Congress to draft appropriate legislation but made it clear that he was prepared to craft executive actions if such legislation was not forthcoming.

In June 2013, *The President's climate action plan* was published (White House, 2013). In the document, Obama reiterated the commitment to reduce US greenhouse gases to 17% below 2005 levels by 2020. It also said that his administration would work 'intensively to forge global responses to climate change' through a series of international agreements and negotiations (White House, 2013, p 17). On 22 June, in a speech at Georgetown University, Obama outlined in clear terms his strategy for tackling climate change. This included his decision to bypass Congress and issue an executive memo to the EPA calling for rules to curb greenhouse gas emissions from power plants. The speech was, as Grunwald (2013) argues, 'a notification of actions taken and actions to come, actions that don't require help from Congress'. In October 2013, for example, Obama issued an executive order setting up a Task Force on Climate Preparedness and Resilience.

In the face of continuing opposition from Republicans in Congress, President Obama told the assembled students that he refused 'to condemn [their] generation and future generations to a planet that's beyond fixing' (*The Guardian*, 26 June 2013). However, despite the president's promise of major developments to support and promote renewable energy sources (White House, 2013), he welcomed the US natural gas boom, brought about by the fracking of shale gas (see Chapter One), as a transitional fuel.

The US is in the middle of an unprecedented gas and oil drilling rush with the use of fracking. In Texas, for example, the Eagle Ford shale geological formation is 400 miles long and 50 miles wide, stretching form East Texas to Mexico. It is said to contain one of the largest recoverable oil deposits in the US. In Monterey County California, proposals to frack an area of some 1,750 square miles have proved very controversial. Indeed, they have been subject to a legal challenge in respect of the environmental impact. The shale reserve in Monterey contains an estimated 15 billion gallons of oil.

Professor William Press, a member of the president's Council of Advisers on Science and Technology, has argued that the climate change goals outlined by President Obama can be achieved by supporting further wide-scale fracking over the next few years (quoted in *The Observer*, 17 February 2013). However, as we noted in Chapter One, there is a body of scientific evidence highlighting the impact of fracking on the environment and attempts to tackle climate change. Furthermore, the EPA has been conducting its own research into the potential negative impacts on the environment and human health of fracking. Its report is due to be published in 2014.

Action at the state and local level

The relative lack of action at the federal level of government with respect to tackling climate change has created a policy space and a regulatory vacuum that a number of individual state governments and localities have sought to fill. For example, in 2006, the California state legislature passed into the law the California Global Solutions Act. The Act has been highly contested and has been the subject of much lobbying, notably, from the automobile industry. Nonetheless, it is a significant piece of legislation. It caps greenhouse gas emissions in key sectors of the Californian economy, with a target to cut greenhouse gases by 25% by 2020, based on a market system of trading credits. Furthermore, California has put in place regulations to reduce greenhouse gas emissions from automobiles, using the Clean Air Act as the legal underpinning for this. This matter has been the subject of much legal wrangling and political conflict, but in June 2009, the EPA, following an intervention from President Obama, granted California a so-called 'waiver', thus enabling the state to enforce its greenhouse gas emission standards for new vehicles.

The Regional Greenhouse Gas Initiative was signed by seven states in the north-east of the US in December 2005. They included New York, New Jersey and New Hampshire. It sets mandatory greenhouse gas emission targets on the electricity-generating sector within the framework of a market-based trading regime. It aims to stabilise greenhouse gas emissions at current levels through to 2015 and reduce emissions by 10% by 2019. The Initiative has faced many challenges, not the least of which was the decision of the state of New Jersey to leave the scheme in May 2011.

At the local level, Cohen and Millar (2012, p 47) refer to the 'far sighted' climate change policies of a number of US cities. There have been a myriad of such local initiatives, such as the introduction of local climate action plans. These range from San Francisco in the west and Chicago in the Midwest, through to New York City on the eastern seaboard.

The city of San Francisco came first in the US and Canada Green City Index in 2011, with New York, Seattle, Denver and Boston rounding off the top five US cities. The index analyses the environmental sustainability of 27 major cities in both countries in areas such as carbon dioxide emissions, energy, transport, air quality and environmental governance.

City governments in the US have direct policy responsibility, independent of the federal government, over renewable energy, energy-efficiency measures and public transportation. In addition, as Cohen and Millar (2012, p 45) observe, 'cities tend to be free from the heightened political polarisation seen at the federal level'. As a result, cities are able to 'create localised solutions' (Cohen and Millar, 2012, p 45). Let us take the example of New York City. More than 75% of the city's carbon dioxide emissions come from energy use in buildings. As a consequence, PlaNYC (New York City's sustainability strategy) has a principle focus on energy efficiency in buildings. In 2009, the city introduced 'ambitious building energy efficiency legislation', covering 22,000 buildings and representing 45% of New York City's greenhouse gas emissions (Cohen and Millar, 2012, p 45).

Conclusion

The 1992 Rio Summit, the accompanying Climate Change Convention and the subsequent Kyoto Protocol on climate change were, or so it appeared at the time, significant steps on the road to a more sustainable world, with global agreements to tackle climate change and reduce greenhouse emissions. Paradoxically, in the US domestic context, the decade of the 1990s was one of retrenchment of environmental and sustainability policy and legislation on climate change, particularly so within sections of Congress. The 'golden age' of 1964 to 1980, underpinned by a cross-party consensus, gave way to a conflicted and partisan polity in which policies came under sustained attack, principally from conservative Republicans and supporters of the Tea Party. It was an attack that took on an increased intensity under the presidency of George W. Bush, with the undermining of the science around climate change, the promotion of policy initiatives that supported mining and drilling interests, and the weakening of a number of the environmental gains of the 'golden age'. This attack on the science of climate change was also supported by powerful lobby groups. Former US Vice President Al Gore (2008, p 201) has spoken about Exxon Mobil's 'brazen efforts to try to manage public perceptions of the reality and seriousness of the climate crisis'. The UK-based Royal Society formally requested that Exxon Mobil stop putting 'very misleading' and 'inaccurate' information into the public domain (Gore, 2008, p 201).

With regard to the record of the Obama presidency, the jury still remains out. In his first term, there was some fine rhetoric but substantive policy action was more limited, thanks in part to a divided Congress and the intensification of political partisanship.

Since Obama's re-election in November 2012, there have been some signs that he is pushing the issues of climate change and the sustainability agenda up the policy agenda. Climate change got a key mention in his January 2013 inaugural address and in his February 2013 State of the Union address. There is a view that as a second-term president and no longer subject to the exigencies of re-election, the normally cautious Barack Obama may become more emboldened to shape and deliver a more substantive and bold climate change and sustainability agenda. Such a scenario may turn out to be correct. We can only wait and see. However, the route that the US decides to take has not only domestic consequences, but global ones as well. For, as Dernbach (2009, p 5) observes, the US global ecological and economic footprint 'is so large that is difficult to imagine how the world can achieve sustainability unless the United States does'.

References

Bailey, C. (2010) 'Environmental politics and policy', in G. Peele, C. Bailey, B. Cain and B. Guy Peters (eds) *Developments in American politics*, Basingstoke, Hants: Palgrave Macmillan.

Borick, C., Lachapelle, E. and Rabe, B. (2011) 'Climate compared: public opinion in the United States and Canada', *Issues in Governance Studies*, April, no 39.

Cohen, S. and Miller, A. (2012) 'Climate change 2011: a status report on US policy', *Bulletin of the Atomic Sciences*, vol 68, no 39, pp 39–49.

Dernbach, J. (2009) *Sustaining America*, Washington, DC: Environmental Law Institute.

EPA (Environmental Protection Agency) (2008) *EPA report on the environment*, Washington, DC: EPA.

Farley, M. and Smith, Z. (2014) *Sustainability: if it's everything, is it nothing?*, London: Routledge.

Flavin, C. and Engelman, R. (2009) 'The Perfect Storm', in Worldwatch Institute, *State of the world 2009 – confronting climate change*, London, Earthscan, pp 5–12.

Gertner, J. (2007) 'The future is drying up', *New York Times*, 21 October.

Gore, A. (2008) *The assault on reason*, New York, NY: Penguin Books.

Grunwald, M. (2013) 'Beyond the keystone pipeline', *Time*, vol 182, no 4, pp 22–4.

Guber, D. (2003) *The grassroots of green revolution*, Cambridge, MA: MIT Press.

Klyza, C. and Sousa, D. (2008) *American environmental policy, 1990–2006: beyond gridlock*, Cambridge, MA: MIT Press.

Mazmanian, D. and Kraft, M. (2009) *Towards sustainable communities: transition and transformation in environmental policy*, Cambridge, MA: MIT Press.

McKay, D. (2009) *American politics and society*, Oxford: Wiley-Blackwell.

Mooney, C. (2006) *The Republican war on science*, New York, NY: Basic Books.

NCADAC (National Climate Assessment and Development Advisory Committee) (2013) 'US National Climate Assessment Report'. Available at: www.globalchange.gov/what-we-do/assessment/ncadac

NOAA (National Oceanic and Atmospheric Administration) (2012) *State of the climate report*, Washington, DC: NOAA.

NRDC (Natural Resources Defense Council) (2005) *Rewriting the rules; the Bush administration's first- term environment record*, New York, NY: NRDC.

Reich, R. (2008) *Supercapitalism: the battle for democracy in an age of big business*, New South Wales, Australia: Allen and Unwin.

Revkin, A. (2008) 'New climate report foresees big changes', *New York Times*, 28 May.

Rosenbaum, W. (2007) *Environmental politics and policy*, Washington, DC: CQ Press.

Stern, N. (2006) *Stern review on economics of climate change*, London: HMSO.

Storey, W. (2010) *US government and politics*, Edinburgh: Edinburgh University Press.

White House (2009) *New energy for America*, Washington, DC: The White House.

White House (2011) *Blueprint for a secure energy future*, Washington, DC: The White House.

White House (2013) *The President's climate action plan*, Washington, DC: The White House.

FIVE

'Greening' the European Union? The Europeanisation of European Union environment policy

John O'Brennan

Introduction

In parallel with its development as a deeply integrated economic zone, the European Union (EU) has evolved as a space where a cumulatively significant pooling of sovereignty around environmental issues has developed apace. From a position in the early days of the European integration process where the environment hardly featured, the EU of 28 member states of today has highly developed policy competences across a range of environmental areas and is a signatory to more than 60 multilateral international environmental agreements (Vogler and Stephan, 2007). Since at least the mid-1980s, the EU supranational space has contended with and, to a significant degree, displaced the national level as the preferred locus of activity for its member states on environmental issues. This process of evolution and adaptation has not been a linear one: contestation of, and resistance to, a muscular EU presence within the environment has been a permanent feature of the politics of the environment in Europe and of inter-institutional relations in Brussels. But the stark reality of climate change, in particular, has moved the member states towards tacit acceptance of the need for a strong EU environmental *acquis* as the key mechanism for managing cross-border externalities of different kinds and for maintaining leadership within the international domain.

The key turning point in moving Europeans towards enhanced environmental action came in 1986, when the principle of substantive environmental integration was introduced into the treaties by the Single European Act (SEA), which stated that environmental requirements *shall* be a component of the European Community's other policies (Article 130r(2)). This commitment was further sharpened by the Maastricht

Treaty in 1992, which stated that environmental protection requirements *must* be integrated with the definition and implementation of other European Community policies (Article 130r(2)) (Koch and Lindenthal, 2011, p 981). Successive treaty changes have thus taken the environment from exclusively the intergovernmental arena to a decision-making system that combines national and shared EU competences. This should not surprise students of integration. After all, environmental problems do not stop at national boundaries; their intrinsic elements demand complex technocratic arrangements supported by pooled sovereignty and international cooperation. Thus, environmental policy within the EU now:

> conforms to a set of guiding principles, has its own terminology, is the focus of significant activity amongst a dedicated network of environmental actors, is underpinned by a binding framework of environmental laws, and has an explicit basis in the founding treaties. (Benson and Jordan, 2013, p 326)

It thus constitutes a 'mature system of multilevel governance', as 'virtually all environmental policy in Europe is now made in, or in close association with, the European Union' (Benson and Jordan, 2013, p 326).

This chapter examines the development of EU environmental policy over six decades of European integration. It assesses the contributions of individual actors and institutions and the progressive constitutionalisation of environmental concerns. It evaluates the extent to which the environment has been the subject of 'Europeanisation' of both politics and policy and the degree to which the EU as a supranational actor has influenced the real and substantive internalisation of progressive norms of environmental governance among its member states. It analyses the internal dynamics of EU climate change politics and how coherence is (or is not) achieved in international negotiations. The EU 'toolkit' for environmental governance includes capacity-building aid and instruments of compliance, persuasion and socialisation; competitive and reputational dynamics are also much in evidence. Supranational regulatory frameworks frequently push up against resistance at the national level and it is thus in the space between the Europeanised environment sector and the national administration of policies that we learn most about the efficacy and reach of EU activity. Europeanisation 'hits home' through both politics and policy, legislative and non-legislative activity, individual and collective action, and strategic and normative calculation. But this impact is far from uniform; there are myriad ways in which 'Europe fails to hit home' both within the EU and globally. 'Differential Europeanisation' thus emerges as the most important feature of the evolution of EU environmental politics; it reflects different patterns in the cognitive internalisation of environmental issues, as well as the structural realities of bargaining power among economic actors across the EU. It suggests that, although the European integration process has come a long way in managing environmental problems, there remain significant challenges if a truly sustainable model of living is to be achieved in the EU.

A trajectory of deepening integration

In its foundational period and early activity, the EU demonstrated little interest in, or capacity to administer, a common approach to the environment. Indeed, the Treaty of Rome (1957) did not even mention the word 'environment' (Benson and Jordan, 2013, p 325). The early EU (or 'European Community' as it was then styled) was primarily an economic organisation, the organisational logic of which was rationalist and intergovernmental; it would take decades before the 'environmental impulse' asserted itself in the treaties and in the normative understanding of the European integration process. And while early initiatives amounted to very little, the European Commission gradually assumed a prominent position as an advocate of environmental integration and, in alliance with a 'leadership group' within the Council (Denmark, Germany, Netherlands), adopted an approach that cumulatively rendered environmental policy more comprehensive in scale and scope.

It is from the early 1970s that we see a more acute ecological and environmental consciousness begin to build at the European Community (later EU) level. In retrospect, we can now identify institutional flexibility and the capacity and willingness of the European Commission, in particular, to interpret the treaties liberally as a space for action on the environment, as important phenomena that helped to shape the policy mix that eventually emerged. One way to trace this historical trajectory is to focus on the successive environment action programmes (EAPs) produced by the Commission. The first EAP (1973–76) emerged out of a request by the member states to the Commission to prepare an environmental policy and establish a directorate with responsibility for environmental issues. It established several key principles (including a rudimentary form of the 'polluter pays' principle), which subsequently evolved into treaty-based norms.

Table 5.1: Glossary of European Union institutions and decision-making

Council of the European Union	The main legislative institution of the EU, representing the executives of all 28 member states. Sometimes referred to as 'the Council' or the Council of Ministers.
EU directives	A directive is a legislative act of the EU that requires member states to achieve a particular result without dictating the means through which the result is to be achieved.
European Commission	The executive body of the EU, which is responsible for tabling legislative proposals, implementing EU decisions and upholding the treaties across the EU.
European Council	Group of Heads of State or Government, which is the pre-eminent political actor in the EU
European Court of Justice	The highest court of the EU in matters of EU law. Tasked with interpreting EU law and ensuring its equal application across all 28 member states of the EU.
European Parliament	The elected assembly of the EU. It exercises the legislative function of the EU alongside the Council and has become increasingly powerful within the EU governance architecture.
Intergovernmentalism	A mode of decision-making in which national governments are in the ascendancy and where each member state retains a veto on EU proposals. The EU institutions play only a minor role in decision-making.
MFF	Multi-Annual Financial Framework – the EU's budget.
OLP	Ordinary Legislative Procedure. Under the Lisbon Treaty, the OLP became the main legislative procedure used by the EU. The OLP gives equal weight to the Council of the EU and the European Parliament.
Supranationalism	A mode of decision-making in which the member states of the EU pool their sovereignty and where decisions can be taken by qualified majority vote. The EU institutions are significantly more powerful than in the intergovernmentalist mode of decision-making.
TEU	Treaty on European Union (1993). Sometimes known as the Maastricht Treaty.
TFEU	Treaty on the Functioning of the European Union, introduced by the Lisbon Treaty (2009).
Treaty of Rome	The 'founding treaty' of the EU, signed in Rome in 1957.
UNFCCC	United Nations Framework Convention on Climate Change.

It also formed the basis for a multi-year plan for action, including legislative and non-legislative options. The second EAP (1977–81) 'emphasized the need for scientifically informed decision-making through procedures such as environmental impact assessment (EIA)'

(Benson and Jordan, 2013, p 327) and asserted the Commission's desire to insinuate itself into the global policymaking sphere.

Moving in a more thoroughly programmatic direction, the third (1982–86) and fourth (1987–92) EAPs delivered a much more ambitious overall strategy for both protecting the environment 'before problems occurred' and identifying many more priority areas for collective action (Benson and Jordan, 2013, p 327). By 1987, environmental action by the EU required a secure treaty base. The SEA identified protection of the environment as an explicit objective of the European Community (Cahill, 2010, p 8). The significant boost to the integration process delivered by the Act boosted the competences of EU-level actors considerably, enabling a shared approach to the environment to emerge, driven by the new EU 'Centre'. The new environment policy emerged with a task enshrined in the treaties (now Article 191) of protecting the environment 'through the prudent and rational utilization of natural resources' such as oil products, natural gas and solid fuels (Solorio, 2011, p 401) and called for European Community action to 'be based on the principles that preventive action should be taken, that environmental damage should be rectified at source, and that the polluter should pay' (Solorio, 2011, p 401). The fourth EAP (1987–92) also signalled a clear ambition by declaring that the 'integration of the environmental dimension in other major policy areas will be a central part of the Commission's efforts' (Owens and Hope, 1989, p 97; see also Solorio, 2011, p 402). Actions based on single market-based measures were governed by qualified majority voting (QMV) and the new Cooperation Procedure, involving for the first time the European Parliament, introduced by the SEA (Cahill, 2010, p 8). By contrast, environmental policy not related to the single market continued to require unanimity within the Council and was not covered by the supranational procedure.

The fifth (1993–2000) and sixth (2002–12) EAPs coincided with and helped substantiate the expansion in EU competences enshrined in the Maastricht Treaty and heralded 'a shift to a more strategic and cross-cutting approach' (Benson and Jordan, 2013, p 327). Maastricht would also introduce significant procedural changes regarding environmental legislation. Perhaps its most important element was the extension of QMV to cover most environmental decisions and not just those related to the single market (Weale et al, 2000). Maastricht also made the environment an explicit policy responsibility of the European Community, 'giving the Commission greater powers to represent Member States in international organizations and with third parties, and calling upon it to promote measures to deal with regional and worldwide environmental problems' (Schreurs and Tiberghien, 2007, p 27) .Of major significance also was the decision to give the European Court of Justice (ECJ) the power to impose fines on member-state governments if they failed to comply with EU environmental laws (Cahill, 2010, p 8).The fifth EAP (1993–2000) provided another leap forward, placing the pursuit of environmental integration within every EU policy area, and called for sustainable development to be placed at the heart of the integration process. It also explored policy implementation through the use of non-legislative instruments and identified new methods through which to embed greater environmental policy integration within the EU space (Benson and Jordan, 2013, p 327).The sixth EAP articulated seven key strategic themes for EU policy – air pollution; the marine environment; sustainable use of resources; prevention and recycling of waste; sustainable use of pesticides; soil protection; and the urban environment – and was accompanied by significantly enhanced legislative force, having been adopted by the EU Council and European Parliament (Benson and Jordan, 2013, p 327).The Lisbon Treaty then formally incorporated energy policy into the formal competences of the EU (Article 194(10) of the Treaty on the Functioning of the European Union [TFEU]), with the establishment of a catalogue of exclusive and shared competences between the EU and its member states (Solorio, 2011, p 410). In parallel, the European Council adopted the first EU Sustainable Development Strategy (SDS) in Gothenburg in 2001, which set out policies to tackle key trends judged to be unsustainable, including the interconnections between climate change, energy and transport (Cahill, 2010, p 3). Since the 1990s, there has been a step change in the nature of EU environmental policy instruments, with some movement from the use of regulation to alternative instruments, collectively referred to as 'new policy instruments'. New policy instruments include market-based instruments (taxes, charges, emissions trading), voluntary or negotiated instruments, and information devices such as eco-labels. A common feature of new policy instruments is that they involve less intrusive intervention and offer those affected greater flexibility than regulation (Cahill, 2010, p 7).

In June 2013, agreement was reached between the Council and the Parliament on the Commission's proposal for a seventh EAP, 'Living well within the limits of our planet'. It identifies nine priority objectives for the period up to 2020, including: protecting nature and strengthening ecological resilience; boosting sustainable, resource-efficient, low-carbon growth; and effectively addressing environment-related threats to health. The programme sets out a framework to support the achievement of these objectives through, inter alia, better implementation of EU environment law, state-of-the-art science, securing the necessary investments in support of environment and climate change policy, and improving the way that environmental concerns and requirements are reflected in other policies. The programme also aims to boost efforts to help EU cities become more sustainable and improve the EU's capacity to meet regional and global environment and climate challenges (European Commission, 2013).

The most striking phenomenon that this cumulative deepening of EU-level environmental governance reveals is the move away from an initially ad hoc and reactive set of responses to the environment to a more thoroughly ambitious, variegated and strategic approach, co-developed by multiple stakeholders and increasingly vested in the 'mainstreaming' of the environment within the broad ambit of EU policymaking (Benson and Jordan, 2013, p 327). From a position (unsurprisingly) in the 1960s and 1970s where legislative output was extremely slow and contained, output quite literally rocketed in the 1980s and 1990s in response to the new opportunities contained within the SEA and Maastricht Treaty. The European Community enacted more environmental legislation between 1989 and 1991 than in the previous 20 years combined (Vogel, 1997; Cahill, 2010, p 8). EU policy gradually became more sure-footed and targeted and increasingly vested in the legislative process, where competences were increasingly shared. Thus, the trajectory of EU environmental policy is revealed as one of increasing regulation at the EU level, a more pluralistic institutional space and a gradualist path of constitutionalisation of environmental norms.

Europeanisation

Europeanisation is a concept that seeks to explain 'how Europe hits home' in both the policymaking sphere and the political arena. In short, it is the process through which EU-level activity impacts upon domestic policy and politics. The classic definition of the phenomenon is that put forward by Bulmer and Radaelli (2004), who define it as consisting of:

> processes of [a] construction, [b] diffusion and [c] institutionalization of formal and informal rules, procedures and policy paradigms, styles, 'ways of doing things' and shared beliefs and norms which are first defined and consolidated in the EU policy process and then incorporated in the logic

of domestic (national and subnational) discourse, political structures and public policies.

Europeanisation is thus 'concerned with what happens once EU institutions are in place and produce their effects' (Radaelli, 2000). This understanding of Europeanisation flows from a view of institutions as social artefacts and systems of rules, both formal and informal. Organisations are 'formal institutions with written rules and procedures prescribing behaviour'; they also encompass informal understandings such as 'bureaucratic routines and cultures' (Börzel and Risse, 2012, p 4). Europeanisation emerges, then, as the key mechanism of change, which modifies and somewhat attenuates the formal practice of national sovereignty across the EU.

Europeanisation has a dual function as an independent variable in national politics and 'as the processes by which the domestic structures adapt to European integration' (Caporaso, 2007, p 27). However, it is important to remember that this centralising trajectory is somewhat tempered by the structural prerogatives of local- or national-level public administrations in implementing rules agreed collectively in Brussels. Contestation and non-compliance are a constant presence (and problem) in the EU environmental arena, as national-level jurisdictional politics collides with the EU supranational juggernaut. Merely 'downloading institutional designs from one context into another is likely to lead to less behavioural compliance with the rules and regulations than active adaptation and alteration of institutional features to a given domestic or regional context' (Börzel and Risse, 2012, p 4). Furthermore, while some aspects of national policy have become more similar, 'no long-term convergence towards a common European model is apparent' (Benson and Jordan, 2013, p 331; see also Jordan and Liefferink, 2004). For the moment, national politics, and the cultural and historical specificities that frame national systems of public administration, militate against the uniform adoption of EU policies within the 28 member states of the EU. Or, as Weale et al (2000, p 468) put it: 'Growing multilevel environmental governance has therefore not yet created more universal environmental governance'.

So, what patterns of Europeanisation can be identified within the EU environmental space? Following Bulmer and Radaelli (2004, p 5) and Börzel (2001), we can locate three specific models of Europeanisation. In order to explain variation in Europeanisation mechanisms, the literature generally distinguishes between hierarchical and non-hierarchical mechanisms (Radaelli, 2000). This distinction allows the analysis of when the EU position is hierarchically equal or superior to the one of the member states. Frequently, we can find that the hierarchical mechanisms occur predominantly in policies where the EU regulatory capacity is enough to impose conditions on the member states; this would be the case for the internal market or environmental policy. The non-hierarchical mechanisms, on the other hand (the second and third models outlined in the following), occur regularly in those policy areas where the EU does not have any regulatory capacity or a limited one, for example, in energy policy (Solorio, 2011, p 7).

The first significant model of Europeanisation is known as 'governance by hierarchy' (Bulmer and Radaelli, 2004). This relates to those circumstances where the supranational institutions have a considerable amount of power delegated to them. In particular, the European Commission enjoys a pre-eminent (early) role through its right of policy initiative and crucial ability to frame the legislative agenda. At the end of the negotiation phase, the Council typically will have agreed new legislation to be transposed and implemented in the member states. The implementation stage is particularly important as 'enforcement mechanisms are designed to build trust by limiting the scope of individual states to cheat on the negotiated agreements' (Bulmer and Radaelli, 2004, p 6). This form of 'positive integration' requires the introduction of an active, collectively binding policy. That measure then has to be 'downloaded' to the member-state level. The Commission must ensure that legislation is properly implemented, and it can (where necessary) refer a non-compliant state to the ECJ. According to Benson and Jordan (2013, p 329), the Commission 'deserves the bulk of the credit for developing an EU environment policy'. Because of its right of initiative and its special role as 'guardian of the EU treaties', the Commission exerts significant influence on the environmental policy of the EU (Koch and Lindenthal, 2011, p 980; see also Lindenthal, 2009). At numerous critical points, the Commission and its environmental Directorate General (DG) wielded substantive agenda-setting power, 'developing and promoting new policy ideas and blueprints of agreements or reinforcing other actors' demands' (Schreurs and Tiberghien, 2007, p 33). Given that the original Treaty of Rome contained no environmental provisions, the Commission had to rely on a certain legal and institutional flexibility in seeking to gradually incorporate the environment into EU activity. It did this mainly by relying on Article 100 EC (now Article 115 TFEU), relating to the internal market, and Article 235 EC (now Article 352 TFEU), which allowed the EU to move into new policy areas in order to accomplish treaty-consistent goals. For the Commission, Article 100 'proved legally more secure and politically less contested than Article 235; hence the tendency for early measures to target traded products' (Benson and Jordan, 2013, p 329). The first key early directive, dealing with standards for classifying, packaging and labelling dangerous substances, was based on Article 100. Other environmental directives that were adopted absent an explicit legal basis in the treaties include a 1970 directive on air pollution from motor vehicles, the Birds Directive (1979) and the Drinking Water Directive (1980). Just as in other areas of policy arguments about the validity and legitimacy of such measures, these were subject to sometimes intense contestation. What is not in question is that a trajectory was established that helped to better insinuate environmental concerns into evolving EU policy and politics. In all these cases, the supranational entrepreneurship of the Commission emerges as a key variable in driving EU environment policy forward.

Although it was, and remains, far from a monolithic actor within the policymaking process, there has been a consistent willingness on the part of the Commission to think creatively about EU environmental policy, to follow unorthodox routes to enactment of decisions and to make the normative and declaratory case for a maximalist approach to the environment. The 'DG Environment learnt to exploit opportunities and colonize institutional niches in the EU', and Benson and Jordan term this 'the very essence of Monnet's neo-functionalist method' of institutional engineering 'by stealth', whereby incremental integration by the EU in key economic sectors creates so-called 'spillover' incentives for further and deeper cooperation in other areas (Benson and Jordan, 2013, pp 329–30). The environment DG initiates and legalises environmental policy and ensures that these policy measures are implemented effectively by the EU member states. Further, it aims to contribute to a better integration of environmental issues into other European Community policies (Koch and Lindenthal, 2011, p 981).

There is 'a pronounced coercive dimension to the arrangements within this first mode of Europeanization, consistent with an approach defined by hierarchy' (Bulmer and Radaelli, 2004, p 6). The ECJ has, at times, played a pivotal role in 'establishing the legal importance (and hence legitimacy) of EU environmental policy', mainly via rulings on the direct effect of directives and its role in adjudicating compliance with EU law (Benson and Jordan, 2013, p 330). The ECJ was drawn into 'institutional turf wars' in the 1970s and 1980s, and when asked to adjudicate on the legal basis of EU policy, often resolves disputes in favour of the Commission (Benson and Jordan, 2013, p 330). Once it acquired the means to issue fines for non-compliance with EU environment law, the ECJ cemented its place as a key actor within the system, while helping to provide a level playing field for member states in the 'compliance game'. Thus, this first avenue of Europeanisation can be characterised as one where the EU's supranational institutional regime is most active and influential. It is now the predominant vector of Europeanisation that shapes EU environment policy.

A second mode of Europeanisation revolves around a process of 'uploading' national-level rules to the European level. The open-ended and competitive governance structure of the EU (between EU institutions and individual member states) in an issue of shared competence, such as the environment, has created multiple and mutually reinforcing opportunities for leadership (Schreurs and Tiberghien, 2007, p 24). Although modified by the process of bargaining and negotiation within the Council, it is frequently the case that new environmental rules emerge from a single state or the 'environment leadership states' to form a synthesis that is acceptable to the majority.

The extent of convergence that forms the basis for this kind of Europeanisation will depend upon how far apart the initial preferences of the member states are, the voting rules in the Council and the patterns of learning that take place over multiple and overlapping sessions of negotiation (Bulmer and Radaelli, 2004, p 5). Shared understandings build up over time after the initial process of 'uploading' ideas and the construction of policy. This kind of Europeanisation is referred to as 'governance by negotiation'.

The determinants of national preference formation are complex, and the Council has, at times, been the site of protracted conflict on the environment between 'maximalist' and 'minimalist' states. However, even as early as the 1970s, some national ministers discovered that they could adopt policies in Brussels that were unattainable in their national jurisdictions. This was especially the case when the measures were being driven by the 'troika' of environment leaders comprising Denmark, the Netherlands and West Germany (Benson and Jordan, 2013, p 330). Not surprisingly, it is in the Mediterranean region that we can locate the so-called 'laggard states', those that have either opposed or been very lukewarm towards a proactive collectivist approach to the environment. More recently, eastern enlargement has also complicated the search for a 'progressive consensus', as the states that acceded to the EU brought a problematic environmental legacy with them to the negotiating table. Sbragia (1996, p 237) has identified a distinct 'push–pull' dynamic within the Council, evident from the early 1980s onwards. She argues that this kind of actor constellation was driven by the 'leaders', who would continually push for action in Brussels and usually succeeded in pulling the laggards towards a common destination, which most of the laggards would rather have avoided. Ireland and

Spain especially stand out as this kind of recalcitrant state. In fact, in both of these member states, very little has happened in environment policy over the last 30 years that was not driven by Brussels. The Presidency of the Council also emerges as a key institutional actor, although its importance has varied according to context, and the role has been somewhat diminished by the changes introduced by the Lisbon Treaty. Nonetheless, there have been many instances where the Presidency has mattered greatly to environmental outcomes in the EU. Unsurprisingly, when the Presidency has been held by a 'leader' state, there has been a more proactive agenda and consistent pursuit of objectives. The Presidency's main role is now mediation, but occupancy of the role comes with an existing norm set that helps to frame and shape behaviour. These norms include impartiality, an impulse towards consensus-seeking and solidarity, and a willingness to jettison egoistic national interests in favour of collectivist solutions. In the EU climate negotiations, there have been multiple times when different actors have taken up the leadership ball. For example, the Dutch played this kind of leadership role when they held the EU Presidency in 1992 and 1997. The Germans and the British have quite consistently taken on climate change leadership roles within Europe, and have very visibly done so when they have held the Council Presidency (Schreurs and Tiberghien, 2007, p 25). In summary, this mode of 'horizontal' Europeanisation depicts dynamics that are intergovernmental rather than supranational and where the key actors consist of environmental leader states within the Council.

A third form of Europeanisation takes the form of loose policy coordination. Here, again, national governments are the key actors: unanimity is often the decision-making rule and EU policy remains rather undeveloped relative to the first two patterns of Europeanisation. We can include in this category Commission Green Papers and Communications as tools of policymaking (Braun, 2009, p 430; Solorio, 2011, p 406) and the broad ambit of policies covered by the Open Method of Coordination (OMC), where so-called 'soft law' prevails. This relates to rules of conduct that are not legally enforceable, but, nonetheless, have a legal scope, in that they act as a guide for all participants in the governance regime. The OMC is an instrument designed to aid the spread of best practice, with the aim of achieving convergence towards EU goals. The idea is to use EU structures as a kind of transfer device rather than a rigid law-making system. There is an open, non-determinative dimension to OMC activity and it eschews the imposition of supranational rules in favour of learning processes and peer review systems (Bulmer and Radaelli, 2004, p 11). 'Learning' can occur through the spread of discourse containing new ideas and principles, the transfer of norms through negotiation and practice, the exchange of qualitative and quantitative data, and commitments at the national level to voluntarily pursue harmonisation in non-legally binding spheres of activity. The EU can provide benchmarks, guidelines and timelines but does so with the aim not of regulating, but of *encouraging convergence towards common positions.*

Crucially, here, the supranational institutions have very weak powers: they cannot act as strong enforcing agents promoting Europeanisation. That does not mean that no Europeanisation process is at work. Rather, it can take on a more voluntaristic and non-hierarchical appearance (Bulmer and Radaelli, 2004, p 7). Criticism of the OMC and similar instruments (particularly from rational choice scholars) suggests that there is no real relationship between rhetoric and action. Social learning does not translate into policy change and may be adopted for strategic rather than normative reasons. But Bulmer and Radaelli (2004) argue that this misses the point. Learning processes are, by definition, cognitive exercises and these are used by policymakers to understand the reality they exist in and contend with. The EU also 'Europeanises' its member states through both persuasion and socialisation. Indeed, the EU might be understood as a giant laboratory for understanding how international socialisation takes place, or as a 'gigantic socialization agency which actively tries to promote its rules, norms, practices and structures of meaning to which member states are exposed and which they have to incorporate into their domestic structures' (Börzel and Risse, 2012, p 7). In the famous formulation of March and Olsen, this constitutes a kind of 'logic of appropriateness'. A close relation is the 'logic of arguing' inherent in processes of persuasion. These are situations in which actors try to persuade each other about the validity claims inherent in any causal or normative statement (Börzel and Risse, 2012, p 8).

Combining these three potential avenues through which Europeanisation takes place, Schreurs and Tiberghien (2007, p 22) identify a dynamic process of what they call 'competitive multi-level reinforcement' among the different EU political poles 'within a context of decentralized governance'. EU leadership has depended upon the actions and commitments of a group of pioneering states and the leadership roles played by the European Parliament and, especially, the European Commission. This upward cycle of reinforcing leadership within a quasi-federal system has been triggered by, and been dependent upon, strong public support and normative commitment. Börzel and Risse (2012, p 8) argue that Europeanisation can be regarded as a 'special instance of policy and institutional "diffusion". Diffusion is conceived as a process through which ideas, normative standards, or policies and institutions spread across time and space'. This diffusion can come about through the formation and implementation of concrete legal rules (as per the first model of Europeanisation) or horizontal negotiation and the development of shared understandings of environmental policy within the Council (as in the second model of Europeanisation). But away from the formal bargaining and negotiating space, there is a myriad number of channels through which the informal norms and ideas are also being diffused that also contribute to the deepening of a collective consciousness around environmental protection.

None of these mechanisms of Europeanisation can guarantee that a 'maximalist' (truly progressive) EU environment policy is actually implemented in the member states. Europeanisation does not follow a simple linear logic; the member states at the receiving end of persuasion, socialisation or compliance demands by the European Commission and other institutional actors are not simply passive actors lacking their own agency. Domestic actors and institutions can play a decisive role in 'absorbing, rejecting, or domesticating Europe' (Bulmer and Radaelli, 2004, p 9). Indeed, 'the adoption of and adaptation to EU norms, rules, and institutional models into domestic or regional structures mostly involve active processes of interpretation, incorporation of new norms, rules, into existing institutions, and also resistance to particular rules and regulations' (Börzel and Risse, 2012, p 8). Thus, the now considerable body of literature on Europeanisation demonstrates conclusively that its impact is *differential* rather than *convergent* (Héritier et al, 2001). The extent to which transposition of EU rules will be accompanied by substantive implementation (implying real and irreversible internalisation of EU norms) will depend upon the range of domestic actors and interests aligned with or opposed to the EU measure, the cultural and administrative capacity of the member state, and the extent of political will to implement fully and effectively, as well as the nature of potential sanctions and reputational damage incurred as a result of non-compliance. While some aspects of national policy have become more similar, 'no long-term convergence towards a common European model is apparent (Benson and Jordan, 2013, p 331; see also Jordan and Liefferink, 2004). For the moment, national politics, and the cultural and historical specificities that frame national systems of public administration, militate against the uniform adoption of EU policies within the 28 member states of the EU.

Environment policy is one of the EU policy spheres where there is the most significant divergence between transposition and implementation of EU rules. As Börzel and Risse (2012, p 11) put it, it does not matter how many measures are 'uploaded' at the EU level if member states fail to implement them at the national level; the mere 'downloading' of rules does not guarantee substantive and successful implementation. In fact, it can lead to so-called 'Potemkin implementation', which is to say, an illusory form of implementation. This is especially the case where compliance with EU rules carries significant financial costs for the member state in question. The Commission lacks the robust inspection powers it enjoys in competition policy or fisheries, and, instead, has to rely on civil society organisations (or other governments) to bring cases of non-compliance to the EU level (Benson and Jordan, 2013, p 334). As Fernandez (2012, p 198) maintains: 'the European Union is good at designing measures but it fails on implementation, something consistently acknowledged by the EU authorities'. Thus, the phenomenon of conflict between EU-level common policy and the divergent national levels reveals the enduring difficulties in turning the 'common' rule into a law that enjoys universal application.

Arguments about the exact size of the transposition–implementation 'gap' persist, but nobody denies the negative impact that this has on the pursuit of a universal policy regime. The ironies of this are not lost on international negotiators, who sometimes scoff at the EU's pretensions towards global leadership and point to the continuing gaps between EU global demands and instances of non-compliance by its own member states. Differential Europeanisation of both policy and politics is thus the most striking phenomenon within the EU environmental regime.

Interests: the European economy versus the environment?

Given that the original raison d'être of the EU lay in the progressive opening of markets and the liberalisation of trade, it was always likely that impulses towards environmental protection would run up against business lobbies whose dominant focus was on the pursuit of ever-deeper market integration that privileged and protected specific economic interests. In more recent years, as a deep economic depression has pervaded the Eurozone, ideas about green growth and recovery through harnessing environmental technology have brought the two worlds closer together. Nonetheless, there remain significant tensions between (largely) neoliberal market imperatives and the need to solidly legislate for environmental protection. Deregulatory pressure associated with market opening has often posed direct challenges to the pursuit of a robust EU environmental and sustainability regime. Industrial lobbies, moreover, managed to gain the support of some key politicians, who mainly argued that plans to implement cuts in greenhouse gas emissions posed a severe threat to industry. These included Italian Prime Minister Silvio Berlusconi, EU Commissioner for Transport and Energy Loyola de Palacio and, perhaps most controversially, EU Commissioner for the Internal Market and Services Charlie McCreevy, who had been the author of many of the neoliberal policies that brought about the collapse of the Irish 'Celtic Tiger' economy (Schreurs and Tiberghien, 2007, p 28). And even though the number of environmental pressure groups expanded exponentially after the mid-1980s, the environment lobby remains comprehensively outnumbered by business interests that have long known how to expertly play the 'European game'.

Perhaps the most serious challenge posed to the environment within the integration process is that of agriculture and the deeply embedded interests associated with the Common Agriculture Policy (CAP). Agriculture plays a hugely significant part in the preservation of vital European ecosystems, biodiversity and natural resources and thus looms large in the horizon of environmental campaigners. The EU is the world's largest importer of food and the second-largest exporter of food, and the CAP remains a difficult space for EU environmental advocates, despite a series of reforms that reduced some of its most perverse and wasteful effects. And although EU heads of state and government agreed in early 2013 to cut the overall budget for agriculture by 11.3%, the CAP will still account for 36% of the 2014–20 EU budget, thus remaining the largest part of the Multi-Annual Financial Framework (MFF) (Pardo, 2013). For most of its history, the CAP promoted a hugely intensive model of farming, with manifestly destructive environmental consequences. The sector relies heavily on the use of pesticides and chemical fertilisers containing nitrates, which are significant sources of water pollution. In France alone, the cost of treating water pollution originating from farming is €54 billion a year, most of which is passed on to consumers. Furthermore, the sector produces 9% of EU greenhouse gas emissions and 70% of the nitrous oxide emissions in Europe, despite generating only 1.6% of EU gross domestic product (GDP) and employing 5% of citizens (Pardo, 2013). Thus, the environmental damage wrought by the agricultural sector is out of all proportion to its contribution to output and employment in the EU.

The transport sector also constitutes a serious obstacle to effective EU environmental protection. Together with energy, the transport sector has contributed most significantly to the increase in greenhouse gas emissions in the EU. Transport and industry combined consume more than half the total final energy consumption in the EU, while only a quarter is attributed to households. Energy consumed by transport has strongly increased over the last two decades (by 31%) even though the economic crisis since 2008 has slightly reversed the trend. EU growth and development priorities sometimes clash head on with those of environmental protection; the data on air and road transport, in particular, provide plenty of evidence to support such a contention. But here, too, the EU has belatedly recognised that the environmental opportunity cost of more airports and motorways is just too significant to bear. As early as 1993, subsequent to the enactment of the Maastricht Treaty, the then European Commission Department DGVII (responsible for key areas such as transport policy) stated that transport policy should not solely focus on the demand side of transport, but should also consider the environmental impacts of the sector. Furthermore, it worked to pursue a strategy aimed at reducing – or at the very least containing – the overall impact of transport on the environment.

The extraordinary challenge posed by climate change has provided the Commission with the opportunity for much greater integration of EU-level energy policy specifically tied to the climate change portfolio. Indeed, the energy sector is perceived as crucial in the fight against climate change. It accounts for almost 80% of the EU's greenhouse gas emissions. The EU produces less than 50% of its own energy needs, although energy dependence varies considerably among the member states. Denmark is the only net exporter of energy, while Malta is almost entirely dependent upon energy imports. On the plus side, however, the last two decades have seen a very strong decline in coal consumption. In line with the findings of the United Nations (UN) Intergovernmental Panel on Climate Change (IPCC), the EU aims to reduce greenhouse gas emissions by 80–95% in the EU by 2050 (compared with 1990 levels). This long-term objective implies an almost complete decarbonisation of the EU energy sector (Dupont and Oberthur, 2012, p 233). Competence on energy policy has slowly been shifting to the EU level, even prior to the enactment of the Lisbon Treaty, where an energy competence was specifically established (Jordan et al, 2010; Dupont and Oberthur, 2012, p 233). Energy policy remains, however, a shared competence and member states retain important leverage including, with regard to determining the outcomes of exploiting energy resources, the choice between energy sources and the general structure of energy supply (Article 194(2) TFEU). The EU has also sought to develop a renewable energy policy. Here, the reduction of greenhouse gas emissions is a major rationale but it has also been promoted for geopolitical reasons, principally security of supply and loosening the dependence upon Russia and other external suppliers. The latest EU legislation on renewables is the 2009 RE [Renewable Energy] Directive which outlines the policy framework for increasing the share of RE (biomass, geothermal, hydropower, ocean, wind) in the EU to 20% by 2020. Importantly, this target of 20% is binding under EU law. The potential of carbon capture and storage technology has been much trumpeted but, as yet, continues to appear commercially unviable. The EU target is for the share of renewables to increase by about eight to 10 percentage points every five years up to 2050. However, between 2000 and 2005, the share of renewables increased by only one percentage point and it looks unlikely that this figure will go much above two percentage points in the foreseeable future without large-scale intervention (Dupont and Oberthur, 2012, p 234).

On the positive side, EU policy has increasingly turned towards green energy as part of the solution to continued economic stasis. Indeed, former Commissioner Pielbags describes the EU's shift in energy policy as a 'third industrial revolution'. The context for understanding this 'greening of the EU business environment' is so-called 'ecological modernisation'. This is the idea that economic growth and environmental protection are not mutually opposed. Rather, they can be 'reconciled by further, albeit "greener" industrialization' (Carter, 2001, p 211). Ecological modernisation sees environmental degradation as a fundamental problem and insists that such degradation may require significant adaptation and innovation (Warleigh-Lack, 2012, p 82). Germany has been especially identified as the member state most associated with this approach. As recession turned to depression, policymakers in many parts of the EU turned to ecological modernisation and the green agenda as an instrument for job creation: solar, wind and other renewables became part of the national conversation on economic recovery. Again, there is wide variation in the take-up of renewables among the member states. In Austria, for example, 68% of electricity generation now comes from renewables, while the EU average lies below 18%. At the other end of the scale, in both Estonia and Poland, the vast majority of electricity generation still comes from coal.

Finally, we should also note the role played by civil society organisations and lobby groups within the environmental arena in the EU. In the 1980s and 1990s, the number of environmental pressure groups lobbying in Brussels accelerated apace. The Climate Action Network Europe, the leading non-governmental organisation (NGO) network working on climate change, has over 100 member organisations. They have been ardent supporters of climate action. At the EU level, the so-called Green 9 Group of environmental NGOs (BirdLife International, Climate Action Network Europe, European Environmental Bureau, Environmental Network, the European Federation for Transport and Environment, Friends of the Earth Europe, Greenpeace, International Friends of Nature, and the World Wide Fund for Nature [WWF] European Policy Office) has gained advisory status in EU decision-making and all members (except for Greenpeace) receive funding from the Commission to do this work (Schreurs and Tiberghien, 2007, p 30). On the other side of the divide, business groups also ramped up their engagement with environmental issues, if only from a rational approach to their business interests. The dynamic that characterises the divide between the two sides of the lobby is one that has made Brussels the rival of Washington in the lobbying arena.

Tackling climate change at the European Union level: towards sustainability

The EU approach to climate change has evolved out of its own broader approach to environment policy and against a global backdrop of increasing concern about the potentially devastating impact on the planet of greenhouse gases in particular. Thus, EU climate change policy integration has aimed at 'achieving sustainable development and preventing environmental damage; removing contradictions between policies as well as within policies; and realizing mutual benefits and the goal of making policies mutually supportive' (Collier, 1994, p 36). The IPCC has worked out that the earth's average surface temperature has risen by 0.76 degrees centigrade since 1850 and that, left unchecked, it is likely to rise by between 1.8 degrees and 4 degrees this century. In the worst-case scenario, some leading scientists predict that it could soar by up to 6.4 degrees centigrade, but an increase of just 2 degrees may have irreversible and potentially catastrophic consequences for our planet. The EU understanding of climate change takes as a benchmark the scientific consensus that climate governance needs to limit global temperature rise to 2 degrees above pre-industrial levels by 2050; climate policy has long been based on this target.

The EU has been a powerful backer of the precautionary principle in relation to climate change, heeding the warnings of the IPCC that anthropogenic emissions of greenhouse gases are warming the planet and that this could have serious ecological, health and climatic impacts (Schreurs and Tiberghien, 2007, p 24). The EU's position is one that relies heavily on the United Nations Framework Convention on Climate Change (UNFCCC) and the Kyoto Protocol to the UNFCCC. The most important objective of the UNFCCC is 'to achieve stabilization of greenhouse gas concentrations in the atmosphere at a level that would prevent a dangerous anthropogenic interference with the climate system' (Torney and Fujiwara, 2010). The targets agreed at Kyoto amount to an average 5% cut against 1990 levels for the five-year period 2008–12. The EU tried its best to get the Kyoto Protocol into force as soon as possible but it faced a range of opposition from global actors and it was only enacted in February 2005. In 2007, EU member states agreed to go a step further and committed to an average 8% reduction. Under a 'burden-sharing' agreement, this target is shared between the 15 older member states (EU-15), with considerable leverage given to newer and poorer member states to catch up. It is at UN summits that the most important agreements related to environment protection and climate change have been agreed, demonstrating the continuing importance of the international level to EU efforts to fight climate change.

The first EU target for stabilising carbon dioxide emissions was adopted by the Joint Council on Energy and the Environment as early as October 1990 (Skjaerseth, 1994; Solorio, 2011). Gradually thereafter, we saw climate change policy interwoven with energy, transport and environment as EU policy responses were sharpened. The integration dynamic was clearly evident in the Maastricht Treaty. Article 6 of the Treaty of the European Community (Article 11 of the Lisbon Treaty) recognised that the 'environmental protection requirements must be integrated into the definition and implementation of the Union's policies and activities, in particular, with a view to promoting sustainable development' (Solorio, 2011, p 402). Thus, well before climate change moved into the mainstream of global politics, the EU had accelerated its efforts to reduce global warming (Solorio, 2011, p 402). The European Commission's ambitions were also clearly evident in the strong package it presented to the Council in the run-up to the Rio Summit in 1992. The so-called 'Climate Package' included a proposed directive on renewable electricity, regulatory tools to address energy-efficiency issues and a tax on energy-using products (Skjaerseth, 1994; Solorio, 2011, p 402). Notwithstanding the fact that some member states recoiled from such measures and succeeded in diluting the package, we can see clear evidence in the early 1990s of an emerging European Community strategy to fight climate change and the emergence of the core of an EU agenda (Solorio, 2012, p 402). Indeed, by the end of the decade, the EU had positioned itself as the international agenda-setter in relationship to climate change mitigation (Schreurs and Tiberghien, 2007, p 19).

By 2005, the EU had embarked upon a new, much more intense stage in its climate change programme to prepare and implement a mid- and long-term strategy to confront the challenge (Solorio, 2011, p 403). In this context, the European Council asserted 'the need to demonstrate that the EU's commitment to meet Kyoto ... is practical and not just a paper one' (Piebalgs, 2009, p 2, as cited in Solorio, 2012, p 403). Environmental policy integration (EPI) is a long-standing goal of EU policy, and it is now explicitly linked with the pursuit of sustainable development. In practice, as Benson and Jordan (2013, p 332) attest, integration means 'ensuring that economically powerful sectors, such as transport, agriculture and energy, build an environmental dimension into their policy design and implementation processes'. In other words, the environment is being 'mainstreamed' into EU economic and industrial policy, with the aim of ameliorating the worst excesses of some parts of industry and gaining acceptance for the objective of normalising environmental concerns within the dominant economic model. This logic underpinned the decision to add sustainable development as an objective of the EU in its external relations in the Lisbon Treaty, and, similarly, international action on climate change has been added as an objective of EU policy on the environment (Article 191 of the Lisbon Treaty). In 2010, a new DG for climate action was created in the European Commission (Cahill, 2010, p 3).

The protracted economic crisis in Europe has meant a significant reduction in EU-15 emissions but this has largely been the result of falling economic output (and especially industrial output) rather than success in tackling emissions. The EU's share of global greenhouse gas emissions currently stands at about 13% of the global share but is decreasing fast and will fall to around 10% in 2020 (Egenhofer and Alessi, 2013, p 6). This compares with respective shares for China and the US of about 20% each. Thus, EU reductions are necessary but far from sufficient to tackle the global problem of greenhouse gas emissions. At present, the EU 2020 target for emissions reduction is legally binding in EU law. The EU may also raise the ambition from 20% to 30% if other major economies take equivalent measures (Torney and Fujiwara, 2010). The crisis has coincided with an assertive new presence within EU environmental governance in the shape of the Central and Eastern European member states. The so-called 'big bang' enlargement of 2004 brought into the EU a large number of states wholly unconvinced about, and unprepared to act seriously on, climate change issues. Many of the newly acceding states had a legacy of environmental damage. During the adoption of the climate–energy package in late 2008, Poland led a group of eight Eastern European states that called for their relatively weak economic positions to be taken into account at a time of deep austerity. This was 'the first occasion on which the new entrants had acted as a negotiating bloc in the environmental sector' (Benson and Jordan, 2013, p 335). The addition of 10 new member states may not have triggered the institutional stasis that many had predicted for the EU negotiation system, but it certainly made the 'eternal EU search for consensus' that bit more difficult in environment policy simply because of the significant costs attached to the 'catch-up' process for Central and Eastern European states. Worries about competitiveness, in particular, feature prominently in the calculus of Central and Eastern European policymakers in the environment Council. All of this makes it difficult for the EU to achieve consensus when it negotiates with other powerful global actors at the UN and in other fora.

Conclusion

Almost six decades after the EU was founded, environmental policy is well entrenched in the supranational governance architecture across the continent. It is 'broad in scope, extensive in detail and stringent in effect' (Weale et al, 2000, p 1). This rapid and enduring transformation in regulatory scope and behavioural norms has made the EU the pre-eminent actor in the 'greening of global politics'. Over time, the focus has moved from an exclusivist, narrowly focused environmental agenda to a 'mainstreaming' approach that has sought to stitch environmental concerns into the broad fabric of European integration activity. Thus, the focus has changed from remedying problems to 'designing them out of' sectoral policies in accordance with the sustainability and environmental integration principles (Benson and Jordan, 2013, p 336). Climate change, in particular, has been a catalyst for major changes in attitudes to the environment and, in functional terms, to transforming the modes of EU environmental governance. The settled consensus on the extraordinary dangers to European society presented by global warming beyond two degrees, has facilitated the breaking down of barriers that traditionally hindered the supranational capacity to achieve concentrated integration. Combating climate change on a global level is now a specific goal of EU environment policy, and sustainable development is enshrined in the treaties as one of the EU's fundamental objectives in its relations with the wider world.

Yet, there remain fundamental challenges, not least within EU borders, where the gap between the transposition and implementation of commitments entered into remains far too high. Compliance with EU laws is still significantly short of what one might expect and this reflects varying degrees of national resistance to, and contestation of, the proactive positions on the environment championed by leaders within the Council and by the Commission and European Parliament. The European Commission, in particular, has played a leading role throughout different periods of environmental integration. Beginning with somewhat of a 'tabula rasa' and frequently taking advantage of the weak policy coordination among member states, the Commission was able to act in the manner of a classic policy entrepreneur and even to behave in an opportunistic manner in its 'environmental ghetto' (Benson and Jordan, 2013, p 336). 'Europeanisation' has had a deep and profound impact upon the public policy functions of the member states of the EU (Bulmer and Radaelli, 2004). However, the Europeanisation of the environment has proceeded in a far from uniform direction. While there is no doubting that European integration has encouraged a fundamental change in consciousness on environmental protection among its member states, there remain significant challenges in moving 28 different sovereign states towards a single destination in a deeply challenging economic landscape. 'Differential Europeanisation' thus emerges as the most accurate conceptual explanation of how EU environment policy has evolved. Europeanisation of the environment is strategic and normative, constitutional and legislative, developing along both vertical and horizontal tracks, both voluntary and involuntary and through uniquely European and universal or global pressures. But it does not produce uniform outcomes in the policy and politics of its member states. Contestation and non-compliance feature as strongly as adaptation and internalisation. For sure, the introspection and infighting triggered by the Eurozone crisis has also presented the EU with an 'existential moment'. But the environmental *acquis* survives and there is little evidence of any significant pushback against its fundamental tenets. The EU remains a global leader in the fight against climate change and an important exporter of environmental norms. The 'greening of Europe' remains a partial and incomplete project. But it is also a story of significant achievements, of a deepening commitment to collective action and 'thick' constitutionalisation of progressive environmental governance.

References

Benson, A. and Jordan, A. (2013) 'Environmental policy', in M. Cini and N. Perez-Solorzano Borragan (eds) *European Union politics*, Oxford: Oxford University Press, pp 325–37.

Börzel, T.A. (2001) *States and regions in the European Union. Institutional adaptation in Germany and Spain*, Cambridge: Cambridge University Press.

Börzel, T.A. and Risse, T. (2012) 'From Europeanisation to diffusion', *West European Politics*, vol 35, no 1 (special issue), pp 1–19.

Braun, J.F. (2009) 'Multiple sources of pressure for change: the Barroso Commission and energy policy for an enlarged EU', *Journal of Contemporary European Research*, vol 5, no 3, pp 428–51.

Bulmer, S. and Radaelli, C.M. (2004) 'The Europeanisation of national policy?', Queen's Papers on Europeanisation, No 1/2004.

Cahill, N. (2010) *The impact of European environmental policy on Ireland*, Background Paper No 5, Dublin: National Economic and Social Council (NESC).

Caporaso, J. (2007) 'The three worlds of European integration theory', in P. Graziano and M. Vink (eds) *Europeanization: new research agendas*, Basingstoke: Palgrave.

Carter, N. (2001) *The politics of the environment*, Cambridge: Cambridge University Press.

Collier, U. (1994) *Energy and environment in the European Union*, Aldershot: Avebury.

Dupont, C. and Oberthür, S. (2012) 'Insufficient climate policy integration in EU energy policy: the importance of the long-term perspective', *Journal of Contemporary European Research*, vol 8, no 2, pp 228–47.

Egenhofer, C. and Alessi, M. (2013) *EU policy on climate change mitigation since Copenhagen and the economic crisis*, 5 March 2013, Centre for European Policy Studies working documents: Brussels: Centre for European Policy Studies.

European Commission (2013) *Living well within the limits of our planet*, Brussels: European Commission.

Fernandez, R.M. (2012) 'European Union and international negotiations on climate change. A limited role to play', *Journal of Contemporary European Research*, vol 8, no 2, pp 193–209.

Héritier, A., Kerwer, D., Knill, C., Lehmkuhl, D., Teutsch, M. and Douillet, A.C. (2001) *Differential Europe: European Union impact on national policymaking*, Boulder, CO: Rowman & Littlefield Publishers.

Jordan, A. and Liefferink, D. (2004) 'The Europeanization of national environmental policy', in A. Jordan and D. Liefferink (eds) *Environmental policy in Europe: the Europeanization of national environmental policy*, London: Routledge.

Jordan, A., Huitema, D., Van Asselt, H., Rayner, T. and Berkhout, F. (eds) (2010) *Climate change policy in the European Union: confronting the dilemmas of mitigation and adaptation*, Cambridge: Cambridge University Press.

Koch, A. and Lindenthal, A. (2011) 'Learning within the European Commission', *Journal of European Public Policy*, vol 18, no 7, pp 980–98.

Owens, S. and Hope, C.W. (1989) 'Energy and environment: the challenge of integrating European policies', *Energy Policy*, April, pp 97–102.

Pardo, R., (2013) *The green light for a modern CAP?*, Brussels: Centre for European Policy Studies. Available at: http://www.epc.eu/pub_details.php?cat_id=4&pub_id=3384

Piebalgs, A. (2009) 'How the European Union is preparing the "third industrial revolution" with an innovative energy policy', EUI Working Papers, RSCAS 2009/11. Available at: http://www.dauphine.fr/cgemp/masterindustrie/cours%20geopolitics/cours%20geopolitics%202009/Commeau%20Yanoussis/Article%20de%20Piebalgs.pdf

Radaelli, C.M. (2000) Whither Europeanization? Concept stretching and substantive change', European Integration Online Papers 4 (8). Available at: http://eiop.or.at/eiop/texte/2000-008a.htm

Sbragia, A.M. (1996) 'Environmental policy', in H. Wallace and W. Wallace (eds) *Policy-making in the European Union* (4th edn), Oxford: Oxford University Press, pp 293–316.

Schreurs, M. and Tiberghien, Y. (2007) 'Multi-level re-enforcement: explaining European Union leadership in climate change mitigation', *Global Environmental Politics*, vol 7, no 4, pp 19–46.

Skjaerseth, J. (1994) 'The climate policy of the EC: too hot to handle', *Journal of Common Market Studies*, vol 32, no 1, pp 25–42.

Solorio, I. (2011) 'Bridging the gap between environmental policy integration and the EU's energy policy: mapping out the "green Europeanisation" of energy *governance*', *Journal of Contemporary European Research*, vol 7, no 3, pp 396–415.

Torney, D. and Fujiwara, N. (2010) 'National commitments, compliance and the future of the Kyoto Protocol', CEPS Policy Brief (226), November, Centre for European Policy Studies, Brussels.

Vogel, D. (1997) 'Trading up and governing across: transnational governance and environmental protection', *Journal of European Public Policy*, vol 4, pp 556–71.

Vogler, J. and Stephan, H.R. (2007) 'The European Union in global environmental governance: leadership in the making? International environmental agreements', *Politics, Economics, Law*, vol 7, pp 389–413.

Warleigh-Lack, A. (2012) 'Greening EU studies: an academic manifesto', *Journal of Contemporary European Studies*, vol 20, no 1, pp 77–89.

Weale, A., Pridham, G., Cini, M., Konstadakopulos, D., Porter, M. and Flynn, B. (2000) *Environmental governance in Europe: an ever closer ecological union?*, Oxford: Oxford University Press.

SIX

Rethinking globalisation through convergence: active learning for social movements

Jenneth Parker

... collective action is nourished by the daily production of alternative frameworks of meaning, on which the networks themselves are founded and live from day to day. (Melucci, 1996, p 70)

Introduction

This chapter aims to explore ways of facilitating effective collaboration between environmental and development organisations (as social movements) to meet the political challenges of global sustainability. It will discuss the framing of a new way of thinking, using the convergence concept, which could facilitate the development of global equity within planetary boundaries.

The chapter is placed in the context of a wider inquiry about the conceptual frames, principles and processes that groups and organisations could use in order to guide joint approaches to sustainability. It will demonstrate how issues in political science regarding globalisation and equity can be explored with citizens using active approaches for learning for sustainability.

Convergence is based on an approach to global eco-justice that was developed during the Kyoto climate talks by Aubrey Meyer (2001). This combines the concept of equal rights of all citizens to use the earth's atmosphere with a per capita allocation approach. This would mean that rich countries would contract their use of carbon, leaving poorer countries to continue to develop. Convergence would occur when equal levels of development are achieved with sustainable carbon emissions. The CONVERGE project (funded by the EU) is exploring the potential of this approach to act as a unifying frame to address local-to-global sustainability questions. The CONVERGE project involves a number of partners, including the Bristol-based Schumacher Institute for Sustainable Solutions and the University of Bristol. CONVERGE focuses on 'rethinking globalisation' and is developing a convergence platform as a policy base for steering globalisation towards sustainability. The convergence concept has been developed to provide an overall frame of reference based on the latest sustainability science and a toolkit will provide tools and approaches to help to develop joined-up strategies for 'equity within planetary boundaries'.

The convergence approach developed by the project will be the focus here, in particular, the potential of convergence to act as a 'unifying framework' and to inform sustainability practitioners in contributing to the process of developing the new Sustainable Development Goals (SDGs). These goals are being discussed as the follow-on global plan when the deadline for the Millennium Development Goals (MDGs) is reached in 2015. The CONVERGE project reported here aims to bring together initiatives, organisations and constituencies with both environment and development approaches. A key question to be considered is whether and how citizen 'framing' of desirable futures can be assisted by research and how this might be tested and evaluated. This is part of the unpicking of the implications for research cultures of research *for* sustainability.

Developing effective alliances and partnerships for sustainability: social movements and active learning

Social movements are considered here as involving a broad range of actors, including civil society organisations, individuals, experts and business. The primary focus for the workshops was related to organisations working in environment and development, including not-for-profit consultancy organisations, local government representatives, charities and independent groups working on sustainability issues. There are, of course, important differences between particular organisations and the wider movements within which these organisations can be seen as embedded or subsisting (Eschle and Stammers, 2004). Here, we consider these organisations as part of the wider sustainability movement, with a focus on working across these smaller and more specific groupings to achieve wider common ends. The CONVERGE researchers were also testing the role of common ideas or 'frames' for collaboration. This involved developing sessions using various participatory techniques combined with some input of information.

There is a very large range of participatory techniques that form the toolkit for community developers and participatory researchers

(Wates, 2000; IIED, 2011). Experienced facilitators are aware that it is a matter not so much of which technique is best overall, but of which technique can help to achieve which purposes at which time. The main issue with all participatory techniques, which is well known in adult and community education, is that the balance often has to be struck between input of information and the participatory process. This issue arises in particularly acute form when the topic is sustainability because it requires a foundation of broad understanding of sustainability, social science and other knowledge.

One central question that provides an undercurrent to the forthcoming analysis is whether we can advisedly use these techniques without thinking more deeply about the accompanying social and learning theory – indeed, about the accompanying politics of knowledge. Awareness of this broad issue conditions our sensitivity as researchers and citizens to the wider ethical and social justice issues inherent in our current social organisation and the validation of different kinds of knowledges and different approaches to learning and research (Alcoff and Potter, 1993; Scheurich, 1997). This links to the critical literature on participation, its degrees and its pitfalls (Rahnema, 1992; Kothari and Cooke, 2001).

Some critical reflections on sustainability research practice would include questioning the extent to which, in the current context, researchers and social movement facilitators often use techniques from the participatory 'toolkit' without reflecting upon the deeper methodology and ethos. For example, how well do approaches developed in the context of challenging colonialism translate to sustainability contexts? One very important question that is raised by sustainability is how these liberatory elements of participatory learning can be linked to the necessary scientific expertise in order to develop a 'people's sustainability research' approach. This is particularly the case with sustainability workshops and initiatives. For example, experience with Local Agenda 21 has shown that simply asking people for their responses to surveys about local priorities cannot provide sustainability-related outcomes unless respondents are first aware of the real issues comprised in sustainability (Raimonds, 2003, pp 318–20).

One approach to sustainability has tended to pragmatically define sustainability movements and organisations as those that can *combine* environment and development perspectives – often represented by different groups of actors and having their own languages and favourite concept sets. At times, these differing priorities and concerns have been impediments to shared understanding and joint action (Wade, 2008, p 11) and there is a real need to move towards a shared vocabulary of sustainability. In this situation, and in view of the enormous challenges of local-to-global sustainability, it is often asked how we can develop effective alliances and partnerships. There is a quite highly developed discussion of 'partnership' for sustainability – including those between non-governmental organisations (NGOs) and civil society, and business and state agencies (Waddell, 2005; Wals, 2007). The preconditions and guidelines for effective partnership to achieve joint goals usually focus on certain key objectives and/or areas – such as river basin joint management or management of fisheries resources, for example. At times, research enters into these arrangements in various ways – to help develop knowledge and engagement across the different groups involved and/or to establish different perspectives that can inform partnership agreements before or while these are being established. Sometimes, research can be concerned with the normative questions of what a more overarching agreement or set of principles for practice *should* look like – but this is more unusual. This is part of the broad conceptual territory of the CONVERGE project.

Social movements, cultural action and the framing of meaning

This section considers some theoretical resources that help to think through the relationships between the concepts that organisations and individuals use and different kinds of action for change. CONVERGE aims to be a cultural intervention, as well as providing policy guidance to the EU and to other policy actors: 'Today, acting on things means acting on symbolic codes; effectively operating on things depends on the cultural models which organize our day-to-day social relations, political systems and forms of production and consumption' (Melucci, 1996, p 163).

One key issue for bringing in sustainability science and, indeed, politics is that some movements are arguably more comfortable operating in the cultural sphere. Alberto Melucci tackles the issue of the cultural forms of action of more contemporary movements. He argues that in the media age, change in values, images and narratives can be more important than more traditional forms of action aimed at directly challenging power and political structures. For Melucci (1996), this is one key difference between 'old' and 'new' movements. However, others argue that we do need a spectrum of movement activities, including both 'expressive' and 'instrumental' aspects (Eschle and Stammers, 2004).

New social movements are considered to be more interested in cultural action, such as ethical change and narrative interpretations, than in instrumental action, such as calling for particular political reforms and challenging regulatory frameworks. We can see these kinds of actions in the ways that various NGOs attempt to encourage us to value nature, for example, the World Wide Fund for Nature (WWF), but also in the ways that others attempt to develop a sense of outrage against injustice, such as Action Aid. One reason for cultural activities in more contemporary movements is identified by Melucci as part of the strategy to keep movements constituted as actors. The issues that combine people to act have to be identified and analysed, and information has to be distributed, in order to help constitute the movement as a collective actor (Melucci, 1996). In order to keep oppositional movements in being, it is argued that these must involve some shared beliefs, identities and emotional engagement, which can be placed more in the sphere of culture than of politics as conventionally understood, in order to keep participants motivated, but also in order for participants to benefit subjectively from their engagement in terms of a sense of 'belonging'. However, shared meanings and information from research are also a precondition of effective joint action that can be seen as more instrumental. Thus, from a more trans-disciplinary perspective, the opposition of 'old' and 'new' forms can, in fact, be more of a complementarity (Stammers, 2009, pp 36–7).

Research on 'framing'

The ways in which different kinds of ideas can help people to form new alliances and a common sense of belonging have been studied by social movement researchers. The concept of 'frames' was developed by researchers as a way of discussing movement actors' use of moral and cognitive resources and the degree of agreement between actors necessary for collective action (Carroll and Ratner, 1996). Framing as a concept seems a possibly helpful way of categorising shared understandings, beliefs and orientations, which leaves space for interpretation and diversity (Druckman, 2001). The concept has also been used to discuss the use of 'justice frames' in the US environmental justice movement (Sachs, 1995; Taylor, 2000). Furthermore, the concept of 'discursive frames' invokes the notion of a relatively open speech community sharing key vocabularies and terms to support collective action. Carroll and Ratner (1994, p 14) have also expressed the need for a frame 'that makes collective action possible, simultaneously avoiding a collapse into either relativism or an authoritarian imposition of order' (Carroll and Ratner, 1994, p 14).

The subjective framing in individual thought and the more social framing of movements can exist and develop in a mutually supportive relationship – one way in which movements have the capacity to link the personal and institutional worlds, and hence engage emotional commitment (Stammers, 2009, p 248). This linkage can help to provide the motivation for personal commitment to movement values and actions, even at the risk of considerable personal danger and discomfort. The development of frames should be seen as part of a wider process of development and change, which Melucci links to the ability of social movements to take action, to communicate their message and to recruit new members with a mobilising vision. In other words, frames can fulfil several roles: they can emphasise a particular message by tapping into existing frames of thought or they can build new frames by resonating with popular culture or a particular stakeholder perspective (Melucci, 1996).

The 'frames in communication' concept refers to a broad landscape of ideas with plenty of scope for different responses and approaches. In this way, it is suited to movements rather than the more specific sets of beliefs associated with political parties. Frames can be seen as a lens through which to approach a range of issues. Frames are useful when the approach is joint learning and this is particularly relevant when considering the stakeholder engagement and dissemination strategies of CONVERGE. Frames can also be part of diagnostic and advocacy processes: 'collective action frames provide diagnostic attribution, which is concerned with problem identification, and prognostic attribution, which is concerned with problem resolution' (Ayres, 2004, p 14).

Convergence as a platform for sustainability movements also provides a diagnosis and hopeful prognosis for positive change. Furthermore, convergence provides a legitimising set of arguments based on current science and interdisciplinary knowledge, including broad ethical stances consistent with global human rights commitments.

In order to have joined-up action for sustainable global change, it may well be highly necessary to have a mosaic of initiatives and movements doing what they do best – but, equally, there is a strategic necessity to have some overall frame that can enable more effective joint action. Arguably, in order to achieve global action for our futures and our planet, we need to construct aspirational identities and frames that people can 'buy into', such as that of global citizenship (Oxfam, 2013; Pontin and Roderick, 2007).

One approach taken in research into framing is to study the development of discourses and produce analyses of how these operate to frame debates. For example, the volume entitled *Framing the global economic downturn: crisis, rhetoric and the politics of recessions* (Hart and Tyndall, 2009) reviewed the competing interpretations made by key public figures using discourse analysis. However, these studies are always retrospective and do not seek to provide new frames that could help enable movement action, except, by implication, through critique. This tradition of 'value-free' scholarship rather than the engaged scholarship demanded by research *for* sustainability is increasingly challenged by those who see an urgent necessity for research to serve the broad purposes of civil society (Schumacher, 1979). The action research approach taken by CONVERGE falls into this category in seeking to provide frames and supporting elements that can help to enable social movement thought and action for positive change for sustainability.

CONVERGE: providing a key frame for rethinking globalisation

The purpose of the CONVERGE project is to devise a frame that facilitates effective collaboration between environmental and development organisations (as social movements) to meet the political challenges of global sustainability and address issues of social and ecological justice. It is supported by the latest sustainability science, which recognises the interdependence of the elements of the earth system and its boundaries and vulnerability to human over-exploitation. It is based on principles of equitable access to the life-support resources of the earth system – but it is also acceptable to a variety of progressive movements and can act to help to frame negotiations between these for a joint vision for the future of humanity.

The CONVERGE project seeks to rethink globalisation by developing the implications of a convergence approach to global development based on equitable access to the life-support capacities of the planet and fair livelihoods within planetary boundaries while taking a trans-disciplinary, systems approach (Fortnam et al, 2010). Systems approaches look at phenomena as interacting and in process, and also recognise the ways that feedback loops can be established (Meadows, 2008). In this respect, the project builds on existing sustainability science, in particular, the earth system science of which climate science is a dynamic part (Cornell et al, 2012).

The project was designed to develop and test the implications of an equity-based approach to planetary resources inspired by the contraction and convergence approach developed by the World Resources Institute for the Kyoto climate summit (Meyer, 2001). Contraction and convergence concentrated on the equitable per capita allocation of the use of the atmosphere to inform climate agreements – but CONVERGE was initially concerned with the concept of per capita 'allocation' of the whole range of the planetary commons. A systems perspective problematises the whole concept of the boundaries of private property in an interdependent and dynamic interconnected system, thus casting doubt on neoliberal strategies to privatise the commons.

As the CONVERGE research developed, and in response to the growing realisation of planetary interdependence, the initial 'allocation' approach has moved towards an emphasis on developing the common use of planetary goods to the betterment of sustainable livelihoods for all of humanity. This has resulted in a focus on how to engage various stakeholders, but particularly civil society as the key agent of change that could be capable of demanding global eco- and resource justice. The challenges to current forms of economy and governance of these demands are also considered by the project. Questions of governance across the scales of the local-to-global system are considered in the CONVERGE policy recommendations, which are to be designed as complementary across the local-to-global scales. An agenda is being developed that summarises the challenges of reorienting the global economy for convergence, with the intention that this should be taken up by the convergence observatory – a research network with a monitoring and policy function. A convergence alliance will continue the linked work with social movements, bringing together environment and development organisations to jointly develop the best ways to support processes of convergence.

Although the differences between 'old' movements and 'new' movements have been exaggerated, it is certainly true that fast communication of new kinds of information and artistic responses to change and issues is changing the landscape of political beliefs, allegiances and ideas. Our intention 'in the CONVERGE project is to find out whether this may open up new opportunities for movements to develop cross theme alliances for social and ecological change that can work for "equity within planetary boundaries"' (Rockstrom et al, 2009). Movements and organisations with more limited agendas may succeed in attaining partial objectives, but systemic approaches indicate that solutions need to be considered in a more holistic manner in order not to create problems elsewhere in the system (Meadows, 2008). Furthermore, a strong uniting ethos and overall vision for an alternative future is arguably a psychological and cultural necessity to support the development of an inspiring agency for change. This kind of approach can draw on scenarios that help strategy development for short-, medium- and long-term change. Convergence is just one of a number of globally available approaches that have potential for the sustainability movement – for example, the Earth Charter initiative is another such approach (Earth Charter, 1994). The intention and hope is that a convergence framework will be able to assist in bringing something extra to the table. The aim of the CONVERGE project is a more unified sustainability movement that can achieve the critical mass required for the major social changes needed to bring humanity into a sustainable relationship with planetary resources and life-support systems.

Convergence principles under discussion

1. In a converging society, every global citizen has the right to a fair share of the earth's biocapacity and social resources to enable him or her to live a fulfilling life.
2. A converging society uses its resources effectively, recognising the critical value of services from natural systems and limiting its harmful impacts upon them. It recognises interdependence among human societies and with nature.
3. A converging society invests positively in human, social and environmental resources, and cares for, maintains and restores them (Kristinsdóttir, 2013).

The convergence framework is still developing but will include: examples of initiatives available in e-book form; a set of principles for convergent societies; systems modelling approaches to assist convergent decision-making (forthcoming at: www.convergeproject.org); and a toolkit for those wishing to engage in convergence and more.

A number of workshops with sustainability practitioners were held as part of the 'testing' of the convergence concept to see if the concept overall was thought to be a useful framing of the issues at this point in time. They had a particular focus on finding out whether the convergence frame was thought to be helpful in bringing together environment and development concerns, as applied to the specific example of the SDGs.

The need for such collaboration across environmental and development constituencies is particularly stark at the level of global agreements for sustainability, which have so far often pitted the human development and the conservation lobbies against each other. Convergence hopes to defuse this logjam by providing a way forward that is based on agreements to achieve an equitable sharing of the earth's resources and the right of the poor to an equitable share of development (Sen, 1999). This involves a commitment on the part of the richer developed world to take urgent action to reduce resource use and to aim for greater equity both within and between societies.

Testing out the CONVERGE approach

The 'mapping' of initiatives has provided a quick way to understand the different emphases of organisations across the environment and development spectrum. The quadrant diagram in Figure 6.1 enables a rough characterisation of any event, initiative or policy according to its support for equality and/or decreasing or increasing resource use. For example, in responding to climate change and human development imperatives, Social and Community Development (SCAD), a CONVERGE partner in India, has a tree-planting programme that also provides food, energy and animal fodder for some of the poorest villages. This initiative would be placed in the top-right quadrant. This diagram has been used as an engagement tool to discuss the positioning of different environment and development organisations and to help individuals reflect on their own positioning and commitment. The approach does not claim to produce answers as to how different positions and organisations might cooperate, as these will need to be highly specific and contextualised.

A range of environment and development initiatives that were all situated in the top-right quadrant were studied and analysed in order to assist in developing the convergence principles and framework. A description and analysis of these initiatives revealed differences in the degree of concern with equity and limits within the top-right 'convergence quadrant'.

The governance perspective taken by the project has not yet been fully elaborated, but tends to a deliberative democracy approach supported by the best sustainability and social science, and linked to participatory learning processes and capacity development. It is part of the role of a convergence framework to present a clear formulation of human rights to the planetary commons as an ethical position that could be used to frame global agreements.

The more technical support for this framework consists in the development of engagement techniques, including systems modelling and tools suitable for different scales of activity – from local communities

Figure 6.1: The convergence quadrant

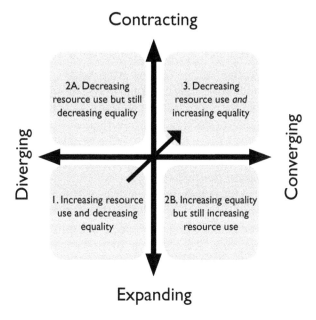

to gatherings of transnational policymakers. The development of indicator sets to support accountability in judging the success of moves towards local-to-global forms of convergence 'goals' is also a key part of the framework that the project will provide. It is intended that the quadrant diagram will be even more useful for analysis if used with the mapping system to be found in the associated e-book (Vadovics et al, 2012). The wider convergence toolkit will also contain systems approaches to assist with joint problem analysis and decision-making. In addition, convergence principles aim to help to provide a common basis for agreement to work on the questions and the ways forward in collaboration.

Addressing the challenges and obstacles

In order to develop effective collaboration for sustainability, we need to remember that NGOs and organisations who often have very similar goals are usually in positions of some competition for funding, members and legitimacy (Parker, 2005). In addition, it must be said that larger players in the NGO arena who are transnational and/or supported by key figures jostle for position to be the coordinators in such cases, and such struggles could derail the convergence approach. Real issues of power and influence exist in the NGO arena – NGOs do not just fight unjust forms of power, they also deploy power in various ways. In this context, we consider forms of soft power, such as the ability to set agendas and discourses, in addition to harder forms of power, such as access to legislative and government power and seats at the table when global and regional agreements are being formulated. The convergence strategy is to bring together the urgency of the planetary bio-system crisis and the worsening crisis of global inequity and injustice as key areas for cross-organisation debate, rather than to seek direct political leadership. In the convergence alliance, we will test if a looser network approach with supporting materials will be able to help broker more effective alliances that could overcome some of this structural oppositional positioning.

A systems approach to goals indicates that goals should be expected to move and change in the sustainability group learning process. In addition, it is possible that the achievement of some pre-set goal is less important than the development of the governance capacity necessary to achieve it (Senge, 2006). This is a critique of functionalist goal-setting as a policy activity, as this tends to assume that the basic structures and agency to achieve the goal already exist, whereas a more process-oriented approach might identify that there are systemic blocks to goal achievement.

A convergence perspective on the SDGs would be that it is necessary to consider the SDGs in the context of a systemic critique of current forms of globalisation and to take due account of the systemic blocks to SDG achievement, such as the form of the global economy and the lack of effective civil governance of this global economy. Therefore, a perspective on the achievement of the governance capacity to achieve SDGs might be considered a key contribution from a convergence frame. Rather than generating a wish list, participants might be expected to think more deeply about the structural conditions for change within the 20-year time frame proposed for the SDGs.

The workshops were designed to engage a range of actors in the environment and development fields in order to discuss ways to unite agendas more fully in the context of debates on the SDGs. The aims of the workshops were to develop a joint set of recommendations to contribute to the SDG process and to test the convergence frame as a possible umbrella concept for further collaboration through the convergence alliance.

Action research is a form of research that engages participants in the co-creation of knowledge. Participation is subject to different levels and degrees of involvement (Rahnema, 1992), ranging from fully negotiated events and outcomes through to participation in discussing agendas and activities. Action research usually means that the motivations of participants have to be considered in order to encourage them to attend and to give up the time involved – and also to really engage their creativity and attention.

In the CONVERGE workshops, the motivation for participation was the desire of the invited participants to engage with the SDG process. For some, the meeting and its outcomes might be the only way to engage with the processes; for others, who might be quite central actors in SDG consultations and processes, the meeting would help them deliver their current objectives and get an idea of where other groups and individuals stood on the SDGs.

It is well known that collaboration requires a focus to be really engaging (Waddell, 2005), and so it was decided to focus on the debates on the completion of the MDGs in 2015. Many environmental and development organisations were engaged internally in developing responses and positions, so it was a good opportunity to try convergence approaches as this would help these organisations to fulfil some existing internal goals.

The input of information prior to the workshops was achieved by circulating some background papers. This approach was chosen for this audience as they are all sustainability practitioners to some degree and would therefore be able, and hopefully sufficiently interested, to engage with the documents presented. The event was not advertised to the general public and was not intended to be at the level of public engagement, but was rather the 'practitioner-informed review' identified in the project activities as needed at this point in the CONVERGE research. The first workshop was conceived as action research because the CONVERGE team were both introducing the convergence frame and asking for feedback on this frame from participants in the form of questionnaires. The design was also influenced by adult education theory and included the following key elements:

- Motivation – recognising that adult learning motivation is usually directed towards achieving some ends or goals, including being updated on current issues, such as the SDGs.
- Existing knowledge – rather than working from a 'deficit' model, working from the presumption that participants have much to bring to the event and to share with each other.
- Participation and respect – the time and energy that participants bring is respected and acknowledged as part of the process.

- Learning processes and agency of participants – including time for participants' reflection upon processes and opportunities to add to and influence the final report.

The event was a mixture of input and discussion in order to keep attention and energy levels high. The mixed approach also served to produce the mix of reflection upon information provided and strategic planning intended in the event.

In accordance with action research approaches, participants were invited to view and comment on the research results, were asked to fill out a short questionnaire regarding their views on the potential of convergence to act as a unifying framework in the context of such events, and to comment on the proposed aims and objectives of the proposed alliance and observatory.

> ## Sample response to the questionnaire
>
> Question: 'Do you find the convergence approach a generally useful one?'
>
> Sample of respondents:
>
> "Yes. I like this idea of coalition-building which convergence suggests. Civil society has its maximum public impact working in coalition."
>
> "Yes. Learnt a lot from the discussion and presentations about sustainability and really got thinking!"
>
> "Yes – because it corresponds to our reality. The world is complex and we need to make connections between the fields."
>
> "It seems to have promise in linking top-down and bottom-up approaches and foregrounding equity issues."
>
> "In terms of resource reduction, this seems to be a very strong and workable approach."
>
> "Yes – but a bit abstract/idealistic."
>
> "Yes – but struggle to understand how to make it practical/relevant to most people/organisations."

Reflections and challenges for the future

Some key points emerged from the evaluations and debriefing:

- Multiple objectives are hard to handle and require thought and analysis, preferably in advance of meetings – but, revisited afterwards, will always yield new insights as well.
- Practitioners have a great deal of varied kinds of knowledge, including contextual, technical, social and traditional. Workshop

activities should make clearer which kinds of knowledge are being accessed at the time.

- One of the structural difficulties of focusing on the SDGs from a systems perspective is that any process that continues over time should be adjusted at regular intervals – but international goals are politically agreed and, hence, difficult to change. This also makes it difficult to develop a short-, medium- and longer-term strategic plan. In the event, the workshops did deliver a set of goals that were very generic and this felt like the beginning of the analysis rather than a definitive set.

One key focus for CONVERGE was to explore how the different scales and levels of the global system could potentially work together for 'equity within planetary boundaries'. Further discussions could focus more fully on how different kinds of aims could be achieved by organisations and movements in a convergence approach, which could be complementary across scales. One key area of difficulty and confusion that needs further examination is that of how to work with the idea of synergies between policy and action at different scales of the global system. In this context, the European level seemed to be appreciated as a helpful intermediary to the global level.

The first CONVERGE workshop did not really research or engage with the individual level or discuss subjective aspects with participants. Therefore, the more subjective or psychological dimensions of convergence were not discussed. Questions of identities, subjective meaning of individual lives and narratives of success and well-being would be important to pursue further. For example, future events might seek to cover more personal motivations and implications for change processes and strategies.

Testing the perceived value of the convergence frame is not the same thing as testing the learning of participants. The workshop set out to test if participants thought that the convergence frame is a useful one. The learning from the workshop overall is a wider question that was not fully addressed. Again, the self-reported evaluation of the event was very positive, although participants were not specifically asked about active learning as such, nor how the frame used may have helped or hindered this.

The testing of the convergence framework was, thus, a more indicative survey of the acceptability of the overall frame to a limited range of self-selected and invited participants. The survey tested the *perceived* usefulness of the frame in bringing together environment and development from the participants' perspectives. However, these data are valuable, as they indicate that the majority of these practitioners valued this research and are keen to be kept informed and to participate in an alliance based on the convergence approach.

Conclusions

Action research to help to develop ways forward for cross-sectoral work on the highly political issues of global sustainable futures is a much-needed development. Many existing sustainability practitioners are often fully stretched in delivering and developing their own existing areas of work. The convergence workshop described earlier demonstrates that participants welcomed the chance to be engaged in a ready-framed approach to bigger-picture thinking and debate on more global issues of sustainability. The approach needed to work with movements and practitioners is one that takes a broader definition of politics as involving both cultural and instrumental forms of action. The complex nature of sustainability does mean that research drawing on sustainability science and interdisciplinary knowledge to develop analysis and tools for engagement is valuable to these actors. A deeper and more systematic study in relation to convergence and to developing issues of *global earth system governance* could inquire more fully into ways to engage citizens fruitfully in participatory research and events. The experience of the workshops reinforces the belief that citizens are keen to engage and have the capacity to develop new ideas to contribute to the radical changes needed for all our futures.

Politics as a 'science' should be challenged by these considerations to spend more effort in active research, attempting to find ways forward rather than just producing suggestive critical analyses – this could potentially be of great assistance to the wider sustainability movement. This is a challenge to the current 'detached' research culture (Flinders, 2012) but also finds support in new demands to demonstrate the 'impact' of research. The CONVERGE project attempts to rethink globalisation, and in order to assist others to do so, it has employed the group 'modelling' and small group work elements of the participatory research toolkit. This project work has also identified some new or sharpened challenges with regards to the current context of work on sustainability and globalisation. These concern the tensions between the need to communicate the basics of sustainability science and an overview of global sustainability challenges which include ethical arguments and principles and the need for localised actions and agendas. This is a very large challenge. However, consider the enormous capacity in politics and political science departments throughout the world.

Even if only 10% of that time was spent on these agendas, that would make an impact! This book demonstrates the diversity of interest to be found in sustainability issues – it only remains for you, dear reader, to take up the challenge.

References

Alcoff, L. and Potter, E. (1993) *Feminist epistemologies*, London: Routledge.

Ayres, J.M. (2004) 'Framing collective action against neo liberalism: the case of the anti-globalisation movement', *Journal of World Systems Research*, vol x, no 1 (winter), pp 11–34.

Carroll, W.K. and Ratner, R.S. (1994) 'Between Leninism and radical pluralism: Gramscian reflections on counter-hegemony and the new social movements', *Critical Sociology*, vol 20, no 2, pp 3–26.

Carroll, W.K. and Ratner, R.S. (1996) 'Master framing and cross-movement networking in contemporary social movements', *The Sociological Quarterly*, vol 37, no 4, pp 601–25.

Cornell, S., Prentice, C.I., House, J.I. and Downy, C.J. (2012) *Understanding the earth system*, Cambridge: Cambridge University Press.

Druckman, J.N. (2001) 'The implications of framing effects for citizen competence', *Political Behavior*, vol 23, no 3, pp 225–56.

Earth Charter (1994) www.earthcharterinaction.org/content

Eschle, C. and Stammers, N. (2004) 'Taking part: social movements, INGOs and global change', *Alternatives*, vol 29, no 3, pp 333–72.

Flinders, M. (2012) *Defending politics: why democracy matters in the twenty first century*, Oxford and New York, NY: Oxford University Press.

Fortnam, M., Cornell, S., Parker, J. and the CONVERGE Project Team (2010) 'Convergence: how can it be part of the pathway to sustainability', CONVERGE Discussion Paper, Department of Earth Sciences, University of Bristol.

Hart, P. and Tindell, K. (2009) *Framing the global economic downturn: crisis, rhetoric and the politics of recessions*, Australia National University, Canberra: ANU E Press.

IIED (International Institute for Environment and Development) (2011) *Participatory learning and action*, Stevenage: Earthprint. Available at: http://pubs.iied.org/pdfs/14606IIED.pdf

Kothari, U. and Cooke, B. (eds) (2001) *Participation: the new tyranny?*, London: Zed Books.

Kristinsdóttir, S.M. (2013) 'The convergence process', PhD dissertation at the University of Iceland, Reykjavik.

Meadows, D. (2008) *Thinking in systems*, London: Chelsea Green Publishing.

Melucci, A. (1996) *Challenging codes: collective action in the information age*, Cambridge: Cambridge University Press.

Meyer, A. (2001) *Contraction and convergence: the global solution to climate change*, Cambridge: Green Books.

Oxfam (2013) 'Why promote global citizenship?'. Available at: http://www.oxfam.org.uk/~/media/Files/Education/Global%20 Citizenship/Why_promote_global_citizenship.ashx

Parker, J. (2005) 'Cooperation and conflict: an analysis of political legitimacy claims in lobbying for education for sustainable development', *Contemporary Politics*, vol 11, nos 2–3, pp 169–77.

Pontin, J. and Roderick, I. (2007) *Converging world: connecting communities in global change*, Schumacher Briefings, Bristol: Green Books for the Schumacher Society.

Rahnema, M. (1992) 'Participation', in W. Sachs (ed) *The development dictionary*, London: Zed Books.

Raimonds, E. (2003) 'Local Agenda 21 process facilitation', University of Latvia. Available at: http://ec.europa.eu/ourcoast/download. cfm?fileID=1502

Rockström, J. et al (2009) 'Planetary boundaries: exploring the safe operating space for humanity', *Ecology and Society*, vol 14, no 2, p 32. Available at: http://www.ecologyandsociety.org/vol14/iss2/art32/ (accessed 1 July 2011).

Sachs, A. (1995) *Eco-justice: linking human rights and the environment*, Washington, DC: Worldwatch Institute.

Scheurich, J.J. (1997) *Research method in the postmodern*, London: Falmer Press.

Schumacher, E.F. (1979) *Good work*, London: Jonathon Cape.

Sen, A (1999) *Development as freedom*, Oxford: Oxford University Press.

Senge, P. (2006) *The fifth discipline*, Doubleday: London.

Stammers, N. (2009) *Human rights and social movements*, London: Pluto Press.

Taylor, C. (2000) 'The rise of the environmental justice paradigm', *American Behavioural Scientist*, vol 434, pp 508–80.

Vadovics, E., Milton S. and the CONVERGE Project Team (2012) 'Case studies ("initiatives") illustrating contraction and convergence. Equity within limits in theory and practice', CONVERGE Deliverable 33, GreenDependent Institute, Hungary. Available at: http://www. convergeproject.org and http://intezet.greendependent.org/en/ node/162

Waddell, S. (2005) *Societal learning*, Sheffield: Greenleaf.

Wade, R. (2008) 'Journeys around education for sustainability: mapping the terrain', in J. Parker and R. Wade (eds) *Journeys around education for sustainability*, London: London South Bank University.

Wals, A.E.J. (2007) *Social learning: towards a sustainable world*, Wageningen: Wageningen Press.

Wates, N. (2000) *The community planning handbook*, London: Earthscan.

Part Three

What is to be done? Case studies in learning for sustainability from across the globe

The challenge of sustainability in sub-Saharan Africa – the implications for education policy and practice

Ros Wade, with Vincent Muhumaza,
Chikondi Musange and Heinrich Rukundo

Introduction

This chapter will highlight some of the key sustainability challenges faced by countries in sub-Saharan Africa (SSA) and their implications for education and learning in relation to some key social and ecological issues. It will present extracts from three case studies by postgraduate researchers in education for sustainable development (ESD) in Uganda, Malawi and Rwanda. Reference will be made to the importance of context and appropriacy and to the relevance of local and indigenous knowledge.

This body of research is a rich resource for ESD in Africa and has already enabled many scholars to make changes to and impacts on their organisations and countries. A number of scholars have also contributed to cross-regional initiatives, such as UNEP's (United Nations Environment Programme) Mainstreaming Environment and Sustainability across Africa (MESA) programme, which seeks to mainstream ESD across all African universities. It is unfortunately not possible to do justice to the full range of work by this group, so we have drawn out some key themes and extracts from their research to illustrate the range and importance of this regional contribution. Africa as a continent and as a region is frequently marginalised or even left out of international discussions and debates and African voices are still not given the attention that is deserved or needed. An examination of most academic literature in political science or ESD will illustrate this absence and this is even more evident in international peer-reviewed journals. There are a variety of reasons for this that are beyond the scope of this chapter to investigate but these case studies will be set within the framework of the politics of knowledge and the challenges that dominant global knowledge systems pose to ESD.

This group of African postgraduate researchers has emerged from the learning community of practice in ESD generated by the master's programme in ESD at London South Bank University. As recipients of prestigious UK Commonwealth Scholarship awards for master's distance learning courses, they were selected for their leadership potential for development impact, as well as their academic ability. The ethos of the ESD programme has promoted a strong community of practice, which was firmly embraced by the scholars themselves. Over the past eight years, they have been working and researching in ESD across a wide range of countries in SSA and a considerable body of work has now been completed. The ESD programme aims to develop effective agents of change through an emphasis on praxis; hence, applying theory to practice has been a key component of their endeavour. Their research has informed a variety of contexts and practice at a local and global level, from educational policymaking to formal sector curriculum development, community development, HIV AIDS awareness training, conservation education and the role of non-governmental organisations (NGOs).

Each selected extract seeks to enable the authentic voices of the scholar to be heard, so, as far as is possible, it makes use of his or her own words. The work of these scholars is all the more impressive as it was carried out during their other work commitments and many of them were also writing in a second or even third language.

Key issues of sustainability in the context of sub-Saharan Africa

These three studies have been chosen as they highlight some very key issues and concerns with regard to sustainable development in the African context, in particular, they look at the role of ESD in helping to balance ecological and social concerns in relation to human development.

As Bush (2007, cited in Carmody, 2011, p 2) puts it:

> African development is defined by the 'paradox of plenty' ... it is a very resource rich continent, but economically poor. Africa is thought to contain 42 per cent of the world's bauxite, 38 per cent of the world's uranium, 42 per cent of its gold, 73 per cent of its platinum, 88 per cent of its diamonds and 10 per cent of its oil.

Carmody argues that 'the deepening process of globalisation ... has unleashed a new scramble for African resources and to a lesser extent, markets' (Carmody, 2011, p 1). Despite some trends towards rapid urbanisation (eg in Nigeria and Kenya), to a great extent, most African countries are still based on rural agricultural communities, so this scramble for resources raises some real challenges. According to the United Nations Development Programme's (UNDP's) 'Human development report 2013. The rise of the South: human progress in a diverse world':

> as global development challenges become more complex and transboundary in nature, coordinated action on the most pressing challenges of our era, whether they be poverty eradication, climate change, or peace and security, is essential. As countries are increasingly interconnected through trade, migration, and information and communications technologies, it is no surprise that policy decisions in one place have substantial impacts elsewhere. The crises of recent years – food, financial, climate – which have blighted the lives of so many point to this, and to the importance of working to reduce people's vulnerability to shocks and disasters. (UNDP, 2013, p ii)

The UNDP (2013) report underlines the fact that the Millennium Development Goal (MDG) target to reduce extreme poverty by 50% will not be met and neither will attempts to eliminate hunger – both goals having been affected by the impact of climate change-related shocks, which have led to an increase in food insecurity.

High levels of poverty and illiteracy abound in SSA despite the gains made by the MDGs. And while achievements have been made in relation to Education for All (EFA), 'Sub Saharan Africa is the region that is lagging most behind, with 22% of the region's primary school age population still not in school in 2011' (UNESCO, 2014, p 2). The GMR also reveals that the number of illiterate adults has risen since 1990 by 37% in SSA. 'By 2015, it is projected that 26% of all illiterate adults will live in sub-Saharan Africa' (UNESCO, 2014, p 3). This, in turn, affects the abilities of communities to understand or claim their rights and to advocate and lobby for change.

Without a substantial change in global and national power imbalances and governance, these key sustainability challenges are likely to lead to increased instability and conflict over land, food and natural resources. Leadership from politicians at both national and global levels has fallen very short in addressing these issues so far. The first case study extract in the following illustrates some of these.

Case Study 1: Highlighting some of the key sustainability challenges in the Albertine region, Uganda, sub-Saharan Africa (extract from the research of Vincent Muhumaza, Uganda, 2011)

Vincent was a former child soldier who was able to acquire formal education through his work as a member of the Uganda Peoples' Defence Forces. During his master's studies, he had a wide range of duties, including working with local communities on conservation in the Bwindi National Park and front-line work in Somalia. He was a resourceful and inspiring person and this chapter is dedicated to his memory.

Vincent's research in 2011 highlighted some of the acute challenges and potential conflicts that are already playing out in the context of the discovery of commercially viable oil in the Bunyoro region in mid-western Uganda. This is predominantly an agricultural economy, with fishing activities along the rivers and in Lake Albert. It includes two major national parks with two tropical forests, where tourism is another source of income. Vincent examined whether it is possible to balance ecological and social concerns in relation to human development. In particular, he examined the possible effects of oil field exploitation in relation to agricultural practices in this region. He recognised that the oil is accessible and he acknowledged that exploitation of it is proceeding ahead. This has raised hopes and expectations among communities that they are going to share in the benefits of the oil boom, and fears that if not well governed through an accountable, transparent and people-centred system that ensures equity in revenue sharing, the resource could become Uganda's curse rather than its blessing. In order to ensure equity, Vincent felt that oil production activities should espouse forms of development that guarantee the integrity of society, the economy and natural systems. Additionally, he felt that it was essential that local communities should participate in local natural resource management and that their participation should convert into improved community livelihoods.

Vincent's research identified that oil production activities were already causing a range of conflicts between local communities, the government and those involved in oil production, as well as leading to threats to ecological resources and, hence, to agriculture. Vincent conducted a qualitative, multi-level survey, focusing on the Buseruka sub-county, interviewing community and youth leaders, a local government official, and the local Member of Parliament (MP). Through the voices of Ugandans who are directly affected by oil exploitation, his interviews reveal a high level of distrust in the government and powerful elites. Their key concerns are highlighted by the following extract from Vincent's research.

Highlighting some of the key sustainability challenges in the Albertine region, Uganda, sub-Saharan Africa
Vincent Muhumaza

Land grabbing
All respondents projected the occurrence of conflicts arising from land grabbing by individuals who pose as government agents. All respondents complained about government officials who have fraudulently leased land along oil exploration areas to themselves or to foreign investors. Community elders reported that local government representatives (LGRs) at district levels connive with central government officials to lease community land without the consent of the local communities. According to two respondents, issues pertaining to illegal possession of land are most likely to cause serious commotion when the 'new landowners' attempt to evict poor legitimate owners or occupy the acquired land. According to all respondents, the scramble for access to land, leading to rapid transition of customary and communal land into leasehold and the subsequent exclusion of communities from common lands and resources, is likely to cause conflicts.

Displacement of local crop growers
It was brought out that the most fertile lands in the Bujaawe forest reserve have already been grabbed from local individuals who own tree plantations therein. The major impact expressed here is that the indigenous population will soon have no land to cultivate, yet they do not have the required education to get jobs in oil production. Crop growers anticipated that the jobless situation is likely to cause insecurity, which may subsequently lead to conflicts. This group sees new land occupants introducing new plants such as palm oil and castle nuts, which cannot help to ensure food security in the region. The youth leaders referred to fraudulent land possession as oppression that calls for physical confrontation. All respondents complained that migrations to oil production areas might negatively intensify tribal and cultural consciousness of the arriving migrants, especially where newcomers are seen to benefit from oil production job opportunities more than local

people. All respondents concluded that resulting conflicts might lead to problems such as internal displacement and constant fighting.

LGRs believe that their power is embedded in the economic stability of the people they represent. It is therefore a concern that any instability caused by land grabbing will lead to the destruction of agriculture, which is the economic base underpinning political and social arrangements. They further condemned district LGRs who connive with foreigners to lease out land without consulting grass-roots authorities. They referred to this as a new era of colonialism that must be challenged. One of them anticipated the use of force to deter unwarranted land grabbing in the region. This category held an opinion that pressure over the sharing of revenues and other benefits from oil between national and local levels might result in political clashes between supporters of different politicians.

Lack of compensation from government

LGRs also observed that conflicts might occur because of compensation-related problems. According to Uganda's Land Act 1998, the government has powers to reallocate individuals or compensate them if their land is found to be strategic to government programmes. The community elder respondents were pessimistic of this view. They complained that Ugandan resettlement and compensation procedures are very weak. All respondents expressed little trust in the government in connection to this matter. They anticipated that only government officials and strong politicians might be fairly compensated.

Another problem raised was that the government embraced privatisation programmes. One youth leader, who is also a teacher, observed that "the government acquires strategic land from local owners at a laughable price and it is then sold to private investors at 'a real' price". The youth leaders and elders observed that poor compensation procedures are likely to cause mistrust within communities. People may resort to resistance to vacating their lands no matter how strategic their lands may be to the government. Youth leaders anticipated a likelihood of force being applied by the government in order to successfully access such lands. The local population may then engage the government in physical confrontations in order to defend their legitimate land.

Degradation of agricultural and forest land

All respondents held to two strong opinions: first, that agriculture is likely to be affected because fertile lands may be taken away in order to develop industries related to oil production, like refinery construction or other ventures that are not related to agriculture; and, second, that the anticipated confrontations are likely to send people into constant 'hide and search'.

Related to the preceding perspective, according to community elders, LGRs have so far taken some of what used to be government forest reserves. Elders reported that these people come with government powers to evict local populations, and when locals leave these areas, such officials take away the land for their personal ventures. One elder reported that in an area where he had planted rice and cassava, after eviction, the land was taken over by one of the officials who evicted him, claiming that it is a forest reserve. Surprisingly, the same official has planted rice and cassava on the same piece of land. Respondents from the Fishing Association were concerned that army officials grab land in the name of constructing military encampments. After a short time, soldiers are withdrawn from these encampments and the land formally occupied by soldiers is left to senior army officers for their personal gain. All respondents concurred that the grabbing of land is associated with oil production activities, and that rich government officials are partitioning local community land aiming to develop it to suit personal development.

Job scarcity and food insecurity

Job scarcity-driven conflicts are more likely to come with a decline in agricultural employment and an increased rate of migration. Uganda is faced with unemployment problems (Bainomugisha et al, 2006) while jobs are expected in oil-related industries. Accordingly, there may be a massive influx of job seekers in this oil-rich region. However, according to youth leaders, jobs are likely to be the major cause of conflicts herein. One youth leader pointed out that the current job allotment in the country is unfairly distributed with one or two subregions dominating "fatty and juicy jobs". He observed that such a trend is anticipated to escalate in oil production activities. There was a unanimous observation that indigenous people have no representation in oil production so far. Eight out of 10 youth leaders agreed that oil companies' recruitment processes and access to business prospects are perceived as inequitable and dishonest. According to this group, this undermines confidence and breeds resentment towards supposedly beneficiary groups.

Nineteen respondents observed a problem that the government seems to be blindfolding the local community by disingenuous claims that the members of the local community have been prepared for oil production related-jobs. They gave an example of one politician from what one youth leader called a 'well-eating' region who overtly lied to locals over a radio station. The political hoaxer told his listeners that many local people have already been trained. He gave an example of one famous indigenous member as a beneficiary of such training, but this turned out to be someone from the Ministry of Energy and Mineral Development who had been trained before the present government even come to power. Twenty-one respondents interpreted this to mean that the government is not ready to involve locals.

Nine out of 10 youth leaders felt that this implied that only expatriates from oil-producing countries will be employed. The exclusion of the local community from oil production job opportunities is likely to cause a rift between the communities and the oil workers, which may result in instability in the area, the MP respondent concluded. Therefore, the agricultural resources that are essential to the daily survival of thousands living in Buseruka are under threat. People may then have no means of survival and the only option may be "death in struggle or survive to suffer", as one youth leader respondent strongly observed.

Respondents from the fishing community considered themselves as unlucky because of oil production activities. The problem is that fishing is distinguished as a customary life-support activity for the region. All Fishing Association respondents observed that in the event of reallocation, the fishing community is not skilled in cultivation. Second, all observed that the existing traditional quarrels between landing sites makes it difficult to resettle the affected communities within a rivalling entity. One respondent complained that an attempt to do this might lead to physical confrontation and, subsequently, protracted civil conflicts. All observed a decline in fishing because of constant lights from flaring. In their opinion, oil production is a threat to their survival because local communities lack the education to enable them to get jobs in oil production, yet their traditional source of survival is already under threat of extinction. When taking over a particular fish landing site, it remains difficult to get proper and satisfactory compensation because valuing income from fishing is difficult due to lack of daily income standardisation. The woman in charge of one landing site observed that if dwellers on landing sites are resettled to areas of cultivation, this will exert more pressure on land, and agricultural sustainability will not be achieved due to land fragmentation.

Some possible positive effects were also noted, however. The local MP did note some possible positive effects, but these all depend on good governance and transparency. A few discussants did observe some positive aspects of oil production activities. The MP respondent held a view that revenue originating from oil can lead to farmers being able to acquire advanced agricultural equipment. They will thereafter increase production due to improved methods of farming, he anticipated. One youth leader also felt that farmers would gain capacity to compete in markets since acquired agro-processing industries will help to add value to local agriculture products. Nine out of 10 youth leaders, however, contested this opinion. They argued that corruption in Uganda cannot allow effective oil revenue management. They project massive corruption in oil revenues. Six youth leader respondents suggested that the adoption of an "all-inclusive approach" in the planning, implementation and spending of oil incomes is essential if the agricultural and other sectors are to benefit from oil production.

The MP respondent further observed that agricultural products would gain markets due to the increased population in the region. All respondents felt that a population increase is projected due to oil-related ventures. Influxes of people translate into demand for food. The MP strongly maintained that with projected increased agricultural production capacity, a market for foodstuffs will be available. But one LGR noted a problem with the expected overwhelming population influx, whereby the available suitable land may not provide the required foodstuffs.

Lack of meaningful consultation

Some consultation meetings were held between stakeholders and oil company representatives. However, the meetings left out concerns about agriculture and food security, which is the major grass-roots stakeholders' concern. In a meeting held on 19 July 2007, there was an emphasis on the establishment of a benefit-sharing mechanism (BSM), which must be transparent to all stakeholders and at all levels. According to one manager in that meeting, the BSM will establish who earns what and what percentage goes to whom. However, after three years, the BSM has not been established, yet early oil production is expected soon.

According to the minutes of a meeting held on 15 August 2007, one oil company operating in the region suggested giving employment opportunities to economically displaced persons. In their meetings, there was no defined procedure for providing employment opportunities to this category, observed one female Fishing Association respondent. They are most concerned over whether any suggested employment can provide equal livelihoods compared to what the fishing industry has been offering. Additionally, all 16 respondents observed that these meetings have been silent about the health-related effects resulting from eating contaminated fish and wondered who would bear the responsibility.

Implications for educational policy and practice

Overall, the potential for increased conflicts between various interest groups was seen to be almost inevitable, and the local communities are left with the most to lose and the least power to effect change. There is a lot of evidence across Africa to show where conflicts over resources can lead, for example, in Uganda's neighbour the Democratic Republic of the Congo. Where powerful interests converge and governance structures are weak or failing, these conflicts can rapidly become armed conflicts and escalate exponentially. Peace and security is one of the most essential prerequisites of sustainable development and Vincent's research underlines the crucial importance of good governance, regulation and transparency. It also highlights the importance of rights education for local communities who are most affected by these issues.

Vincent highlighted the lack of education as a disadvantage for local communities who are ill-prepared to take on the more highly skilled jobs in oil production. At the same time, this lack of education and knowledge left people unclear of their rights and legal position and also left them at a disadvantage in consultations. Therefore, it was not merely the lack of education, but the type of education, that left communities at a disadvantage.

In addition, 'by removing indigenous groups from their lands or recklessly exploiting natural resources such as minerals and forests, corporations and governments are effectively erasing thousands of years of practiced traditional ecological knowledge' (Adamson et al, 2012, p 212).

Case Study 2: Extract from a study of 'The role of indigenous knowledge in fisheries management: a case of Mbenje Island, Lake Malawi', by Chikondi Lydia Manyungwa

The next case study illustrates the relevance and importance of local and indigenous knowledge. This research was important to Chikondi because it is related to her work as a planning officer responsible for providing guidance to other technical units of the Department of Fisheries in Malawi and also because of her own values in relation to ESD. Chikondi took an action research approach and envisaged this study as a pilot for further development. She worked with three focus groups and three key informant interviews to collect her data. The participants included indigenous inhabitants of Chikombe village who have accrued vast indigenous knowledge (IK) over the years, as well as some migrants, especially those involved in fisheries. An extract from Chikondi's research is found in the following.

The role of indigenous knowledge in fisheries management: a case of Mbenje Island, Lake Malawi, *Chikondi Lydia Manyungwa*

At the national level, the fisheries sector in Malawi plays a major role in providing the population with employment opportunities in fishing, processing or trading activities. In addition to their subsistence importance, small-scale fisheries in Malawi provide principal livelihoods for a large number of its rural households. The sector offers direct employment to about 500,000 people and supports about 14% of the Malawi population that resides along the lakeshores of Lake Malawi through fishing, processing, marketing, fish gear construction, boat building and other ancillary activities (Malawi Government, 2001, p 3). Men dominate fish-catching activities and women participate in shore-based fishing activities and fish processing, while marketing engages both men and women. Although the fisheries sector only contributes about 4% to the country's gross domestic product (GDP), in terms of nutrition, fish forms the principal source of dietary protein, providing over 70% of the total animal protein consumed in the country (Njaya, 2009, p 10).

This research sought to demonstrate the powerful benefits and lessons that IK can offer for sustaining fisheries resources. It looked at fisherfolk beliefs, methods and practices. The results of the research show the interdependence between social behaviour and the environment, and between IK and the environment: how the local communities relate their behaviour to their use of environmental resources and the extent to which they can sustain local methods in relation to fisheries management. The research aimed at generating knowledge that influences change in values and practices in technical fisheries, training officers by using local knowledge to engage communities in solving fisheries-related challenges.

However, the research also indicated that while IK is a vital and precious resource for planetary survival, it is important not to take a non-critical approach. Tanyanyiwa and Chikwanha (2011, p 140) highlight a critical assumption of IK approaches that local people have a good understanding of the natural resource base since they have lived in the same environment for many generations and have accumulated and passed on knowledge of natural conditions, soils, vegetation, food and medicinal plants. However, under conditions where local people are recent migrants from a quite different ecological zone, they may not have much experience with the new environment. In such situations, some people's IK may not be helpful. Hence, it is imperative when dealing with recent migrants to evaluate the relevance of different kinds of IK to local conditions. That is why IK, being part of global knowledge, can be adapted to particular conditions.

Grenier (1998, p 41) noted that wider economic and social forces can also erode IK. Pressure on indigenous people to integrate with larger societies is often great, and as they become more integrated, the social structures that generate IK and indigenous practices break down. He further asserts that the importation of educational and religious systems and the impact of development processes are leading more and more to homogenisation of the world's cultures. Hence, indigenous beliefs, values, norms, know-how and practices may be altered.

Another key feature of IK that has to be taken into consideration is that the knowledge that the local people rely on is sometimes wrong or even harmful. Practices based on mistaken beliefs or inaccurate information can be dangerous and can be a barrier to the well-being of indigenous people.

Evidence of traditional fisheries management in Malawi during the pre-colonial period is scanty. However, Allison et al (2002, p 53) observed that attempts to limit access to fishery resources in southern Lake Malawi were an instrument used by traditional authorities or rival ethnic groups to exercise power rather than a measure to conserve fish stocks. However, Msosa (1999, p 56) noted a conceptual basis for resource conservation among the Tonga people in northern Lake Malawi and also observed that traditional fishing gear designs indicated an appreciation of the conservation imperative in fisheries management. Lowe (1952, p 48) also encountered the survival of traditional conservation measures whereby local rules were set by the Native Authorities, such as banning the use of seines (or dragnets) near river mouths at certain times of the year to conserve spawning runs of fish or nursery grounds for juveniles.

The development and management of fisheries in Malawi has taken place in the context of considerable political and economic changes. According to Hara et al (2002, p 31), the last two decades witnessed a paradigm shift in fisheries management from state-centric strategies to co-managerial ones. Malawi's fisheries policy was framed to include various issues on fisheries extension, with a focus on participatory fisheries management (Njaya, 2009, p 12). Njaya further highlights that the concept of co-management was introduced in the fisheries sector, with recognition that user groups have to be more actively involved in fisheries management. In the context of fisheries co-management, it meant that fishers and fisher groups and other agencies are actively involved in the management of fisheries resources through various types of structures. Co-management is based on the premise that local people must have a stake in conservation and management of resources. This links with the notion of ESD that educational programs should be rooted in the actual experiences of people in their own communities. It is an opportunity to consider the use of IK since the sector has already embraced co-management, which involves ideas from communities.

At the national level, the Fisheries Management and Conservation Act 1997 recognises that fisheries management has to be implemented using participatory approaches that provide for local community participation in the conservation and management of fisheries (Malawi Government, 1997, p 10). Furthermore, the Act also emphasises that fishery management for fishing and breeding shall consider local customs and practices, as well as community involvement. The reflection of such statements in the Act can be seen as a basis for the country's policy commitment to develop the fisheries sector by involving local participation and utilising their traditional knowledge. The Fisheries and Aquaculture Policy of 2001 also recognises the role of community participation in identifying, planning and implementation in order to achieve sustainable fisheries development (Malawi Government, 2001, p 7).

The Malawi constitution endorses the concept of IK in its concern for the preservation of natural resources. In article 13(d)(iii), it reminds the state and citizens that the environment has to be managed responsibly in order to accord full recognition to the rights of future generations by means of environmental protection and the sustainable development of natural resources (Malawi Government, 1997, p 14).

Knowledge on the status of fisheries

Respondents of the fisherfolk and a focus group discussion with members of Mbenje Management Committee (MMC) indicated that:

> "we recognise that there is a tendency of decline in the catches compared to the past. We could go fishing twice per day and get good amounts of fish but nowadays they don't get similar quantities. However, compared to other islands close by, Mbenje Island has more resources."

They attributed this trend to the management regulations that they instituted locally based on ecological knowledge. They claimed that "most fishers and traders flock to Chikombe once the fishing season begins since the fishers harvest a lot of fish which are traded across the country". This was also ascertained by the women's focus group, who indicated that "Mbenje becomes a centre of attraction at the opening of the fishing season with fishers from different areas patronising the area". The Traditional Authority (TA),[1] however, singled out heavy siltation as a result of unsustainable land use practices as contributing to the decline of fish stocks. The focus groups expressed their interest in learning how to collect data so that the local committee members could use it to help track production trends. They felt that this would also be helpful to the Fisheries Department as it would provide up-to-date data.

The role of indigenous knowledge on fishing around Mbenje Island – the regulation on the closed season

It was reported by the TA and Chief Nyangulu that:

> "closed season for the island was initiated by the ancestors in the early 1950s. The closed season runs from December to April annually and the decisions on the dates to close and open come from the local people through the chief. During closing and opening of fishing season, they perform a ceremony called 'kuteta', where they offer sacrifices on the graves of the ancestors. During closed season, fishing on waters 5km around the island is totally prohibited with whatsoever fishing gear."

It was reported that:

> "the ancestors set aside this season when they observed that during the period December to April they catch many fish but most of which were very small fish. Considering that this was rainy season, it was becoming difficult to properly manage the catch. Then they thought of establishing this season."

The other reason that was also cited was that this closed season was aimed at allowing the people to concentrate on crop-farming activities. By the time the fishing season starts, people are waiting for the field crops to ripen. They hinted that "we feel the benefit of such a regulation is that there is abundant fish soon after the closed season in April every year which gives us the motivation that our practices are working in managing the fisheries resources".

Rule enforcement

The TA, MC and Chief Nyangulu said that "we established sanctions to deal with those who violate some regulations.... Such regulations include observation of closed season, fishing using unacceptable gears, breaching of the set norms and fishing during closed season." It was found that through the local leaders, communities enforce rules through sanctions that are applicable to the violators of the rules and regulations. These sanctions include fines and the banning of fisherfolk from access to fishing for the rest of the season. The TA, MMC and Chief Nyangulu highlighted that "communities comply with the set rules by the local leaders". The committee indicated that:

> "when it comes to fishing gears, we ensure that there is an inspection of the mesh size for each and every net that is set to go fishing. The Management Committee is also responsible for registering the fishers to go fishing for the season."

To what extent are the communities involved in resource management based on their knowledge?

The MMC, Chief Nyangulu and the TA indicated that "the management regime is a centrally traditional management system. This is a system whereby institutional arrangements are locally established and institutionalised by the communities through the local leaders". The chief further alluded to the fact that Mbenje Island has a status that conducts particular regulations based on customary law. This is a typology of co-management that is centrally facilitated by local people. They emphasised that there is no government interference in any regulations set by the communities. The TA hinted that:

> "all along, we were embarking on celebrating the closing and opening of the fishing season by ourselves. It was in 1996 when we engaged government in our interventions and we saw that it only came in with supportive measures. Like the Department of Fisheries bought us a patrol boat to be used by the Mbenje Management Sub Committee for patrolling. Having listened to the long history of the traditional practices of managing the resources, it is understood that it came into being as a way of trying to avoid depletion of the resources."

In general, the TA considered that "We adopted practices for the conservation of the fish resources after we acquired extensive experience with fishing operations, learning from our ancestors". Indeed, as a result of this, it seems that local knowledge and traditional regulatory frameworks have considerably more authority than the government. In fact, the subsistence fishery of Mbenje is not subject to government regulations. Government regulations are only applicable when the MMC identifies usage of illegal fishing gear.

Challenges to the future use of traditional practices

When asked how they view the conservation of their local knowledge, Chief Nyangulu and the MMC members reported that:

> "We would love as much as possible to preserve our traditional way of managing the fisheries resources. This is with the motivation we have gotten with time when we receive visitors from all over to learn about we do in managing our resources."

However, they indicated that "we also foresee some challenges to the sustainability of the same, with HIV and AIDS as one stumbling block which is affecting the productive age group, which is critical". The mother of Chief Nyangulu also expressed concern over the HIV and AIDS scourge, saying that:

> "I am very worried with the alarming rate of deaths of the young ones. Unfortunately, it is that age group which is heavily affected. Like, myself, I have lost four children in a space of one year, which is so devastating."

The other challenge that was alluded to by the MMC and Chief Nyangulu was the political interference in the installation of chiefs at TA level. They fear that the government may decide to install someone who may not be willing to continue with the traditional practices. However, they indicated that "we will ensure we give the necessary guidance to government on the right successors for the chieftaincy so that they do not conflict with their traditional way of managing and conserving the fish resources".

The study highlighted that the traditional fisheries management system on Mbenje is one of the oldest systems in managing fisheries in Malawi. It has also been documented that the MMC undertakes their tasks and duties based on customary rules to regulate fishing activities on waters around Mbenje Island. Its role has been deeply rooted in the community of Chikombe since early 1952. It is a traditional mechanism worth securing. Hence, the recommendation being made is that such norms and practices regarding the sustainable management of fisheries should be well documented and shared among the younger generations for its sustainability.

Implications for the training of fisheries managers and workers

It has been observed that the adoption of IK in fisheries management is still in its infancy. However, the Malawi government's commitment to embrace IK in resource management is reflected in national policies. Educational approaches that foster real and complex integrated spiritual and physical relationships between people and other living things should be enhanced in order to shift from mechanistic ways of learning. Apparently, it is being suggested that efforts need to be undertaken to establish an extension training delivery system that upholds IK to increase efficiency and effectiveness in resource management.

Having gone through the analysis, there is need for a paradigm shift of extension approaches with regard to the nature of training of extension workers. Sustainable fisheries management may require extension personnel to have a greater understanding of the interaction between the physical and socio-economic fishing environment so that they are able to adapt technical advice to specific circumstances and local environments. The learning and teaching methods in the training institutions also need to be brought in line with the requirements of ESD and should thus be focused on interdisciplinary approaches. From a gender perspective, women have a particularly important role as environmental managers, and extension service providers should take account of and build upon women's environmental knowledge and tasks within the communities.

The role of education policy and practice in addressing the challenge of social and ecological sustainability

The case of the Albertine valley and of Mbenje Island can be seen as a microcosm of the challenges involved in balancing social and ecological issues across all of SSA, and this raises many issues for the prospect of sustainable development in Africa. The current neoliberal paradigm of market-led development and the weakening of state power cannot ensure social and ecological sustainability. Indeed, without stronger environmental and social regulation of activities such as oil production, it seems likely that powerful groups and elites will be the only beneficiaries while ecological degradation is likely to continue apace. However, a strong state is not a panacea, as without good governance and accountability, state power can also be abused in the interests of the powerful. These studies highlight the need for a new kind of big picture politics that addresses local, national and global issues of sustainable development. This is not a simple task, of course, and will rely on politicians with integrity, values and a moral compass to promote policies that address social and ecological justice. These two studies have also illustrated the need for increased local and regional governance that, wherever possible, involves a policy of subsidiarity. This has implications for the educational needs of local communities and of politicians at all levels.

Many social actors and social movements are engaged in challenging the current neoliberal hegemony but there are many obstacles to this. As already mentioned, one of these is education, both formal and non-formal, and how this is constructed. Vincent's research illustrates that equal access to education is an obstacle, but the relevance, appropriacy and, hence, quality of education is also a key issue. Chikondi's research underlines this by highlighting the importance of valuing local and indigenous knowledge.

As David Orr (2004, p 8) points out:

> Education is no guarantee of decency, prudence or wisdom. Much of the same kind of education will only compound our problems. This is not an argument for ignorance but rather a statement that the worth of education must now be measured against the standards of decency and human survival – the issues now looming so large before us in the twenty-first century. It is not education but education of a certain kind that will save us.

Some commentators go so far as to say that education itself is a negative idea that merely divides people by creating 'two classes of people everywhere: the educated and the uneducated or undereducated' (Esteva et al, 2005 , p 20). They feel that education is often a new means of colonisation of the mind and that it denigrates local and indigenous knowledge and skills.

The rest of this chapter will explore the kind of education that is needed in order to address the challenges of sustainability in SSA.

The challenge of education

One of the key elements of the MDGs was the emphasis on education through the EFA targets. Education was, and still is, seen as an important lever to eliminate poverty and inequality. The goals of EFA included:

- Goal 1: Early childhood care and education: Expanding and improving comprehensive early childhood care and education, especially for the most vulnerable and disadvantaged children.
- Goal 2: Universal primary education: Ensuring that, by 2015, all children, particularly girls, children in difficult circumstances and those belonging to minority ethnic groups, have access to complete, free and compulsory primary education of good quality.
- Goal 3: Youth and adult learning needs: Ensuring that the learning needs of all young people and adults are met through equitable access to appropriate learning and life skills programmes.

Some impressive achievements have been made in SSA with regard to these goals. However, without embedding ESD within the future education goals and policies, there is a danger that we will just replicate the same kind of learning that has led to current patterns of unsustainable development. While no one can doubt the importance of education as a human right for all people and the need to ensure access to this for all, especially the most disadvantaged and marginalised, at the same time, it is important to recognise that formal education is not ideologically neutral. Indeed, formal education has often been used in an instrumental way by ruling elites (eg as in apartheid South Africa) to try to control their populations. In the case of South Africa, it was the attempt of the apartheid regime to force the study of the Afrikaans language on the black population that provided a catalyst to the Soweto uprising of June 1976. This is an extreme case and it is to be hoped that democratic processes will generally ensure that checks and balances are in place to avoid such exigencies. However, formal education has long been a site of struggle for competing views and interests and the last 25 years have seen increasing attempts by central governments to take control of the agendas and curricula (Bowe et al, 1992; Apple, 1996).

As Apple (1993, p 1) puts it:

> The curriculum is not simply a neutral assemblage of knowledge, somehow appearing in the texts and classrooms of a nation. It is always part of a selective tradition, someone's selection, some group's vision of legitimate knowledge. It is produced out of the cultural, political and economic conflicts, tensions and compromises that organise or disorganise a people.

In the past two decades, the dominance of neoliberal policies has helped to shape formal education in many countries, both in relation to the increasing trends towards the privatisation and marketisation of education and also in relation to the shape of the curriculum (Blewitt, 2013). These are the very same policies that have led us to rely on current models of unsustainable economic growth, overproduction and overconsumption patterns, and degradation of the natural environment on which we all depend. New ways of thinking, new skills and new competences are needed if we are to build sustainable livelihoods for the future. Therefore, it is not education per se, but the *quality* and kind of education, that really matters.

Mary Pigozzi (2003) eloquently describes a vision of 'quality education', which takes into account both EFA and ESD:

> A quality education must reflect learning in relation to the learner as individual, family and community member and part of a world society. A quality education understands the past, is relevant to the present and has a view to the future. Quality education relates to knowledge building and the skilful application of all forms of knowledge by unique individuals that function both independently and in relation to others. A quality education reflects the dynamic nature of culture and languages, the value of the individual in relation to the larger context and the importance of living in a way that promotes equality in the present and fosters a sustainable future.

Both EFA and ESD are concerned with the quality of learning and education systems that are needed for sustainable development in the 21st century. Although EFA and ESD agendas have different starting points, they share broad aims and objectives to promote learning that enables human and ecological well-being for both present and future generations. While it is, of course, necessary to acknowledge the different constituencies and histories of both EFA and ESD, there is now a growing consensus that synergies between ESD and EFA will strengthen both agendas and bring them mutual benefits (Wade and Parker, 2008; ACCU, 2012).

EFA has achieved a great deal towards the MDGs, but its focus on primary and basic education has understandably been limited in achieving this much broader vision of quality education, as outlined earlier by Mary Pigozzi. The reasons for this have been well documented elsewhere (eg Wade and Parker, 2008; ACCU, 2012), but ongoing concerns about educational quality persist. When it comes to quality education, it would seem that a false dichotomy has been made in the past between EFA and ESD. Among educational practitioners, there is considerable agreement around the pedagogy and approaches that underlie an effective curriculum. This growing consensus could be expanded and developed to bring into EFA the additional dimensions of ESD, which are currently missing. This would help to ensure that education was appropriate, relevant, contextualised and underpinned by the need to balance ecological and societal needs for current and future generations.

This is not to imply that this will be an easy process or a quick fix, as illustrated by the third extract. The role of ESD in the curriculum is addressed in this research by Heinrich Rukundo.

Case Study 3: An extract from the research of Heinrich Rukundo, 'Using education for sustainability to analyse the system barriers and bottlenecks to the implementation of the Nine Year Basic Education policy in Rwanda'

Heinrich formerly worked in the National Curriculum Development Centre – Rwanda, where he was involved in curriculum design and review, and then in the Ministry of Education project for promoting science education in Rwandan primary and secondary schools. He now works for UNICEF (United Nations Childrens' Fund).

This was a qualitative piece of research using a multilevel approach. Purposive sampling was used to identify a team of policymakers and educational planners from the Ministry of Education, and then a case study was conducted of a specific school – Kacyiru Primary School.

Heinrich's research in Rwanda in 2012 had a focus on the most disadvantaged children. He examined, in particular, how an ESD approach could facilitate inclusive education for all in the context of Rwanda's new Nine Year Basic Education (NYBE) policy. Rwanda has made great strides in education in the last five years, but, as Heinrich points out, its problems are manifold, with a much greater proportion of damaged and disadvantaged children as an ongoing legacy of the 1994 genocide.

ESD and the challenges for basic education in Rwanda
Heinrich Rukundo

Equity of learning opportunities and development outcomes has emerged as critical to the discourse leading up to 2015, when the world will assess the extent to which it has achieved the MDGs and the targets of EFA, and determine what new goals and targets will be set for the future. Equity has become particularly important in Rwanda's refocused agenda because current assessments of progress point to two results:

- that many disadvantaged children are excluded from or not reached by schools because schools seem not to be responsive to their needs; and
- that where achievements have been made in reaching disadvantaged children, they have not been equitably distributed (Ministry of Education, 2011).

The study established the importance of ESD as a key element of quality education. However, it identified that some opportunities to enrich the curriculum and embed ESD were not being taken up. Given that, according to the Ministry of Education, Rwanda's future economic development hinges upon how it develops its human resources (Ministry of Education, 2003). Education in Rwanda is viewed alongside other social institutions as working to create and maintain a stable society. The country looks forward to having an informed, involved citizenry with creative problem-solving skills, scientific and social literacy, and commitment to engage in responsible individual and cooperative actions about their lifestyles for today and tomorrow.

In order for these skills to be ensured, the learning processes at the school classroom level need to be stimulating to suit the learning needs of children. It is clear in the literature that ESD is viewed as playing a transformative role, which signifies an emerging change in the educational paradigm that is sufficiently strong in terms of its philosophy, methodology and pedagogy to challenge the dominant educational paradigm. ESD learners develop social contextual skills and creative and critical thinking skills. ESD encourages interdisciplinary and holistic thinking and the analysis of issues in context. For instance, ESD brings issues of society, environment, economics and culture to the fore in education and learning. The ESD perspective also strengthens the equity agenda by targeting disadvantaged children so as to ensure equity in the community.

Sterling (2005, p 12) underlines that 'ESD is the product of changing thinking about the relation between learning and the wider world, between education and society, and between the human and natural worlds and this thinking is itself a learning process which still continues'. Particularly in Rwanda, this learning is in line with how the country can better achieve its refocused agenda of ensuring education for the disadvantaged children.

In line with this argument, the systems view of a school context has been used in this critical analysis to establish the relationship and connection between the Kacyiru community of parents, students and teachers and NYBE implementation so as to bridge the gap for ESD, while also aligning to existing development and decentralisation policies that focus on empowering people at local administrative levels to implement important education policies such as NYBE.

Participation and engagement of local communities – a key success factor?

As Sterling (2005, p 92) points out, 'top down and participatory approaches do not necessarily form a dichotomy and ... both can have value as long as the assumptions driving them are clarified'. In relation to this argument, using a more community-based approach and taking an integrated approach has been viewed as good practice for fast-tracking NYBE, and it is clear from the study that ownership of the community in relation to the education of their children has been significantly improved. However, how far this translates well for disadvantaged children requires deeper research.

The case study of Kacyiru Primary School found that a number of ESD approaches were being employed as part of the NYBE. A key part of the NYBE strategy has been the active involvement and engagement of communities, especially with regards to building infrastructure and maintaining schools, but also in contributing to management and planning. For many years, education in Rwanda has been considered a role of the state in terms of establishing schools, training and paying salaries for teachers, and providing all pedagogical materials, in addition to uniforms for all children. However, as highlighted by one parent, who was also part of the local administration leadership:

> "This perception is changing and the communities are now willingly being part of their children's education, this has been realised in the community participation in constructing their school, but also participating and contributing in the planning and day-to-day management of the school."

The NYBE came up as the policy of the government to ensure that all children in communities access schools and learn through nine years of education.

In order to ensure that the policy was implemented at community levels, parents were called upon to work with community leaders and provide the labour, using locally available resources to ensure the construction of additional classrooms. The government provided essential materials such as cement and iron sheets and parents provided labour for bricklaying and classroom construction. In some ways, this development is the foundation for the community and parents to start getting involved in the student learning process.

Changing the role of children in learning

In the interviews with the school-level community, the head teacher underlined that children have long been treated as passive recipients of knowledge rather than as active participants in their own education, with their own voices neglected. Furthermore, their families and the community surrounding the school were explicitly or implicitly kept out of the school unless, of course, their contribution or funds were needed.

Encouraged by government policy, one of the teachers felt that Kacyiru Primary School, on the other hand, welcomed and promoted the participation of children, families and communities through focusing on the following:

- Being child-centred, promoting the participation of all students in school life, including school governance.
- Being community-focused, working to strengthen the family as a child's primary care-giver and educator and helping children, parents and teachers establish collaborative relationships.
- Activating community-based initiatives for encouraging local partnerships in education with the community for the sake of children, such as collaborative parent–teacher school committees (with gender balance) and school-based management.

The following two elements were of particular importance to disadvantaged children:

- Peer-to-peer support mechanisms involving children supporting other children. These helped to promote inclusive teaching and the provision of care and support in order for them to participate in learning and interacting.
- Psychosocial and school guidance and counselling services. These have been established at the school to ensure that support for all children is strengthened.

Effective school management and leadership

In line with the education quality standards of the NYBE, all schools are required to institute an effective school management and leadership system that is inclusive of parents, teachers and children. Specifically for Kacyiru Primary School, the existing management aspects included the following:

- a management team, including a functioning Community Education Development Committee (CEDC) with effective leadership and management skills to undertake school-level planning and support the school management;
- a head teacher who seeks to encourage the staff at the school to work in a holistic approach, recognising the importance of education to socio-economic development, and takes a leading role in the promotion of education within the broader community and in ensuring that learning provided at the school is locally relevant;
- staff involvement with sound knowledge of government policies that can then be put into practice in planning for inclusive school development; and
- a student management information system, including student portfolios, which are used by teachers to improve the students' learning both at school and at home.

Conclusion

Each of these case studies, in their different ways, has illustrated the potential for building on community involvement and support in moving towards sustainable development. Heinrich's research highlighted the potential for schools to offer a more relevant and appropriate curriculum and, by maximising the human resources of teachers, parents and children, to enable increased access and support for disadvantaged children. However, a note of caution does need to be struck as his case study was of only one school and further research will be needed in order to establish to what extent this model is transferable. Nonetheless, it offers us some optimism that with goodwill and through the use of the enhanced social capital of local communities, a great deal of positive change can be achieved. Of course, this model does have many implications for policymakers at national and global levels. The last 20 years has seen increasing centralisation and control of education policies, while Heinrich's model involves the need for much more subsidiarity and trust in local communities and local government.

This need is also demonstrated in Vincent's and Chikondi's research, which further highlight the need for good governance, accountability and transparency. Vincent's research in Uganda has indicated the dangers of not paying attention to the urgent needs of local communities for food security, employment and education. His study pinpointed the real fears of local communities and indicated the potential for increasing conflicts over resources and livelihoods. Chikondi's research in Malawi took a more optimistic tone and demonstrated the value of involving local communities in relation to fisheries management. All these case studies illustrate the important links between politics, education and learning in achieving sustainability.

A moral framework of shared values centred around human and ecological rights is a prerequisite of this – which requires a step change by politicians of all levels and in all countries. It also requires a more informed public that embraces these values; hence the need for more engaged educationalists and academics.

Education policy and practice cannot, of course, be divorced from other areas of social and economic policy and any discussion must therefore, of necessity, sit within this context. As economic models are so central to our current world view, and as all people on earth need a livelihood in order to survive, we cannot afford to ignore a central question: what kind of society do we need to build in order to achieve sustainable living? These three case studies have not just provided some food for thought, but proposed some practical actions for a change towards such a society. Through their engagement, this growing learning community of ESD activists in Africa presents a vibrant pool of talent to take forward a future vision of sustainability for organisations and their countries. Through their scholarship and research, they have the potential to reach influential positions in their relatively young countries. For the academic staff who have been teaching them, it continues to be an inspiring and energising experience. Their commitment and dedication certainly lend hope to the possibility of a more sustainable future world.

Note

[1] The area of indigenous geopolitical and socio-economic jurisdiction; an indigenous state (customary sovereignty) sometimes of a single lineage descent group that represents the source of authority of the chief as the *primus inter pares*.

References

ACCU (Asia Pacific Cultural Centre for UNESCO) (ed) (2012) *Tales of HOPE 111: EFS-ESD linkages and synergies*, Japan: ACCU

Allison, E.H., Mvula, P.M. and Ellis, F. (2002) 'Conflicting agendas in the development and management of fisheries on Lake Malawi', in K. Geheb and M. Sarch (eds) *Africa's inland fisheries: the management challenge*, Kampala, Uganda: Fountain.

Apple, M. (1993) 'The politics of official knowledge', in *Discourses 14.1*, Australia: University of Queensland.

Apple, M. (1996) *Cultural politics and education*, Milton Keynes: Open University Press.

Bainomugisha, A., Kivengyere, H. and Tusasirwe, B. (2006) 'Escaping the oilcurse and making poverty history. A review of the oil and gas policy and legal framework for Uganda', ACODE, Policy Research Series No 20.

Blewitt, J. (2013) 'EfS: contesting the market model of higher education', in S. Sterling, L. Maxey and H. Luna (eds) *The sustainable university: progress and prospects*, Abingdon: Routledge.

Bowe, R., Ball, S. and Gold, A. (1992) *Reforming education and changing schools*, London and New York, NY: Routledge.

Bush, R. (2007) *Poverty and neo liberalism: persistence and reproduction in the global South*, London: Pluto Press.

Carmody, P. (2011) *The new scramble for Africa*, Cambridge: Polity Press.

Esteva, G., Stuchul, D.L. and Prakash, M.S. (2005) 'From a pedagogy for liberation to liberation from pedagogy', in C. Bowers and F. Apffel-Marglin (eds) *Rethinking Freire: globalisation and the environmental crisis*, New Jersey, NJ: Lawrence Erlbaum Associates.

Grenier, L. (1998) *Working with indigenous knowledge. A guide for researchers*, Ottawa, Canada: International Development Research Centre.

Hara, M., Donda, S. and Njaya, F. (2002) 'Lessons from Malawi's experience with fisheries co-management initiatives', in K. Geheb and M. Sarch (eds) *Africa's inland fisheries: the management challenge*, Kampala, Uganda: Fountain Publishers Limited.

Lowe, R.H. (1952) *Report on the tilapia and other fish and fisheries of Lake Nyasa. Part II 1945–47*, London: Crown Agents for the Colonies.

Malawi Government (1997) *Fisheries conservation and management Act 1997*, Lilongwe: Ministry of Natural Resources and Environmental Affairs.

Malawi Government (2001) *National fisheries and aquaculture policy*, Lilongwe: Ministry of Natural Resources and Environmental Affairs.

Ministry of Education (2003) *Education sector policy*, Kigali, Rwanda: Ministry of Education Rwanda.

Ministry of Education (2011) *Education management information system datas*, Kigali, Rwanda: Ministry of Education Rwanda.

Msosa, W. (1999) 'Fishery culture and origins of the Tonga people of Lake Malawi', in H.G.W. Kawanabe and A.C. Coulter (eds) *Ancient lakes: their cultural and biological diversity*, Ghent, Belguim: Kenobi Productions, pp 271–80.

Njaya, F.J. (2009) 'The Lake Chilwa fishing household strategies in response to water level changes: migration, conflicts and co-management', PhD (Economic and Management Sciences) thesis, University of Western Cape, South Africa, September.

Orr, D. (2004) *Education, the environment and the human prospect*, Washington, DC: Island Press.

Pigozzi, M.J. (2003) 'Reorienting education in support of sustainable development through a focus on quality education for all', paper presented at GEA conference, Tokyo, 25 October, UNESCO.

Sterling, S. (2005) *Unit 7 study guide: education for sustainability: education in change*, London: Distance Education Centre, South Bank University.

Tanyanyiwa, V.I. and Chikwanha, M. (2011) 'The role of indigenous knowledge systems in the management of forest resources in Mugabe area Masvingo Zimbabwe', *Journal of Sustainable Development*, vol 13, no 32, pp 1520–5509.

UNDP (United Nations Development Programme) (2013) 'Human development report 2013. The rise of the South: human progress in a diverse world', UNDP. Available at: http://hdr.undp.org/en/

UNESCO (2014) *Education for All global monitoring report 2013/14*, Paris: UNESCO, Available at: http://unesdoc.unesco.org/images/0022/002256/225660e.pdf

Wade, R. and Parker, J. (2008) *EFA–ESD dialogue: educating for a sustainable world*, UNESCO ESD Policy Dialogue 1, Paris: UNESCO.

EIGHT

Regional centres of expertise as mobilising mechanisms for education for sustainable development

Roger A. Petry, Lyle M. Benko, Takaaki Koganezawa, Tomonori Ichinose and Mary Otieno, with Ros Wade

Introduction

This chapter will examine the role of regional centres of expertise (RCEs) in promoting and delivering change towards sustainability through education and learning. It will take a number of case studies from different global regions and identify some key challenges and opportunities. The central core text for these case studies is provided by one of the very first regions to adopt this RCE model, that of RCE Saskatchewan in Canada, which was started in 2005. Lyle Benko and Roger Petry from RCE Saskatchewan have highlighted a number of key elements and issues for their RCE and have identified some key enabling factors that have led to examples of effective mobilisation. Although every RCE is different in the challenges that they face, as well as in their development and structure, nonetheless, some interesting comparisons can be made with the other two case studies of RCE Greater Sendai in Japan (contributed by Takaaki Koganezawa and Tomonori Ichinose) and RCE Greater Nairobi in Kenya (contributed by Mary Otieno). Each RCE has grown up organically, developed by the various concerned social actors in their regions. They all have different focuses and have responded in different ways to the challenges of their regions. This is an example of a kind of subsidiarity in terms of policymaking and practice in education for sustainable development[1] (ESD) and will be considered in relation to their effectiveness as mobilising mechanisms for ESD. Acccording to Professor Hans Van Ginkel, one of the founders of the RCE initiative while Rector of the United Nations University (UNU):

> 'Education *for* Sustainable Development' means what it says: it is not just environmental education or even sustainable development education, but 'education *for* sustainable development'. Only when we are successful in pooling all available people and resources, can we do an appropriate job. We must 'walk the talk' in order to transform all education and transcend all existing divisions to achieve our ultimate goal of a better future for all. (Van Ginkel, 2013, p 92)

What is a regional centre of expertise?

RCEs were set up to achieve the aspirations of the United Nation's (UN's) Decade of Education for Sustainable Development (DESD), 2005–14. The UNU Institute of Advanced Studies (UNU–IAS) intends that the network of RCEs around the planet will become part of a global learning space for sustainable development. In 2013, there were over 100 RCEs worldwide, including over 20 in Europe. Their purpose is to mobilise individuals and communities towards sustainable development, using the most appropriate expertise, knowledge and skills, and they are founded on the principles and values of ESD in relation to social and ecological rights and justice, locally and globally. Aspiring RCEs have to apply to be accredited by the UNU through a rigorous, peer-reviewed application process. The concept of regional centres of expertise is 'firmly based on the principles of respect, self-organization and participation' (Van Ginkel, 2013, p 92).

An RCE is a network of formal, informal and non-formal organisations mobilised to act as a catalyst for the delivery of ESD to local and regional communities. The network is made up of schools, community and voluntary groups, the business sector, universities, non-governmental organisations (NGOs), local authorities, and other interested individuals. Most (though not all) RCEs were founded and coordinated by higher education institutions (HEIs).

An RCE is about information sharing, networking and collaborating on projects and programmes that enable all sectors of the community to benefit from the skills and knowledge of educators that have sustainable development at the core of their teaching. It is about adding value to existing networks and, where appropriate, creating synergies between them:

> An RCE is not a physical centre but an institutional mechanism to facilitate capacity development for sustainable development. An RCE is a network of existing local–

regional institutions mobilised to jointly promote all types of learning for a sustainable future. RCEs, both individually and collectively, aspire to achieve the goals of DESD. (Mochizuki and Fadeeva, 2008, p 372)

The RCE initiative of the DESD aims to develop a global knowledge network for transformative education to promote sustainable communities. RCEs have largely developed organically in response to regional contexts and needs, while, at the same time, being part of a wider global network.

Common to most RCEs is their emphasis on volunteerism, their engagement with a wide range of community actors, their flexible structures and their emphasis on innovation and action based on sound science, local knowledge and expertise. These elements present both challenges and opportunities for engagement and mobilisation, which are highlighted in the chapter. For example, while RCE Saskatchewan finds positive advantages and virtues in the model of volunteerism, RCE Greater Nairobi struggles with a lack of capacity. It is beyond the remit of this chapter to examine to what extent this relates to the wide differences between the two areas in terms of infrastructure, social and educational resources, and human capital. However, these imbalances between different regions clearly play a big part in the challenges of sustainability. RCE Greater Sendai, on the other hand, was faced with the major ecological and human disaster of the 2011 'Great East Japan Earthquake' and has identified how some of the capacities it has developed played a part in reconstruction and mutual support. This case study highlights the potential role of RCEs and ESD in capacity-building and disaster preparedness.

A case study of Regional Centre of Expertise Saskatchewan, Canada

Organisation of Regional Centre of Expertise Saskatchewan – opportunities and challenges

RCE Saskatchewan intentionally built its organisational structure and mobilisation of activity on volunteerism. The lack of ongoing financial support available for RCE formation and maintenance meant that a non-financial model mobilising volunteers, in-kind contributions from partners, freely available technologies (specifically free/open source software) and targeted financial contributions for specific ESD initiatives was more likely to succeed than a traditional organisational model tied to raising money and paying staff for its ongoing viability. This method of innovation through volunteerism can reasonably include a new range of development options that might be sustainable over the long term.

In the case of RCE Saskatchewan, a lightweight organisational structure was not just demanded by partners, who did not want to see the RCE as a separate organisation depriving them of resources; it was also in keeping with its sustainable development goals – the creation of an organisation that sought to maximise impacts on human well-being and ecosystem health while minimising resource use. A non-market model was adopted, with formal education in Canada being the primary responsibility of the provincial government. The high costs of sustainable development technologies in the commercial sector were also key to adopting a non-market model (Petry, 2008).

However, in a peculiar way, resource constraints are a kind of resource for ESD as a lack of resources requires an intentional focus on local materials available free or at a low cost, low energy use, and freely available technologies. These technologies include free/open source technologies, locally developed low or intermediate technologies tied to the region's historic development and cultures (and not fenced off by intellectual property rights), and technology available through existing publicly accountable HEIs and those with public service mandates. Living within these constraints is typically a goal of sustainable development. A lightweight structure also minimises risks by not being dependent upon a single resource base, which is a further sustainability goal. From a political perspective, this reduces the potential of an RCE being organisationally beholden to powerful individuals, interest groups or organisations providing these resources, and subject to the constraints that this might place upon an RCE's autonomy and ability to pursue its mission.

Regional Centre of Expertise Saskatchewan: the big tent approach

While volunteerism is the primary basis upon which RCE Saskatchewan achieves its various goals, it is the *cause* of ESD through which voluntarily contributed resources are mobilised. Why, then, does ESD *as a cause* serve as such a valuable and useful mobilising mechanism, in particular, within the Saskatchewan region? Unwavering commitment to the cause of ESD allows the RCE to be perceived as a unifying, impartial and apolitical organisation in a region historically known for its extremes on the political Left and Right. At the same time, achieving the agenda of sustainability implicitly advances many desirable political, social and economic aims.

Part of the ability of the RCE to be legitimately perceived as impartial has to do with a non-judgemental attitude towards the reasons individuals or organisations might want to advance sustainable development and ESD. Sustainable development in the Saskatchewan region is a 'big tent' cause appealing to multiple organisational stakeholders. In terms of political organisations, Charles Hopkins (United Nations Science and Cultural Organisation [UNESCO] Chair in ESD at the University of Toronto) has observed that at a broad political level, there is no political party that wants a future that is unsustainable. At a provincial level, even though there was a change of government from the time of the formation of RCE Saskatchewan in 2006, government ministries (whether environment, education or culture) have continued to be supportive of its work. The longevity of sustainable development as a discourse in policy circles is remarkable.[2] Its success in governments, especially at the municipal and provincial level, probably has to do with the constructive critique it provides of traditional development models and a pragmatic concern to avoid previous mistakes. There is a need to understand development at a local level in an integrated way in order to best achieve desired citizen outcomes embedded in the concept of sustainable development. In the case of RCE Saskatchewan, governments of different levels have appreciated the ability to work across governmental jurisdictions (departmental and territorial) and across organisations in advancing sustainable livelihoods in specific regions and communities. This recently included RCE Saskatchewan's participation in the 'Northern Economy Sustainability Team of Action' conference in Nipawin, Saskatchewan, in May 2013. The 'Sustainability in Rural and Remote Communities' event had representation from five HEIs, school districts, First Nations and Métis communities, provincial and municipal governments, and national ESD organisations. Importantly, the natural boundaries for livelihood activities and ecosystems cross into the neighbouring province of Manitoba and, therefore, representatives from organisations from Manitoba were in attendance.

Building on the skills and knowledge of Regional Centre of Expertise Saskatchewan members

The leadership in putting together the application for RCE Saskatchewan in 2005 came from the Sustainable Campus Advisory Group, which was comprised of faculty, students, administration and staff and had informally emerged to develop a campus sustainability policy at the University of Regina. These leaders also drew upon their connections with other organisations to engage, for example, the City of Regina, the City of Saskatoon, the Province of Saskatchewan and smaller communities such as Craik. Mobilisation of resources is tied to targeted advocacy within organisations, deliberately linking the value of ESD as a collective agenda to a specific organisation's own goals and accountabilities while, at the same time, affirming its general appeal to citizens. RCEs, in turn, have been demonstrated to be an important platform for this inter-organisational collaboration, based on their proven successes and rapid growth of their respective networks.

On the other hand, it is the expertise that is found within the RCE network itself that draws other organisations and individuals to seek out its members. By positioning itself as it does, participants in the RCE acquire specific forms of expertise based on the inter-organisational, regional and global collaboration afforded by an RCE. As such, it is not so much the expertise that individuals bring to the RCE that is a primary determinant, but rather, over time, the expertise that they generate from their embeddedness in the new social relationships that an RCE generates and their strategic management of this emerging social capital. RCEs, then, function as originally intended, namely, as centres of expertise, yet 'centres' grounded in those individuals who are willing to take the risk to make connections across traditional divides and who are also dedicated to advancing ESD in a given geographic region. This expertise, once generally known, in turn, draws specific proposals for action to an RCE, specifically where these are not readily accomplished by any single organisation. The structure of RCE Saskatchewan is also meant to be such that individuals and organisations see themselves as part of a regional movement for ESD. The RCE does not have to advocate to other organisations as an outsider, but rather strengthens the advocacy of its members within their respective organisations by externally acknowledging and legitimising their activity.

Developing priorities and areas of focus

Organisational partners of the RCE agree to support the cause of ESD as expressed in RCE Saskatchewan's founding document and assessed by the Ubuntu Committee of Peers for RCEs (representing 14 global educational, scientific and technological organisations). This document was subsequently approved by the UNU as the RCE's constituting document. An RCE's founding document amounts to a quasi-legal, yet primarily ethical, contractual commitment to the functional goals of the UNU-IAS in establishing the RCE network, along with a commitment to its fellow RCEs.

A further 'neutrality' or 'impartiality' is tied to constraints on how sustainable development is understood. While sustainable development has been noted by many as a political and contested concept, the understanding or meaning of sustainable development and ESD as a cause in an RCE context is constrained by several sources. First, as RCEs are established to advance the UN DESD (2005–14), UN documents and conventions related to sustainable development and ESD approved by national governments in UN assemblies legitimately frame RCE goals. At the same time, RCEs have the freedom, latitude and expectation both in their formative documents and through their structural evolution to identify important sustainable development issues related to the goals of sustaining human well-being and ecosystem health (and how this is understood) within their given geographic context. In addition, through its formal connection to the UNU and HEIs in its region, the concepts of sustainable development and ESD are also informed by peer-reviewed scholarship, including, for example, in the areas of ethics, biology and interdisciplinary, grounded theoretical methods. As such, while having potential political ramifications within a region, an RCE's goals have both global and scholarly legitimacy, which are non-arbitrary, allowing it to be viewed as impartial and non-partisan.

In this light, RCE Saskatchewan identified seven areas of focus. These are:

1. adapting cultures for sustainability;
2. climate change, farming and local food production;
3. health and healthy lifestyles;
4. reconnecting to natural prairie ecosystems;
5. supporting and bridging cultures for sustainable living;
6. sustainable infrastructure (including water and energy); and
7. building sustainable communities/sustainable community planning.

The role of higher education institutions and the United Nations University

In terms of non-governmental sectors, HEIs in Saskatchewan see the strategic value of advancing ESD in the region as a common cause. At one level, the RCE allows for innovation in the nature of scholarship by applying the model of volunteerism to how scholarship is conducted and knowledge is thereby generated (Petry, 2012, p 115). At another level, the RCE both legitimises and protects the investigator-driven pursuit of knowledge for ESD, providing academic freedom and legitimacy through the scholarly protections of the UNU, and protection from sanctions by the state through the UN and its agencies (Petry, 2012, p 118). In the case of Saskatchewan (and Canada more generally), the UN also has a high public prestige due to Canada's historic support for the UN and its role as a mid-sized state valuing multilateral political arrangements (versus those of traditional global powers such as the US).

A final value HEIs place on an RCE is in the attainment of long-term objectives of interest across the higher education sector, despite competitiveness between universities, colleges and technical institutes for students and state support. For example, a shared long-term higher education goal has to do with remedying a lack of successful completion of high school, especially among poor and marginalised groups in the RCE Saskatchewan region (such as First Nations communities), and the lack of prerequisite skills for success in higher education (such as certain levels of literacy). This means that *all* HEIs have an interest in increasing high school completion rates and the quality of education within schools; this will increase the future size of the market for higher education regardless of what specific choices these students might make, whether technical or professional training or a general liberal arts and sciences degree. To the extent that ESD is proven to increase both educational quality and student retention rates (eg by increasing the relevance of curricula and engaging a range of learning styles), the higher education sector has a collective economic interest in advancing ESD throughout the region's school systems. HEIs with a regional accountability can then place themselves competitively relative to those outside the region by incorporating further ESD learning experiences desired by students into their programming.

The cause of ESD also works as an important mobilising mechanism because of its focus on the potential productivity of neglected forms of capital, in this case, human capital, natural capital and social capital, especially non-market forms of each. RCE Saskatchewan's annual ESD Recognition Event (which entered its fifth year in 2013) helps showcase what sustainable development actually looks like within communities through a non-competitive awards format that allows recipients a chance to share their own stories and milestones. This, in turn, provides policymakers with a clear view of what community resources and avenues of development are being overlooked or excluded in their own policies and programmes – this despite sustainable development projects typically being low-cost (for reasons cited earlier) and socially desirable. So, for example, in terms of *human capital*, these projects frequently employ volunteerism (whether by employees or individuals), including individuals contributing their own sweat equity to projects. In addition, as *education for* sustainable development projects, they necessarily have an educational component, which amounts to investments in human capital/capability formation. Building up *natural capital* (or minimising depletion of natural capital) means that projects typically use locally available renewable resources. Lastly, *social capital* formation is found in the creation of new spaces and networks for sharing tacit/experiential knowledge and knowledge of who holds particular expertise within a community. ESD projects recognised by RCE Saskatchewan in 2013 through its awards programme often demonstrate all three of these elements simultaneously.

Issues, obstacles and challenges related to education for sustainable development policy and practice

RCE Saskatchewan has encountered a range of issues related to policy and practice that challenge the advancement of sustainable development. A key issue for policymakers in government, but also HEIs, business and NGOs, is a lack of awareness of what sustainability *as a kind of development* looks like on the ground within their region and the diverse forms of education required to advance it through place-based/situated processes. It is not surprising that development built on human capital investments with benefits cutting across multiple sectors and across time (both short-term and long-term), as well as placing an emphasis on building up neglected capital stocks (whether human, natural or social), will frequently start quite small and in unexpected places. Individuals and organisations themselves are typically not aware that what they are doing falls appropriately under what would be called ESD. As such, RCE Saskatchewan has consistently sought to raise organisational awareness of what such development looks like, both by helping groups self-identify projects through its annual ESD recognition event and by initially conducting an inventory of ESD projects in the region through a student-led process (White and Petry, 2011). HEIs who are members of RCE Saskatchewan have also sought to do inventories of their own sustainable development and ESD projects and have constructed their own internal mechanisms for governance, including monitoring and advancement. Lastly, RCE Saskatchewan has brought representatives of other RCEs to Saskatchewan to help profile the nature of ESD and ESD research in their respective RCEs, while regularly making contributions to and circulating the RCE publications of the UNU.

Examples: developing the profile of education for sustainable development

A community health initiative organised by the town of Craik developed a diverse set of fun, engaging, low-cost and seasonally appropriate recreation activities as part of a year of programming. As another example, the Aylsham Fruit and Vegetable Company offers low-cost workshops on greenhouse construction techniques adapted from a Spanish context to a northern prairie climate in Saskatchewan. These greenhouses require low-cost materials to build and offer fresh produce such as strawberries until November, significantly extending Saskatchewan's growing season. Lastly, a straw/light clay workshop organised by Riverstone Studies teaches participants how to build sturdy wall constructions out of locally available materials, in this case, straw and clay, using knowledge of early home construction by pioneers on the prairies.

The University of Regina established its President's Advisory Committee on Sustainability in 2011. The University of Saskatchewan established a sustainability office early on and created an extensive Campus Sustainability Plan with ESD leadership in its Faculty of Education through its Sustainability Education Policy Network (SEPN) and recently established Sustainability Education Research Institute (SERI). The Saskatchewan Institute of Science and Technology (SIAST) also created its own Corporate Social Responsibility committee to focus on sustainability issues in 2011. A main publication of the UNU is the 'RCE-bulletin', which has been issued approximately three times per year since 2007 (UNU-IAS, 2013a).

Key challenges

Given the nature of the ESD projects described, these typically emerge with relatively small, locally sourced, in-kind investments. As such, financial costs to scale these up by a province/state or national authority would be relatively inexpensive. Four barriers to doing so, however, are evident.

First, governments in Saskatchewan (and possibly other regions with economies based on primary resource development/extraction) have thought of 'development' framed within a traditional modernisation paradigm. Here, development is seen as coming from outside the region through specialised resource companies. Provincial and local authorities, then, task themselves with creating accommodating economic, social and environmental regulations and tax policies. In Saskatchewan's case, this mindset is reinforced due to the province's traditional barriers to economic development: distance from navigable waterways, lack of large population centres (and their accompanying markets) and inherent risks associated with its weather-dependent agricultural economy and temperature extremes. This has historically created limited room for local value-added processing or other forms of secondary industrial development. Effectively, this creates an 'eggs all in one basket approach' to development by policymakers despite the risks associated with price fluctuations in resources and increasing evidence that places like Saskatchewan might be very fertile grounds for new types of sustainable development. These sustainable development innovations could, in turn, be highly useful in reducing the adverse natural, human and social capital impacts of traditional agriculture and resource extraction in the province despite sustainable development potentially being viewed as a threat by these sectors (due to its likely support for higher standards related to the treatment of human beings and ecosystems and associated costs for their degradation/depletion). Furthermore, RCE Saskatchewan has found that the goals of sustainable development are quite harmonious with those of aboriginal peoples (whether First Nations or Métis and their communities in Saskatchewan), suggesting a useful, principle-based platform for the resource sector to engage these communities, many of which control important natural resources in the province. To the extent that a significant demand for employees by these sectors is envisioned in the near future, the importance of ESD in engaging students in meaningful learning, thereby reducing dropout rates and allowing for the further specialised skills training required by these sectors, should not be underestimated.

A second challenge for policies and programmes supporting strategic investments in ESD, particularly by business but also government, is the uncertainty associated with ESD projects in achieving sustainable development outcomes (many of which may not be able to be properly evaluated in the short term). This uncertainty (potentially including a higher failure rate) is, however, offset by: (a) the relatively low financial cost of ESD relative to other forms of investment; (b) the ability to mobilise a much greater amount of in-kind and financial resources from other players (given the diverse benefits afforded); and (c) the likely political support from the general citizenry and consumer base across an increasingly polarised and fragmented electorate. A further way of addressing this uncertainty has been to have an initial organisation (such as government) provide resource support on a one-time basis, then, once the risks and potential are known, acquire subsequent support from other organisations (such as the private sector), for which understanding risks is a central part of resource planning and allocation.

A third challenge, however, is linked to problems associated with intentional polarising strategies by political parties and other agents that hinder free-forming relationships emerging across organisations and sectors. These may also be destabilised by political agendas neglecting or targeting partners in such relationships. The formation of these relationships at small geographic scales that foster diverse forms of local sustainable development may also be hampered by organisations (such as transnational corporations or national governments) seeking standardisation at larger scales for their own competitive advantage or control. Once a formal relationship is established, such as a memorandum of understanding between multiple RCE partners, there may also be a lack of willingness to provide sustained resources to help support these fledgling inter-organisational commitments. Organisational investments that might help structurally 'lock in' these social relationships for ESD may be viewed as 'administrative costs' with unclear deliverables, and, therefore, be under-resourced.

A fourth challenge is organisational willingness to give up control to treat collaborative efforts towards specific forms of sustainable development as having their own legitimate autonomy. This requires, for example, the willingness of governments to embrace a kind of gentle (versus coercive) leadership and a willingness to give up power to allow grassroots forms of development that, over the long term, provide additional power and resources to all organisations, including governments.

Regional Centre of Expertise Saskatchewan influence on policy and practice

Despite these challenges, RCE Saskatchewan has had some notable policy successes. In October 2008, the Province of Saskatchewan launched its Uranium Development Partnership (UDP), a committee tasked to 'to identify, evaluate and make recommendations on Saskatchewan-based value added opportunities to further develop [its] uranium industry' (Government of Saskatchewan Ministry of Environment, 2009). In response to strong public concerns related to the pro-nuclear power findings of the UDP report of March 2009, the government launched the Future of Uranium in Saskatchewan Public Consultation Process in April to gather public input. Dan Perrins, the chair of the consultation, was required to submit a report by the end of August 2009. This relatively short time frame was particularly challenging for HEI researchers wanting to provide input. It was further exacerbated by HEIs in Saskatchewan having significant public funding that could be undermined by taking a position on a controversial political issue. In the end, the RCE submission was the only submission from HEIs received, among numerous oral and written submissions. The three authors of the RCE Saskatchewan submission and the document's editor came from four of the HEI partners of the RCE and included disciplines in psychology, biochemistry, physics and philosophy. In the analysis, the authors used the seven sustainability issues identified as a focus for the RCE to constructively critique the UDP report. A strong case was made by the RCE for the need to broaden the energy options being considered in the government's deliberations in order to compare the relative opportunity costs of each energy option. In 2010, the Inquiry into Saskatchewan's Energy Needs was subsequently held by the Saskatchewan legislature's Standing Committee on Crown and Central Agencies, to which RCE Saskatchewan was invited to present. The choice of the provincial government not to develop a nuclear power plant and to expand its energy deliberations mirrored the findings of the RCE submission. The RCE's analytical approach, built on core questions of sustainable development, intended that long-term citizen interest be embedded. This was, in turn, powerfully informed by academic expertise and peer-reviewed scholarship from a variety of disciplines. While the RCE's analysis suggested that nuclear power generation was not appropriate in the current Saskatchewan context from a multidisciplinary and technical basis, the province was likely relieved that it had not pursued this option in light of the subsequent Fukushima Daiichi nuclear disaster in Japan in March 2011.

Future plans and challenges

The RCE network is at a critical crossroads as it approaches the end of the DESD (2005–14) and embarks upon a new phase of work for ESD, having been one of the DESD's major success stories. Having accomplished much at a regional level over the last eight years, RCEs are now in a position to capitalise on the full potential of a global network of RCEs engaging each other. They are also positioned to engage global players, including national governments, UN agencies, global NGOs and global businesses committed to sustainable development, specifically wanting to have an effective partner on the ground to advance ESD in local communities, where these organisations recognise the necessity of these communities themselves shaping and delivering effective ESD programmes. In the case of RCE Saskatchewan, with its proven track record linked to a number of individuals situated within a variety of organisations, a recommitment by organisational partners themselves to internalise ESD within their structures and provide formal supports for basic functions of the RCE on an ongoing basis (eg website support and support for secretariat functions) is now needed to deal with the scope of opportunities presented to the RCE. Local communities seeking to create 'living laboratories' for ESD open to the range of educational partners of RCE Saskatchewan are just beginning to take shape. Structures for governing these community networks need to be developed to maintain the local autonomy expected of these projects, guided by the principle of subsidiarity, while ensuring the value added that a formal connection to RCE Saskatchewan as a networked flagship projects allows.

A case study of Regional Centre of Expertise Greater Sendai, Japan

Educating for disaster risk reduction – the lessons of the East Japan earthquake: the role of Regional Centre of Expertise Greater Sendai

Like RCE Sasketchewan, RCE Greater Sendai was established in 2005 through the liaison of local communities and organisations. Sendai city had long been aware of environmental issues and, for example, initiated a movement as far back as the 1980s to replace studded winter tyres with studless tyres in order to reduce dust pollution. In Kesen-numa city, environmental education for primary schools was established, whereby stakeholders such as the local museum, university and overseas school worked closely with local primary schools to develop awareness of environmental issues and sustainable development. In the Osaki/ Tajiri area, environmental education was promoted to utilise the local aqua life and farmland through methods with a strong focus on sustainability. These experimental programmes were in collaboration with and supported by the Miyagi University of Education. RCE Greater Sendai was born using these regional and university networks.

One of the unique characteristics of RCE Greater Sendai is that each region has its own regional network of stakeholders (schools, private corporations, NGOs, local city council, museum, etc) that aims to build human resources to realise the sustainable development of each area, while each region further collaborates and networks with other regions of Greater Sendai. In other words, RCE Greater Sendai has two layers of network and missions: one within each region's ESD activities and the other in collaboration with RCE Greater Sendai as a whole. For example, Sendai region has an agenda of environmental education and learning activities as an urban area, while Kesen-numa looks at practices of ESD. Osaki region looks at sustainable farming and the Shiroishi/ Shichigashuku area works on sustainable forest conservation. For Greater Sendai, the agenda is to learn from each region's activities and characteristics and to promote ESD and the sustainable environmental conservation of the forest, farmland and ocean in the region as a whole.

The organisation of RCE Greater Sendai is unique in the sense that the universities act as linking agencies to bring each region together, so that critical activities such as information sharing and capacity building in different areas of Greater Sendai can be achieved uniformly while respecting each region's characteristics. RCE Greater Sendai consists of Miyagi University of Education (MUE) linking the activities conducted at Sendai, Kesen-numa, Ōsaki/Tajiri and Shiroishi/Shichigasyuku region. RCE Greater Sendai sets three rules in running the RCE project: first, each region is to set a goal of their own to conduct activities for a sustainable future suited to each region and characteristics; second, all regions are to share their experiences and learn from each other; and, third, RCE Greater Sendai is to set a common goal and work together to achieve sustainable living in Greater Sendai as a whole. Two examples of projects conducted in each region are outlined in the following box.

Projects of Regional Centre of Expertise Greater Sendai

Osaki/Tajiri – sustainable farming and environmental education

This is a network of 19 organisations, including farmers, agricultural organisations, the city council and non-profit organisations, which work together to find ways to achieve sustainable farming practice. They are also working on ecotourism in the region, utilising this farming model.

Tajiri region has a wetland called Kabukuri, which is a contracting wetland to the Convention on Wetlands of International Importance (Ramsar Convention). In order to achieve harmonious living in this area, where migrating birds like swans and geese fly in every winter (as many as 80,000), farmers in the region use no pesticides.

However, ESD activities in the region are limited to the farmers who would benefit directly from the projects and are not expanded to education institutions. Therefore, partnership between the concerned parties needs to be further established.

Miyagi University of Education – teacher training and human resource development

As a teachers' college, it focuses on providing a teacher training programme for ESD at four existing centres: the Environmental Education Centre, the International Education Centre, the Special Needs Education Research Centre and the Centre for Clinical Education. MUE also plays the role in collaboration with four different regions as an organiser of RCE Greater Sendai.

The Great East Japan Earthquake and the role of Regional Centre of Expertise Greater Sendai

Since the Great East Japan Earthquake on 11 March 2011, however, RCE Greater Sendai's activity had to turn to cope with the disaster that the area experienced. Each region worked on restoration and redevelopment and each is now working on their redevelopment programme. RCE Greater Sendai now includes the promotion of education for disaster risk reduction (EDRR) and redevelopment in its agenda.

With a magnitude of 9.0, the earthquake was extraordinarily large and strong, leaving 15,854 dead and another 3,155 missing. After residents had moved from shelters to temporary housing, an important issue arose related to the continued existence of local communities and schools. This is a major challenge as communities in the submerged areas were practically lost. Many residents moved to temporary housing or to new houses that they found themselves far from where they lived. Some schools had to be abandoned because buildings were submerged and could no longer be used, and many students also moved away.

It is difficult to return to and live in flooded areas again because the ground has subsided and, above all, people know that the area will be submerged again if another tsunami comes. The only way to recover local communities in the same place is to raise the ground level. It was revealed that 12 coastal municipalities in three prefectures damaged by the tsunami have a plan to raise the ground level of the submerged urban district. After the ground is raised, lands will be subdivided and housing and business districts will be rearranged. However, there are a number of problems in rebuilding communities in the areas hit by the tsunami. One is the difficulty in building a consensus due to the conflict of opinions between the residents who want to return and those who do not. The other is the relationship with the schools. If there is no prospect for the recovery of local communities, there is no prospect for the rehabilitation of schools. No municipality has yet begun its construction work to raise the ground level at this time. The schools moved from the damaged area have no plan for the future. If they do not return to the original location, more people will move away from the community, making it even more difficult to rebuild the community.

Education for disaster risk reduction and redevelopment

Taking this into consideration, RCE Greater Sendai and its constituent regions have been working on programmes such as EDRR, with a focus on community. Active effort has been put into regions such as Kesen-numa and Sendai city, with much support from both Japanese and overseas organisations. In Kesen-numa, where the city centre was severely damaged by the tsunami, EDRR has been proactively conducting post-disaster at primary and middle schools, but, at the same time, the effect of existing EDRR that was taking place prior to the disaster has been examined. Most primary and middle schools in Kesen-numa city are recognised as UNESCO schools and have been working on ESD and EDRR. After many years of working together, a network of school and local community organisations was well established and communication was flowing smoothly. As a result, even though the area was severely damaged by the tsunami and claimed many lives, everyone at the schools survived as they followed their evacuation instructions. Furthermore, when schools acted as evacuation centres, their organisation and operation went very smoothly as schools have built such good relationships with the local community. Students also actively volunteered to play a part in the operation of the evacuation centre. In the midst of a horrific disaster, these are wonderful achievements as a result of conducting ESD for many years.

As RCE Greater Sendai, we conducted seminars to share experience and learning following the disaster almost every month. An ESD Seminar for Our Future was conducted nine times in 2011 alone. Other seminars included topics such as the rebuilding of ruined areas in Natori-city, student volunteers reporting on their activities, networking activities between Ishinomaki city coastal (tsunami-affected) regions and mountainous regions, and reporting on UNESCO school activities in tsunami-affected Kesen-numa region. At the moment, we are in the process of creating textbooks to share experience in each school and region and to learn from this disaster. At MUE, more than five reports on primary and middle schools from Miyagi prefecture have been published. RCE Greater Sendai is also working on strengthening the network between the 70 UNESCO schools that promote ESD within Miyagi prefecture. As part of this networking, a Miyagi UNESCO school conference has been established and it is now in its third year of operation. In this conference, each school reports on their activities, learns from each other while networking and is given awards as recognition of their hard work.

Future plans and challenges

The concept of sustainable development provides an important framework for relationship building between local communities and schools. We learned through the Great East Japan Earthquake how effective it is to have had a cooperative relationship between the two when we have to cope with a natural disaster, and we have deepened such liaisons and communications. Clearly, the details of the relationship between the two depend upon which concrete community we talk about. For example, for schools in urban areas that are highly fluid, it may be difficult to have the consciousness to contribute to community building in liaison with local people. However, for local communities where residents and students know each other, it is easy for the two to work together to further develop the community. In this region, the networks that have been developed through the RCE and UNESCO have strengthened our resolve and ability to tackle key local issues, strengthened our ability to fight against disasters and contributed to the restoration of local communities.

Case study of Regional Centre of Expertise Greater Nairobi

Key issues and challenges for Regional Centre of Expertise Greater Nairobi

The Regional Centre of Expertise Greater Nairobi (RCEGN) was launched in 2007, with a mandate of mobilising stakeholders around sustainable development goals to support concrete actions that make a difference in people's lives. In particular, RCEGN is a hub for networking among those engaged with communities in city slums and, over time, it should serve as a model from which other such centres can be set up. Unlike the other two case studies, RCEGN is set in a capital city, which brings its own additional complexities and challenges.

The multi-stakeholder make-up of Regional Centre of Expertise Greater Nairobi

RCEGN was established as a multi-stakeholder undertaking, which includes the National Environment Management Authority (NEMA) and other government institutions, universities, the Kenya Organization for Environmental Education (KOEE), the Umande Trust, UNESCO, UNEP (United Nations Environment Programme), and UN-Habitat, among many others. Since its inception, RCEGN has brought a variety of stakeholders on board and has also given birth to other RCEs in the country. Environmental challenges that have been a focus for the activities of the RCE include the loss of biodiversity, the poor management of resources, land/environmental degradation, poor farming practices, forest degradation, pollution due to poor waste management and effluent discharge in the environment. Economic issues have also come under the RCE's purview, including high poverty levels, poor land planning, unemployment, poor infrastructure, corruption, poor living standards and rural–urban migration.

Issues encountered by Regional Centre of Expertise Greater Nairobi in relation to policy and practice

Sustainable development in Kenya is very challenging and complex, encompassing social issues such as peace and security, human rights, gender equality, cultural diversity and intercultural understanding, poor governance and corruption, the increased incidence of diseases, and the erosion of cultural values. The government of Kenya recognises these development challenges facing the country, and being party to many international agreements and conventions, is aware of its responsibilities to implement measures that promote sustainable development through all modes of education. For this, the government views ESD as an opportunity for continuously building its citizen's capacity towards healthy measures for utilising the country's resources to lead productive livelihoods and improve their quality of life. The following nine issues have been identified as key challenges in relation to policy and practice.

Facing the complexity of the sustainable development concept

Sustainable development is a complex and evolving concept. Many partners, scholars and practitioners in the RCEGN network are trying to explain sustainable development and face the difficulties of envisioning how to achieve it at the national and local levels. Components of it appear in the primary school curriculum under 'emerging issues', which is not a compulsory subject, neither is it tested in the national exams; therefore, teachers do not need to give it priority. Because sustainable development is hard to define and implement, it is also difficult to teach. Even more challenging is the task of totally reorienting an entire education system to achieve sustainability in Kenya.

Increasing awareness about education for sustainable development and its importance

In collaboration with RCEGN (which is currently being hosted by Kenyatta University), NEMA is in the process of sensitising university staff and students, government officials, school administrators, and local communities to the critical linkages between education and sustainable development. Reorienting education to address sustainable development will not occur without their support, and awareness is key as the essential first step in the reorienting process. This is a big issue for RCEGN, whose support and resources are limited.

Structuring and mainstreaming education for sustainable development in the curriculum

RCEGN faces a fundamental decision in implementing the national ESD strategy launched by NEMA in 2010, namely, whether to create another 'add on' subject (eg Sustainable Development, Environmental Education or Population Education) or to reorient entire education programmes and practices to address sustainable development. The process of clarifying whether educators are to teach *about* sustainable development or to change the goals and methods of education to *achieve* sustainable development could be another challenge.

Linking to existing issues: educational reform and economic viability

In Kenya, like the rest of the developing world, educational qualifications are used as a screening device to obtain employment. ESD is not currently directly linked to one or more priorities of educational reforms; nonetheless, ESD has the potential of offering transferable skills for both formal and self-employment and it could also make an important contribution to socio-economic development. However, trying to add another issue to an already overburdened system, like the Kenyan education system, is difficult to say the least. Nonetheless, the Kenya Institute and Center for Development (KICD) is in the process of looking into how ESD can be liked to existing curriculum content at the primary level of education. The Kenya government strategy document 'Kenya vision 2030' and the 2010 constitution include some of the milestones that embrace sustainability, but the key challenge is implementation and enforcement in an economically strained economy.

Sharing responsibility

Volunteerism is seen as a big challenge for RCEGN. There are difficulties in gaining the participation of RCE members in the management of RCEGN, as member organisations appointed to host RCEGN have the burden of providing resources for coordination. Most members are volunteer stakeholders who are often expected to sponsor themselves in all the meetings/forums. The RCEGN management structure has not yet been unanimously constituted and agreed upon by all network members and, hence, it is not always clear who plays which role. NEMA appears to be the uniting organisation when something new comes up, such as the RCE Global Conference. Therefore, RCEGN management is still a challenge in relation to day-to-day operations and fundraising , let alone membership expertise as relating to the knowledge and application of ESD.

Building human capacity

The successful implementation of ESD requires responsible, accountable leadership and expertise in both systemic educational change and sustainable development. The big issue is that the RCEGN leadership and membership require enhanced capacity for ESD in order to manage possible implementation challenges. RCE network members also need enhanced capacities for advocacy to enable them to mobilise adequate resources for awareness creation. This may be through enhanced training to conduct research, advocacy and public awareness campaigns, networking, information dissemination, and political goodwill.

Developing financial and material resources

Another key issue for RCEGN is mobilising both financial and material resources to implement ESD. This is not withstanding government efforts through all sectors in sensitising staff to sustainable development. The other good news is that Kenya is now spending a larger percentage of its gross domestic product (GDP) on education.

Developing policy

RCEGN is yet to implement the national ESD strategy. Unpacking the strategy, and the process of every member/stakeholder/sector customising it, is far from being realised. Together, administrators, teachers and community leaders at the local level in Kenya must interpret what the policy should 'look like' locally. NEMA and the Ministry of Environment are taking the lead to support RCEGN regarding this, but the pace is fairly slow and stuttering.

Developing a creative and innovative climate

RCEGN was the first RCE in Kenya. However, its growth has been very slow as a result of management changes and a lack of clear operational activities to facilitate creativity and innovativeness, which is a reason why RCEGN now operates under the umbrella of NEMA. In order to bring about the major changes required by ESD, policymakers, administrators and teachers need to make changes, experiment and take risks to accomplish new educational and sustainability goals.

Regional Centre of Expertise Greater Nairobi as a 'mobilising mechanism' for change towards education for sustainable development

Despite all these issues and challenges, RCEGN has nonetheless achieved some notable successes. The RCE has acted as a mobilising mechanism for ESD in a number of ways, for example:

- Sensitisation workshops for member organisations and stakeholders have been conducted, including 20 government ministries.
- National and international conferences have been organised.
- A new Community MSc in ESD has been developed in collaboration with the UNU, Kenyatta University and the University of Nairobi. The memorandum of understanding has been signed and the process is ongoing for the first group of students to be admitted in the 2013/14 academic year.
- RCEGN has set up an urgent response system, where special meetings have always been called whenever there are urgent issues and matters arising that need urgent attention and deliberation.

Future plans and challenges

There is now a need for RCEGN to be exposed to the work of other RCEs globally for learning purposes and for insights on management, fundraising and capacity building. The ability to network and mobilise resources by working in partnership with other organisations outside Kenya is a logistical problem and there is a need to clarify roles and responsibilities in order to maximise effectiveness.

Conclusion

Despite the range of challenges and obstacles that have been articulated in this chapter, these three case studies clearly identify the potential for RCEs to act as effective mobilising mechanisms for policy and practice change towards sustainability.

The strengths of RCEs include their organisational flexibility, their ability to respond to local conditions within a global framework and their potential to draw on the expertise of the wider RCE global network. From their inception, they have been set up as cross-sectoral, interdisciplinary networks, drawing from scientific as well as local and indigenous knowledge. They bring together actors from the formal, non-formal and informal education sectors and break down barriers between these elements. Compare this model with the picture of ESD described in the UNESCO framework in Chapter Three of this book and it seems to offer a possible way to bring this into being. Notwithstanding the difficulties of operating such a model in a world mainly focused on market mechanisms and hierarchical management structures, it nonetheless seems clear that the RCE approach allows for a creative and innovative space to develop both dialogue and action for policy and practice change. As mentioned in earlier chapters, the challenge of sustainability requires nothing les than a paradigm shift in the way we live together as a species and the way we relate to the natural environment on this small planet of ours. From these case studies, it would seem that RCEs have the potential to cut across some of the structural blocks and obstacles and to mobilise dynamic communities of practice united around the common goal of sustainable development. After the end of the UN DESD, the RCE network can and must continue to build and strengthen into a self-supporting and collaborative local and global network. In this way, RCEs can help to promote the urgent mobilisation of policymakers and practitioners that is needed to achieve sustainability.

Notes

[1] For a fuller discussion of the concept of ESD and its relationship to 'sustainable development', see Chapter Three of this book.

[2] The concept of sustainable development has been the backbone of UN policy and programme development since the World Commission on Environment and Development's (1987) report *Our common future* was released.

References

Government of Saskatchewan Ministry of Environment (2009) 'Uranium development in Saskatchewan – strategic direction'. Available at: http://www.economy.gov.sk.ca/uranium-development

Mochizuki, Y. and Fadeeva, Z. (2008) 'Regional centre of expertise on education for sustainable development (RCEs): an overview', *International Journal of Sustainability in Higher Education*, vol 9, no 4, pp 369–81.

Petry, R. (2008) 'The role of free knowledge at universities and its potential impact on the sustainability of the Prairie Region', PhD dissertation, University of Regina.

Petry, R.A. (2012) 'Achieving sustainable production systems through new multi-sectoral scholarly partnership: parallels between the UN University's RCE initiative and the earlier rise of humanism and science', in Z. Fadeeva, U. Payyappallimana and R.A. Petry (eds) *Towards more sustainable consumption and production systems and sustainable livelihoods*, Yokohama, Japan: United Nations University Institute of Advanced Studies, pp 110–22.

UNU-IAS (2013) 'RCE-bulletin'. Available at: http://www.ias.unu.edu/sub_page.aspx?catID=108&ddlID=369

Van Ginkel, H. (2013) 'RCEs: "An innovative initiative"', in R. Wade 'Promoting sustainable communities locally and globally: the role of regional centres of expertise in ESD', in S. Sterling, L. Maxey and H. Luna (eds) *The sustainable university*, London and New York, NY: Routledge.

White, P. and Petry, R. (2011) 'Building regional capacity for sustainable development through an ESD project inventory in RCE Saskatchewan (Canada)', *Journal of Education for Sustainable Development*, vol 5, no 1 (March), pp 89–100.

World Commission on Environment and Development (1987) *Our common future*, Oxford: Oxford University Press.

NINE

Social media and sustainability: the right to the city

John Blewitt

Introduction

Over half the world's population lives in cities. The 'natural' world is now predominantly urban, as is the global economy. The fate of the planet depends upon the nature of our urban future. Cities are inevitably complex places and spaces, and social (in)justice within them invariably has a spatial dimension. However, spaces and places, social and political action, justice and injustice now also have a third, virtual, dimension, with digital media technologies, smart buildings and smart cities being complemented by new emerging forms of social cognition, literacy (or, maybe, 'electracy') and assemblages of trans-local citizenship. Just as the city is a place and a space, the new media ecology means that the city's environment is truly multidimensional, with justice, politics, action and learning transcending both localities and socio-spatial networks. What is increasingly, and clearly, defining the conditions of possibility for social and environmental justice within the city is, as Henri Lefebvre (1996) argued, the need for a transformed and renewed right to urban life.

The 'right to the city' is therefore a claim to recognise the urban as a producer and reproducer of social relations of power in the city and the (substantive) rights to, and realities of, participating in it. Rights and urban citizenship, and, to a significant degree, social learning for social sustainability, entail active engagement in the public realm, in genuinely public spaces and places. An obvious challenge to realising this possibility and need is the continuing dominance of neoliberalism, the marketisation of the social and the privatisation of spaces and places within the city, which has helped foster a ruling value syntax that deliberately conflates freedom with 'market freedom' and rights with the 'rights of business' rather than those of people or communities. The challenge to public education, public libraries, public culture and public spaces and places is clearly evident in the multidimensional and complex environments of the city where social media have become an integral aspect of everyday life, politics, learning, business, public engagement and trans-local citizenship. This contribution interrogates the interpellation of the social and the spatial, the physical and the virtual, with the politics of justice, democracy, learning and sustainability in realising the right to the city. It will draw on examples from different national and international contexts.

Public space and the digital city

Today's cities are predominantly characterised by the ideological, commercial and economic practices of neoliberalism, dutifully supported by the state, which attempts to regulate, but more often bail out, private capital deemed too big to fail. Urban environments are products of capitalism, trading as they do in goods, services, natural materials and people. Capitalist enterprise of various descriptions enables people to live, even if it harms or kills them in the process. Some business gurus say that there is profit to be made at the bottom of the pyramid or that all the majority-world slum dwellers really need are proprietary rights over the shacks they construct for them to thrive (De Soto, 2001 Hart, 2005). This urban world is a world of market exchange, of ubiquitous connections that enable the affluent to eat strawberries all year round and the poor to survive on US$1 a day in Mumbai. Nonetheless, the city offers windows on a number of other worlds, although these windows are really screens that project an image of reality by 'screening', masking, the reality behind it. The screen is now everywhere – in the living room, in the shack, in the pub, on a department store wall, in the city square, in the subway, in the dental surgery, in your pocket, next to your heart, in your face and in your head. The screen is a lived reality of capitalism, of a commercialised and privatised environment where most things are for sale and everything seemingly should be. Silent images flash by – a car, a smartphone, a tanned body, designer shades, a must-see blockbuster movie – in malls, city precincts, hotel lobbies, public parks and other public spaces that, to put it kindly, are hybrid – social but privatised, energetic but draining, multifaceted but one-dimensional. The architecture of neoliberalism seems to be everywhere and not just in the sleek lines of the latest corporate tower, or the luxury apartment block built ostensibly to regenerate a particular area but only by displacing the poor and unsightly 'problem families'. This neoliberal architecture can be found in the very structure of urban feelings, the culture of the city and the individuated lived experiences of contemporary urban living. It frames and shapes the imagination, the values and metaphors we assume we live by – competition, freedom, success, happiness, wealth, status and power:

> The street screen is also the embodiment of spectacle in its most repressive form. Today spectacle is no longer alone in controlling the inner life, the interior of the alienation of the average TV junkie. The street, the classic stage of modern theatre, is overloaded with marching electronic screens and projections, so erasing the public functions of open space. Public functions become blurred by the flow of light and images drenching us in a fetish of alienating desires as we follow our necessary route through the city, from A to B. (Kluitenberg, 2006, p 11).

Urban space is electronically augmented with moving image billboards and signals that ping off the various smart devices you may carry around with you. Inspired by Las Vegas, star architect Robert Venturi spoke of architecture as communication saturated with 'iconographic representation emitting electronic imagery from its surfaces day and night' (Venturi, quoted in Manovich, 2006, p 232). Another global architect, Rem Koolhaas, designed Prada's flagship store in New York to create a brandscape of religious postmodern intensity. By placing screens exhibiting moving images next to the actual clothes, the designers offer a postmodern irony that everyone feels able to buy into, assuming he or she has the money to do so. It is simply chic to know that it is images and attendant visceral experiences we live and die for. We are losing our sense of place as beings sharing a living planet.

Neoliberalism and the virtual world

We speak of virtual realities, virtual communities, virtual geographies, virtual dimensions, virtual shopping, virtual worlds, augmented reality, avatars, social networked media, cyberwar and attention deficit hyperactivity disorder. Public libraries are now hybrid digiplaces promoting literacy and electracy, heterotopic spaces that connect people with places and spaces throughout the city and beyond (Blewitt, 2012). Wars are also digitised and hybridised, with actual conflicts resembling a computer game (except for those who do actually lose limbs or get killed). Computer games are the militarised training grounds for war itself but the military combat of *Full Spectrum Warrior* has made way for the biopower of *World of Warcraft*, a multiplayer online experience whose game world includes experimentation with nuclear energy, the destruction of ecosystems, biological warfare and the slaughter of whales. Even so, Bainbridge (2010, p 3203) claims that, with their international audiences, such games have the potential 'to become arenas for discussion of global issues in the real world'. The neoliberal urbanism of the emblematic and immersive *Grand Theft Auto* is so 'real' that life seems to imitate art, which seems to show that actually-existing capitalism is just common sense – and exciting too. An addictive game. Exploring this phenomena in detail, Dyer-Witherford and De Peuter (2009, p 163) write:

> Possession unlocks new access to, mobility in, and knowledge of urban territory. They are complexly tied to accumulation's advance: how much city there is for you as player depends on how much money you have. But what makes *Vice City* [one of the virtual cities of *Grand Theft Auto*'s game world] properly neo liberal is that, as your financial tally rises, there is not a hint of labor, just the abstracted, increasing magnitude of accumulated capital.

Neoliberalism operates not only in the space of flows that run through the metropolis, but through the ideology that frames the virtuality of popular gameplay. Over 130 million copies of *Grand Theft Auto* have so far been sold. The game industry has provided opportunities to enfold digital space into the hard concrete paves of main street or the studious quiet of the academic library. Location-based games involve multiple players and traverse real and virtual spaces in search of virtual insects or the subject for a virtual assassination (Avouris and Yiannoutsou, 2012). Of course, many games have vast educational potential and are used for serious and reputable educational purposes, but many do not (De Souza et al, 2006). Games have become pervasive and if life is not yet a game but still a journey, or some other cultural cliche, they will certainly become an increasingly significant element of our lives. Games are what people play, and what anchors them in society is commerce. What gives them meaning is the way that they have been enacted and the values that they confirm, articulate, frame and legitimise.

The implications of digitised space

Digital media have become embedded in much of the social and cultural life of the city, every city, and what is becoming increasingly important is how all this feels, how all this shapes up in the various dimensions of our cognitive and emotional worlds (Couldry, 2004).

We are all cyborgs now; and being cyborgs, we also live in cyburgs. Computer processing, codes, communication, sensing and surveillance are the contemporary enacted urban environment. Walls literally have ears; and lights, eyes; and buildings, intelligence. As cities become smarter, our life-world is further enveloped with digital objects that shape the type of lives we can, should and ought to live. Physical space is now 'data dense'. Software automatically creates or transduces space, establishing new forms of conduct applicable to various specific situations, albeit with appropriate modulations. Software codes direct citizens in what to do, how to do it and where to go (Thrift and French, 2003). Digitised space is a monitored space, containing far more dimensions that the geometric one that human civilisation has grown up with. Geometry is no longer the most important aspect of a citizen's phenomenological urban experience; being watched is. As Cuff (2003, p 46) remarked, 'the usurpation of privacy by means of technology is a modern phenomenon but not a new one'. Closed-circuit television (CCTV) is an integral part of the modern city, particularly in the UK, which is the world leader in citizen surveillance. However, this technology also enables us to buy more stuff, go on more holidays and accumulate more debt. It helps catch criminals but it does not stop crime. Smart technology even tries to make the trains run on time. It renders buildings and cities more environmentally sensitive, even if not necessarily more environmentally sustainable given the huge ecological footprint that the digital technologies have. These new mediated urban ecologies require a holistic learning that combines media with sustainability literacy, skills with understanding and critical engagement with a politics that perpetrates radical alternatives rather than ameliorative accommodations.

There is a danger that smart cities are the brave new world of corporatised, managed democracies. With an estimated 75% of the world's population likely to live in cities, there is unsurprisingly an expanding market in smart systems technology for urban areas. By 2014, the global market value for these products is anticipated to be around US$57 billion and IBM, through its Smarter Cities Unit, is targeting large city governments, such as Rio de Janeiro, as part of its goal to raise its annual revenue to over US$150 billion (Singer, 2012). When corporates are able to customise cities as well as individualise consumer marketing, the self becomes more fully commoditised. We leave a digital audit trail wherever we go, whatever we do and with whatever we buy: 'Privacy is now less a line in the sand beyond which transgression is not permitted, than a shifting space of negotiation where privacy is traded for products, better services and or special deals' (Haggerty and Ericson, 2000, p 616).

Surveillance not only facilitates buying, it facilitates fun too. *The World's Wildest Police Videos*, first aired on Fox Television in 1998, has had worldwide syndication, but this does not alter the fact that anonymity in the city is next to impossible. The surveillance business may have started by working closely with and within the security and defence industries, but since the mid-1990s, it has successfully sought other markets and justifications. Its rhizomatic expansion is hardly limited by the imagination, but digital surveillance, like so many other digital assemblages, has important implications for the future of democratic urban governance. As Sassen (2000, pp 20–2) has consistently demonstrated, economic globalisation and technology has reconfigured power and authority within nation states and of nation states. Corporate economic power harnessed to the affordances of digital technology has unleashed privatising dynamics that are often beyond the controlling or regulatory power of accountable democratic government. The city is the space of global capitalism, and global capital markets hold governments to account by determining the logic of fiscal and economic policy at city, national and international levels. These corporate power dynamics move in and out of electronic and non-electronic space, become entwined in the hollow rituals of parliamentary debate, and are embedded in the spatial topographies and hierarchies of social, employment and other human relationships. There is a crisis of Western democracy. There is a democratic deficit, as more and more people use their mobile phones to vote in TV talent shows than in city elections. The French philosopher Jacques Ranciere (2009) argues in his book *Hatred of democracy* that economic elites have never really liked democracy. It just gets in the way of the all-important business of power, oligarchy and business. Citizen indifference, political disillusion and quietism are therefore just fine. Political action is migrating to other spaces and places – private, public, social and hybrid – which may not be so compromised. This means, as Michael Saward (2003, p 167) has argued, that we probably ought to take a fresh look at democracy's key principles and the devices that make democracies come alive. As Dahl (1967, p 970) wrote in his seminal article 'The city in the future of democracy', it is imperative that we at least attempt 'to develop an urban civilization founded on the democratic city, only consistent this time with the imperatives of modern technology'. In doing this, we will also need to remember the words of Henri Lefebvre (1996, p 158, emphases in original), 'the *right to the city* can only be formulated as a transformed and renewed *right to urban life*', encompassing rights to freedom, to individualisation within socialisation, rights to habitat ('nature') as well as to inhabit, rights to creative labour, and rights to participation in and to the appropriation of the fruits of social and civic well-being.

Recovering public space

'The space that symbolizes the Information age', writes Manovich (2006, p 234), 'is not the symmetrical and ornamental space of traditional architecture, the rectangular volumes of modernism, nor the broken and blown-up volumes of deconstruction. Rather, it is space whose shapes are inherently mutable'. For some, urban screens, billboards and public artwork have the potential to rediscover the public sphere and create a lively, communal, deliberative and harmonious urban space. But this requires such augmented spaces to be appropriated by non-commercial forces, for if they are to nurture the cultural richness and historical complexity of local environments, they must complement the initiatives of proactive citizens rather than calling on them to be 'just law-abiding consumers' (Struppek, 2006, p 178). Public space is a medium of democracy, for it is here, whether real or virtual, that differences can be communicated and accommodated, that free speech and collective action can be allowed and enabled (Sorkin, 1997; Mitchell, 2003; Diamond, 2010). For Kohn (2004), public space necessarily includes three key concepts: ownership, accessibility and intersubjectivity. If citizens are not able to encounter difference, either politically or socially, in their day-to-day lives, then segregation will necessarily follow, mutual fear and suspicion will most like be fostered, and ignorance and prejudice will most likely be reinforced. Our corporatised culture of consumption requires only cosmetic differences disciplined by brand homogeneity, the surveillance camera and the many other coded spaces that make the city but remain largely unseen, unrecognised and unaccountable. In making things happen, software codes also alter the very nature of spaces and places, for they shape social relations and enfold people within things. As Kitchin and Dodge (2011, p 40) write, 'power arises out of the interrelationships and interactions between code and the world', continuing:

> One of the effects of abstracting the world into software algorithms and data models, and rendering aspects of the world as capta, which are then used as the basis for software to do the work in the world, is that the world starts to

structure itself in the image of the capta and code – a self-fulfilling, recursive relationship develops.

It is, therefore, necessary for citizens to be the authors of these codes rather than authored by them. It is surely possible to create physical, digital and hybrid places and spaces that are both public and free, where groups and individuals can learn a new self-respect, assert and refashion their group or individual identities, articulate the values of cooperation and civic virtue, and, as Evans and Boyte (1986, p 17) state, 'act with dignity, independence and vision'. Inevitably, then, they will be, and indeed are, places of informal and formal learning. The newly redesigned public libraries (such as in Birmingham, Worcester, Seattle, Aarhus and Helsinki) are prefiguring the emergence of new heterotopic spaces (spaces used for a varied and unexpected purposes) that are both green and inclusive (Mattern, 2007; Blewitt and Gambles, 2010; Blewitt, 2012). However, these spaces must do more than host disinterested learning and communication or be (relatively) isolated from the suffocating embrace of corporate power and mainstream political institutions. They need to have, or be capable of supporting, a mobilising power defined by a cultural idiom that privileges pro-sustainable, transformative social and political change. As Polletta (1999, p 20) writes: 'what is crucial is the set of beliefs, values and symbols institutionalized in a particular setting'. Libraries are networks and networked, they are places where sharing occurs, that lend and enable borrowing, reuse and recycling, where learning, work and leisure may be combined, and where environmental sustainability and cooperation is, or can be, enacted. But public libraries are also being undermined by a neoliberal market logic that accepts that nothing is more worthy than private profit and private gain. However, they remain a eutopic inspiration to a politics and a learning that aims to reassert not only the cultural commons, but what is indeed common to a democratic and sustainable manner of being. This, now, entails not only a rooted sense of place, but a recognition that being in the world entails physical and virtual manifestations, that technology offers both affordances and invitations, that only politics and learning can create an understanding that a managed democracy is no democracy and that the brave new world is neither brave nor new.

So, what if digital media are harnessed to democracy and to the wider green city agenda? In 2009, the European Union (EU) issued a 'Green digital charter' (European Union, 2009), building on an earlier report identifying the complex relationship between information and communication technology (ICT) and energy efficiency (European

Commission DG INFSO, 2008). The Charter promotes smart cities, smart grids and many other ICT-enabled, often private sector-led, solutions that will reduce the environmental impact of urban areas and of ICT itself, and help create a new technologically enhanced social and political democracy. New media technology is invariably presented by corporations and political groups as the means to deal with important social, environmental and political ills (Crang and Graham, 2007). In so doing, software-sorting applications restructure and re-commodify previously public areas and cultures, operate at multiple levels and scales, and are usually closely linked to neoliberal approaches to public service reform (Graham, 2005). Geographic information systems (GIS), such as Google Maps, enable citizens to find their way in the city, and other smartphone applications enable them to see what other people have recorded about this place, this cafe, this hotel, this store, this product. Neighbourhood information systems provide data that may be actively appropriated and used to sort property markets into the desirable and less desirable. Location-aware technologies and software apps turn locations into tradable entities, commodifying information and enabling locations to develop a power, aura and meaning of their own. Information is attached to place; it can easily be read off your smartphone, effectively creating an interface between the personal, physical, the virtual and the informational. GIS software codes filter and manipulate information, which, in turn, may become further individualised and customised by the user as the user-citizen comes to 'read' the city as a hypertext (De Souza et al, 2012). Users may be able to change and create this digital world by sharing and adding comments, photos, place marks or overlays on the commercially designed and produced digital maps:

> Thus, not only does each individual's ability and cognition shape the DigiPlace [the mixing of code, data and physical space] they inhabit, but their unique code (manifested as a data profile) automatically determines the enclosure of information space in which they operate. In short, DigiPlace represents the situatedness of discrete individuals straddling virtual and physical realities, rather than any sort of shared, objective, and fixed reality. (Zook and Graham, 2007, p 1329)

There are clearly possibilities as well as dangers derived from the seemingly relentless corporate colonisation of the Internet and these DigiPlaces. The free or open software movements, for example, suggest an instability and a resistance to the managed marketised freedoms of cyberspace.

People may alter their behaviour, their travel, leisure, spending and work patterns accordingly; they may move to a location where there are 'good schools' or live in places where there are 'people like us'. Such premium-networked sites and locations may consequently splinter away from the rest of the city. New forms of social spatial zoning or partitioning may get established as informed choices promote processes of gentrification or displacement, social and environmental (in) justice, and the subtly modulated practices of citizenship entitlement. As Burrows and Ellison (2004) argue, individuals who have the capacity to make ostensibly lifestyle or consumption choices in this way tend to be the relatively privileged, seeing it as both possible and desirable to distance themselves from being dependent on goods and services produced for collective ends. With this separation and disengagement comes a revised understanding of duties, responsibilities and obligations. Social capital and cohesion in one area may thus be at the expense of social inclusion more generally, with publicly funded service provision and spaces being for those who are unable to afford ownership, accessibility and interaction. In his study of urban digital divides, Graham (2002) noted that the ICT-facilitated intensification and liberalisation of globalisation has increased social polarisation and fractured the conditions of and for urban solidarity.

Smart cities as entrepreneurial cities

Smart cities are invariably characterised as 'entrepreneurial cities', meaning that the idea of 'the technological smart city becomes a smokescreen for ushering in the business dominated information city' (Hollands, 2008, p 311). City marketing and branding material is stuffed with the iconic accoutrements of fashionable bars, expensive hotels and high-rise developments, with their smart offices and luxury apartments. Odendaal (2006, p 45), writing of digital city initiatives in South Africa, notes that concentrating on economic growth, city marketing, government efficiency and business development often means that the more qualitative benefits of ICT that could more assuredly help the majority population, such as learning, communication and networking, receive considerably less attention. Social inclusion and (tackling) deprivation remain important policy goals for many city and national governments, but the economy and maintaining privilege seems to come first. The riches and the social benefits will trickle down, the neoliberals say. Crang, Crosbie and Graham (2006, pp 793–4) argue that affluent and professional groups tend to use new media technologies as infrastructure and background in sustaining their privileges, whereas less privileged groups tend to use the new technologies episodically and more instrumentally, and these are often organised collectively by the state. Thus, digital technologies and their affordances, together with the Internet and technology and software companies, are transforming the structure of the urban environment and of community and changing the nature of space and place. Remember, Google Earth 'is a private space in which user behavior is regulated and proscribed by corporate policy' (Zook and Graham, 2007, p 1341), and although few people may deny the usefulness of the commercial services Google provides, many fail to note that Google and similar companies have enclosed the Internet with codes and policies determined by corporate managers rather than a well-informed, politically active and engaged democratic citizenry.

This is not to say that Google and other profit-oriented companies do not provide products and applications that can be used for, and are in fact designed to support, active citizenship, democracy and environmental sustainability. If there is a business case and a surplus to be made, then capitalist enterprise will act. There may exist, then, any number of complexities and contradictions, spaces and possibilities for hope and change. Even though News Corporation has vigorously supported climate change denial, particularly on Fox News, through its Global Energy Initiative, launched in 2010, it has simultaneously set a target for the company to become carbon-neutral. The *Futurama* animated TV series was released on carbon-neutral DVDs, and in 2009, Fox's highly successful series *24* became the first carbon-neutral drama on US television (Maxwell and Miller, 2012). The most successful technology company of recent times, Apple, finally responded to powerful criticism from Greenpeace regarding its poor record on sustainability and labour rights issues by developing a smart green profile and greener corporate responsibility strategy. In 2012, writing for the Tree Hugger website, Alex Davies noted that:

> while the 'greenness' of the iPad is debatable, and there are lots of ways to avoid ever 'needing' one, it can still be a really useful tool for living a sustainable life. From helping you get around on your bike to eating veggies to understanding climate change, these 13 awesome apps will all get you on the right path.

These apps include: Gardening Toolkit, Vegan Yum Yum, Bike Repair, Audubon Guide, Solar Checker, My Recycle List and Google Maps. The organisers of Earth Day in 2012 saw it as only fitting 'that we leverage the popularity of mobile phones to help further the cause of conserving planetary resources' (Steele, 2012). The Earth Day website offers all manner of green information, advice and guidance and links to social media groups of conservationists and environmental activists. The website provides details of GreenMeter, an iOS app for the iPhone and iPad Touch, which calculates a vehicle's fuel and crude oil use, helping a driver assess his environmental impact while on the move. Seafood Watch is an iOS Android app that enables consumers to make sustainable choices when purchasing wet fish or eating in fish restaurants. The Treehugger app enables people to keep up to date with sustainability-related news. Green Shine helps consumers replace many commercial cleaners with environmentally friendly, healthier and safer ones. The US company MapCruzin offers a wide range of GIS tools, including environmental risk maps, interactive toxic facility maps and toxic release inventory data, together with online tutorials that enable community groups to locate the big polluters in their neighbourhoods, undertake ecological and habitat assessments, evaluate health risks, form toxic watch groups, publish maps indicating areas of local toxicity, and conduct facility audits. It is interesting to note that many of these green apps are aimed at fostering (green) consumerism, and although this may create a more virtuous and politically green citizenry (Micheletti, 2010), the focus does remain a resolutely commercial one, maintaining aspects of a consumerist ideology.

There are also other possibilities which suggest that all is not yet lost, that politics and the political may in some way come together. Many international agencies and national governments promote the concept and practice of computer-assisted sustainability. In 2010, the World Bank made available many of its data sets relating to the Millennium Development Goals (MDGs), launching a competition inviting participants to design software applications for any device widely available to the public. A sum of US$45,000 was made available in prize money and 107 applications were received from 36 countries. The first prize went to StatPlanet World Bank, an app that is able to explore and analyse over 3,000 indicators through interactive maps and graphs even when Internet connectivity is not available. The Get A Life game app aims to create awareness of different countries through communicating the MDGs and using up to 52 indicators organised into various categories, such as public expenditures, labour, education, health, infrastructure, economic policy and environment. The intention is for the game to offer 'an alternative perspective of the wider world compared to the giant newsgroups we have become so familiar with. *Get A Life* offers a snapshot into the life of somebody, somewhere, whose story is still in progress' (World Bank, no date). In May 2012, the Environmental Protection Ministry in Israel launched the Thinking Green app, designed to promote eco-friendly consumer behaviour.

Grassroots action and the democratisation of digital media

Although large software developers have significant power 'in setting agendas for the ways in which geographical information can be displayed and analyzed' (Dunn, 2007, p 631), the potential for enhanced citizen input is also being realised in a number of ways, such as in participatory research, GIS design and environmental justice campaigning. As Montague and Pellarano (2001) have argued, the development of digital resources has aided many grass-roots community groups in their attempts to alert others about dangers associated with the irresponsible disposal of toxic materials. In some cases, this has led to the formation of public policy articulating principles of precaution, substitution and clean production. Jordan et al (2011) show how citizens in Tallahassee (Florida) collaborated in collecting spatial data from web-based software such as Google Earth, using photos, video and other socio-demographic information to oppose the installation of a biomass facility in a moderate-income minority ethnic group area. A permit had been issued without any prior involvement of the community or consideration of the effects of pollutants on the health of the local population and local environment. Maisonneuve, Stevens and Ochab (2010) have explored how the general public could initiate a low-cost solution to measuring urban noise pollution by just using ordinary commercially purchased smartphones as noise sensors. From the data gathered collectively, annotated noise maps could be created and shared within a community and with local government. GIS and similar digital applications therefore have significant political implications for empowering particular groups, democratising planning and enhancing processes of local democracy. Some observers have even suggested that the utopian impulse to radical action is alive and well and residing in DigiPlaces (Warren, 2004).

Computer hacking is a form of cyber-activism, or 'hactivism'. It has radical and democratic potential when the aim is to subvert autocratic states and other powerfully exploitative institutions and organisations, but is decidedly undemocratic when practised by these autocratic, undemocratic and unaccountable bodies themselves (Taylor, 2005). The revolution may be digitised. Cottle (2011) has shown that Facebook, Twitter, YouTube and other sites have been significant actants in the Arab Spring, although no clear and easy generalisations can be made. Certainly, human rights abuses and state terrorism have been monitored and communicated effectively on a global scale and protests have received a degree of legitimacy that they perhaps would not have done otherwise. There may also be an element of contagion extending beyond national borders, as powerful images of dissent have provided a template for others to do the same. Cottle (2011, p 654) explains:

> It is not only the demonstration of people power, however, that is 'contagious' and communicated via media and communication networks lending hope and inspiration to those embarked on similar struggles elsewhere, or via the replication of symbolic forms of protest such as the occupation of city central squares/plazas or extreme acts of self-immolation by 'martyrs' to the cause – like Mohammed Bouaziz. Also 'contagious' are the constantly evolving communication tactics and creative adaptations of the same communicated around the world by media activists seeking to evade and counter media censorship and imposed media controls.

For Fahmi (2009, pp 91–6), the 'blogosphere' was a crucial element in revitalising Egyptian civil society, mobilising street protests, boycotts, labour action and opposition generally to the Mubarek regime in the period preceding the revolution. Significantly, new media enabled the opposition to assert popular control over Cairo's key public spaces, such as Tahrir Square.

Opportunities for mobilisation and sustainability

Despite this, the relationship between digital media, communication, space and politics remains complex. States can and do use the Internet to censor and repress debate, and many of the big media companies aid them in this (Zook and Graham, 2007; Morosov, 2011). For some, inter-state cyberwars and 'terrorist' attacks seem to be leading to a closing down and/or control of the Internet as a democratic public sphere. Corporate and government weapons of choice include pay walls, copyright and surveillance. The *Kony2012* campaign offers some other salutary lessons to enthusiasts for, and supporters of, cyber-activism.

When the highly emotive 29-minute *Kony2012* video, produced by the campaign group Invisible Children, was posted on YouTube and Vimeo on 5 March 2012, it quickly went viral, gaining over 100 million hits and raising around US$5 million in less than a week (Perrot, 2012). Joseph Kony is a Ugandan warlord whose Lords Resistance Army has for over two decades been responsible for killing more than 100,000 people, abducting more than 70,000, forcing at least 2 million people from their homes and, between 2009 and early 2012, kidnapping 591 children, subjecting many to sexual slavery and forcing others to inflict violence on others (Smith, 2012). His arrest has been demanded by individuals, groups and governments, including the Obama administration, but when Invisible Children attempted to transfer this cyber-activism to real street action in the Cover the Night initiative, where supporters in cities all over the world were asked to plaster posters calling for action against Kony, the response was exceptionally poor. Nothing much happened – anywhere. Those who had criticised Internet activism as being but an excuse for real action had coined the term 'slactivism' and were apparently justified (Morosov, 2011). One tweet referring to the Cover the Night disappointment with the words 'Kony is so last month' seemed to substantiate this view, but this would be mistaken. In his influential book *Here comes everybody*, Clay Shirky (2009, p 54) reminds us that there are reasons to be cheerful:

> Our recent communications networks – the internet and mobile phones – are a platform for group forming, and many tools built for those networks, from mailing lists to camera-phones, take that fact for granted and extend it in various ways. Ridiculously easy group-forming matters because the desire to be part of a group that shares, cooperates, or acts in concert is a basic human instinct that has always been constrained by transaction costs. Now that group-forming has gone from hard to ridiculously easy, we are seeing an explosion of experiments with new groups and new kinds of groups.

Conclusion: sustainability, politics and the public sphere

For political freedom to be established and maintained, there needs to be a literate citizenry and densely connected spaces where citizens can discuss, debate, dissent, make decisions and take action. Libraries offer one such space and place. There are others too, as the Occupy movement demonstrated (Graeber, 2013). As Peter Dahlgren (2005, p 159) writes:

> Democracy must be enacted in concrete, recurring practices – individual, group, and collective – relevant for diverse situations. Such practices help generate personal and social meaning to the ideals of democracy. They must have some element of the routine, of the taken for granted about them (e.g., elections), if they are to be a part of a civic culture, yet the potential for spontaneous interventions, one-off, novel forms of practice, needs to be kept alive. Civic cultures require many other practices, pertinent to many other circumstances in everyday life.

Public and practised places need to emerge to ensure the civil society and democracy continue to exist and be reproduced. These spaces and places may be both real and virtual, spatially located in towns and cities, as well as in the cyber-networks that are increasingly shaping the lives we inhabit. Mobile phone and other new media technologies provide affordances for communal participation and action for social and environmental justice. The new technologies may also enable a certain degree of privatism and disengagement from public space and public conversation. Clearly, the private and the public are, in many ways, converging. People enter their private worlds in commercial wifi cafes and public parks, their own private homes and public libraries. Groups and individuals may immerse themselves in computer games or construct maps of their locality, may create lives and identities from digital data, may analyse their environmental impact as they drive to work. Technology has always shaped cities and people and, unsurprisingly, ICT is doing so too. As Susan Piedmont-Palladinio (2011), writing in *TIME* magazine, observes:

> A cloud of wifi hovers over the park, bringing activities that [Robert] Moses, a truly ambitious urban planner, could not have imagined. Those trees that shaded city dwellers out for a stroll decades ago now keep the glare off touch screens. And despite the fears that mobile communication technology would drive us all into lives of wireless isolation, the opposite seems to be happening. Bryant Park [New York City], like myriad parks and plazas in other cities, is returning to a role it filled generations ago: a place to share, read, write, gossip, and debate … in short, communicate.

There also needs to be public spaces without state surveillance and corporate control or substantial influence. Market dynamics may undermine meaningful civic participation and the capacity to realise a new form of urban life – the right to the city – which must take a public and democratic form. Hybrid spaces, such as public libraries, allowing for and enabling connections of all sorts, which can involve learning and civic engagement, are places and spaces that can be trusted by their users and where trust in others can be assured. Other spaces and places will need to be fashioned that are networked and flexible, even if imperfectly, to enable critique of and resistance to state and corporate power, neoliberal and economistic values, environmental irresponsibility, and socio-political and economic inequality to manifest themselves. The city is predominantly the site of these digital and analogue, real and virtual, spaces and places, since this is where the majority of us live. The public sphere needs to be more than a subject for academic analysis, but it can only become real through the practices people develop, the technologies they use and the values they shape or are allowed to realise. Liestert (2012, pp 443ff) shows how state and corporate surveillance quickly accommodates itself to new forms of cyber-activism and counter-surveillance practice. There is a continuous process of change and becoming, of struggle and resistance. The cyber-cultural commons has been widely recognised as politically and economically valuable, worthy of enclosure but capable of resistance. It is a space where people's minds can meet, can share, can organise, can dispute, can learn and can create. It is a space made for a dialogue on, and of, values, a space for learning and cosmopolitan connection. It is an integral and intimate element of 21st-century sustainability, particularly if democracy and participation is be more than the mediated performances of corporate-sponsored politicians or the continuing circus of consumer materialism. For Zizi Papacharissi (2010, esp ch 5), commercially public spaces may not actually constitute a public sphere in the Habermasian sense, but they do provide areas for civic social interaction, and it is these experiences and practices that are essential to a functioning and vibrant democracy. New media technologies may not in themselves be inherently democratising or sustainable, but they can be made to work towards that goal. The technologies undoubtedly can and do cut both ways. The materiality of these digital technologies means that they are heavy users of energy, are created out of precious metals and toxic substances, and their global ecological footprint is growing and likely to do so for the near future (Maxwell and Miller, 2012). The environmental sustainability credentials of digital media technologies are therefore ambiguous, but they are now so much a part of the world that it is impossible to dismiss or relinquish them in any serious way. They are a part of our urban life-worlds and they may enhance and deepen practice and actions that do make for sustainable change. They are also a part of us, but, like the city and those spaces where sharing and cooperation take place, they offer spaces of hope.

References

Avouris, N. and Yiannoutsou, N. (2012) 'A review of mobile location-based games for learning across physical and virtual spaces', *Journal of Universal Computer Science*, vol 18, no 15, pp 2120–43.

Bainbridge, W.S. (2010) 'Virtual sustainability', *Sustainability*, vol 2, no 10, pp 3195–210.

Blewitt, J. (2012) 'The future of the public library: reimagining the moral economy of the "people's university"', *Power and Education*, vol 4, no 1, pp 107–17.

Blewitt, J. and Gambles, B. (2010) 'The Library of Birmingham project: lifelong learning for the digital age', *Journal of Adult Continuing Education*, vol 16, no 2, pp 52–66.

Burrows, R. and Ellison, N. (2004) 'Sorting places out? Towards a social politics of neighbourhood informatization', *Information Communication and Society*, vol 7, no 3, pp 321–36.

Cottle, S. (2011) 'Media and the Arab uprisings of 2011: research notes', *Journalism*, vol 12, no 5, pp 647–59.

Couldry, N. (2004) 'Theorising media practice', *Social Semiotics*, vol 14, no 2, pp 115–32.

Crang, M. and Graham, S. (2007) 'Sentient cities: ambient intelligence and the politics of urban space', *Information, Communication and Society*, vol 19, no 6, pp 789–817.

Crang, M., Crosbie, T. and Graham, S. (2006) 'Variable geometries of connection: urban digital divides and the uses of information technology', *Urban Studies*, vol 43, no 13, pp 2551–70.

Cuff, D. (2003) 'Immanent domain: pervasive computing and the public realm', *Journal of Architectural Education*, vol 57, no 1, pp 43–9.

Dahl, R.E. (1967) 'The city in the future of democracy', *The American Political Science Review*, vol 61, no 4, pp 953–70.

Dahlgren, P. (2005) 'The Internet, public spheres, and political communication: dispersion and deliberation', *Political Communication*, vol 22, no 2, pp 147–62.

Davies, A. (2012) '13 awesome green-themed apps for your new iPad'. Available at: www.treehugger.com/gadgets/13-awesome-green-themed-apps-new-ipad.html

De Soto, H. (2001) *The mystery of capital*, New York, NY: Black Swan.

De Souza, E., Silva, G. and Delacruz, C. (2006) 'Hybrid reality games reframed potential uses in educational contexts', *Games and Culture*, vol 1, no 3, pp 231–51.

De Souza, E., Silva, A. and Frith, J. (2012) *Mobile interfaces in public spaces: locational privacy, control and urban sociability*, London: Routledge.

Diamond, B. (2010) 'Safe speech: public space as a medium of democracy', *Journal of Architectural Education*, vol 64, no 1, pp 94–105.

Dunn, C.E. (2007) 'Participatory GIS – a people's GIS?', *Progress in Human Geography*, vol 31, no 5, pp 616–37.

Dyer-Witheford, N. and De Peuter, G. (2009) *Games of empire: global capitalism and video games*, Minneapolis, MN: University of Minnesota Press.

European Commission DG INFSO (Directorate General for Communications Networks, content and Technology) (2008) *Final report – impacts of ICT on energy efficiency*, Brussels: European Union.

European Union (2009) 'Green digital charter'. Available at: http://www.greendigitalcharter.eu/greendigitalcharter

Evans, S. and Boyte, H.C. (1986) *Free spaces: the sources of democratic change in America*, New York, NY: Harper and Row.

Fahmi, W.S. (2009) 'Bloggers' street movement and the right to the city. (Re)Claiming Cairo's real and virtual "spaces of freedom"', *Environment and Urbanization*, vol 21, no 1, pp 89–107.

Graeber, D. (2013) *The democracy project*, London: Allen Lane.

Graham, S. (2002) 'Bridging urban digital divides? Urban polarisation and information and communications technologies (ICTs)', *Urban Studies*, vol 39, no 1, pp 33–56.

Graham, S.D.N. (2005) 'Software-sorted geographies', *Progress in Human Geography*, vol 29, no 5, pp 562–80.

Haggerty, K.D. and Ericson, R.V. (2000) 'The surveillant assemblage', *British Journal of Sociology*, vol 51, no 4, pp 605–22.

Hart, S.L. (2005) *Capitalism and the crossroads*, New Jersey, NJ: Wharton School Publishing.

Hollands, R.G. (2008) 'Will the real smart city please stand up?', *City: Analysis of Urban Trends, Culture, Theory, Policy, Action*, vol 12, no 3, pp 303–20.

Jordan, L., Stallins, A., Stokes IV, S., Johnson, E. and Gragg, R. (2011) 'Citizen mapping and environmental justice: Internet applications for research and advocacy', *Environmental Justice*, vol 4, no 3, pp 155–62.

Kitchin, R. and Dodge, M. (2011) *Code/space: software and everyday life*, Cambridge, MA: MIT Press.

Kluitenberg, E. (2006) 'The network of waves', *Open*, no 11, pp 6–16.

Kohn, M. (2004) *Brave new neighbourhoods: the privatization of public space*, London: Routledge.

Lefebvre, H. (1996) 'The right to the city', in H. Lefebvre, *Writings on cities* (trans E. Kofman and E. Lebas), Oxford: Blackwell.

Leistert, O. (2012) 'Resistance against cyber-surveillance within social movements and how surveillance adapts', *Surveillance & Society*, vol 9, no 4, pp 441–56.

Maisonneuve, M., Stevens, M. and Ochab, B. (2010) 'Participatory noise pollution monitoring using mobile phones', *Information Polity*, vol 15, nos 1–2, pp 51–71.

Manovich, L. (2006) 'The poetics of augmented space', *Visual Communication*, vol 5, no 2, pp 219–40.

Mattern, S. (2007) *The new downtown library: designing with communities*, Minneapolis, MN: University of Minnesota Press.

Maxwell, R. and Miller, T. (2012) *Greening the media*, Oxford: Oxford University Press.

Micheletti, M. (2010) *Political virtue and shopping: individuals, consumerism, and collective action* (2nd edn), London: PalgraveMacMillan.

Mitchell, D. (2003) *The right to the city*, New York, NY: Guilford Press.

Montague, P. and Pellerano, M.B. (2001) 'Toxicology and environmental digital resources from and for citizen groups', *Toxicology*, vol 157, nos 1–2, pp 77–88.

Morosov, E. (2011) *The net delusion*, London: Allen Lane.

Odendaal, N. (2006) 'Towards the digital city in South Africa: issues and constraints', *Journal of Urban Technology*, vol 13, no 3, pp 29–48.

Papacharissi, Z.A. (2010) *A private sphere: democracy in a digital age*, Cambridge: Polity Press.

Perrot, S. (2012) 'Kony 2012: 100 million views for a non-event?', *The Independent*, 6 May. Available at: http://www.independent.co.ug/column/comment/5720-kony-2012-100-million-views-for-a-non-event- (accessed 30 July 2012).

Piedmont-Palladinio, S. (2011) 'How wifi is reinventing our city parks', *TIME*, 15 July. Available at: http://www.time.com/time/specials/packages/article/0,28804,2026474_2026675_2083366,00.html (accessed 30 July 2012).

Polletta, F. (1999) '"Free spaces" in collective action', *Theory and Society*, vol 28, no 1, pp 1–38.

Ranciere, J. (2009) *Hatred of democracy*, London: Verso.

Sassen, S. (2000) 'Digital networks and the state: some governance questions', *Theory, Culture and Society*, vol 17, no 4, pp 19–33.

Saward, M. (2003) 'Enacting democracy', *Political Studies*, vol 51, no 1, pp 161–79.

Shirky, C. (2009) *Here comes everybody: how change happens when people come together*, London: Penguin.

Singer, N. (2012) 'Mission control, built for cities: I.B.M. takes "smarter cities" concept to Rio de Janeiro', *New York Times Business Day*, 3 March. Available at: http://www.nytimes.com/2012/03/04/business/ibm-takes-smarter-cities-concept-to-rio-de-janeiro.html?_r=1&pagewanted=all

Smith, D. (2012) 'Joseph Kony kidnapped 591 children in past three years, UN report reveals', *The Guardian*, 7 June. Available at: http://www.guardian.co.uk/world/2012/jun/07/joseph-kony-united-nations-report

Sorkin, M. (1997) *Traffic in democracy*, Ann Arbor, MI: University of Michigan Press.

Steele, C. (2012) '12 Green apps for Earth Day', *PCMag*, 20 April. Available at: http://www.pcmag.com/slideshow/story/296829/12-green-apps-for-earth-day

Struppek, M. (2006) 'The social potential of urban screens', *Visual Communication*, vol 5, no 2, pp 173–88.

Taylor, P.A. (2005) 'From hackers to hacktivists: speed bumps on the global superhighway?', *New Media & Society*, vol 7, no 5, pp 625–46.

Thrift, N. and French, S. (2003) 'The automatic production of space', *Transactions of the Institute of British Geographers*, vol 27, no 3, pp 309–35.

Warren, S. (2004) 'The utopian potential of GIS', *Cartographica: The International Journal for Geographic Information and Geovisualization*, vol 39, no 1, pp 5–16.

World Bank (no date) 'Apps for development'. Available at: http://appsfordevelopment.challengepost.com/submissions/1545-get-a-life-game

Zook, M.A. and Graham, M. (2007) 'The creative reconstruction of the Internet: Google and the privatization of cyberspace and DigiPlace', *Geoforum*, vol 38, no 6, pp 1322–43.

Part Four

Emerging themes and future scenarios

TEN

Emerging themes and future scenarios

Hugh Atkinson and Ros Wade

This book has sought to cover a wide range of themes with regard to sustainability, politics, education and learning. They are too numerous and interlinked to list here, but it would be helpful to identify some of the key themes that have emerged from our analysis. These can be grouped under three main headings.

Policy imperatives

There is a growing realisation that traditional neoliberal growth models are proving increasingly problematic for the people of this planet, with countless millions unemployed and living in poverty. We need a different kind of economy, but neoliberalism, with its emphasis on free markets and consumerism, remains remarkably robust in spite of its clear and apparent failures. However, the increasing inequality between the high-earning super-rich and the rest threatens our very social fabric and sense of a shared public good. A new, fairer, social and ecological contract is needed that enables us to avoid increased social conflicts and unrest and promotes a shared sense of purpose and responsibility. This is in the interest of us all, including chief executive officers (CEOs) of big corporations – after all, it is not in the interest of capitalism to kill the customers!

The constant pumping of greenhouse gases into the atmosphere and the eating up of the world's resources are laying waste to the planet at an ever-increasing rate. We are now in what has been described as the anthropocene era. It is the argument that the impact of human activity on the planet has been so significant as to constitute a new geological epoch. Policymakers and politicians need to publicly acknowledge the overwhelming scientific evidence that climate change is happening and that it is due to human activity. Therefore, it is of crucial importance to tackle climate change if we are to support and strengthen environmental and social justice.

Ecological modernisation and improved technology are part of the solution but there are no quick fixes to sustainability. What is needed is transformative change through a policy agenda that balances social and ecological needs, not merely for present generations, but into the future also. This will require a step change in the way that policy is developed, with much more collaboration between different policy areas and between different ministries. Policy needs to be less driven and led by conventional economic imperatives and more driven by human and ecological well-being. In other words, policymakers need a greater focus on human well-being and happiness, moving to what Tim Jackson has called 'prosperity without growth'. We need to build a 'new normal', so that humanity sees itself as part of the natural world and not separate from it.

There are good examples of policy innovation and action at the local, national and global levels. The European Union (EU), for example, has shown its capacity to develop substantive policy on sustainability and climate change. In addition, there are emerging signs that the US is beginning to 'get' climate change and is prepared to do something about it. However, more integrated decision-making and coordinated policy initiatives are needed at the local, regional, national and global levels. This requires an increase in policy autonomy at the local level, with accountability, transparency and good governance. These are essential components of sustainable development. They will also require a new approach to urban spaces and the city, with more opportunity for public engagement and community. There is a need to challenge the trend towards the privatisation of the public realm, with its focus on the enclosure of public space, whether material or virtual.

Implications for education and learning

Access to education for all should be strengthened as a basic human right but it is essential that sustainable development is at the core of this in terms of values, knowledge and skills. As Sterling (2001) emphasises, this will require a paradigm shift in the way that formal education is currently constructed. There is an urgent need for a more holistic, trans-disciplinary approach to education and pedagogy to prepare us for the sustainability challenges of the 21st century and to support social and environmental well-being. Regional centres of expertise (RCEs) (Chapter Eight) have demonstrated that such approaches can be effective and illustrated their potential to develop effective communities of practice in education for sustainable development (ESD), helping to shape a more sustainable world.

Organisational and social learning are essential components of social and policy change, and there is some encouraging evidence of this starting to happen in the work of the EU (Chapter Five) and among policymakers in the US (Chapter Four).

There is also a crucial role for formal, non-formal and informal education and learning in supporting and promoting sustainable lifestyles. Local community and indigenous knowledge and culture has a great deal to contribute to sustainability and needs to be acknowledged and valued. The case studies from sub-Saharan Africa (Chapter Seven) illustrate the risk of not paying attention to this, as well as the benefits of doing so. They also highlight the potential energy and innovation that can be engendered by engaging communities in developing policy and practice for sustainability.

Social movements from the environmental and development fields are needed to mobilise their energies and understanding to address sustainability issues. The convergence framework seems to offer an effective way of constructing new learning for planetary equity across a range of scales, from local to global.

There are, indeed, many good examples of innovation and action at the local, national and global levels, as illustrated in this book and by the hundreds of thousands of educational activists around the globe who are promoting ESD. We need to learn from these and build on them.

The need for a new kind of politics

There is a need for a more honest engagement by politicians with the public about the challenges of combating climate change and building a more sustainable world. However, this requires a series of brave decisions on the part of politicians. Politicians need to shift the terms of the debate so that meeting the challenge of climate change is seen not in negative terms, but rather as a clear opportunity to build a more sustainable way of life. There is an important role here for the media and for media-smart climate scientists. Politicians and policymakers also need to become better informed about the key challenges of sustainability.

Proactive political action, from the local to the global level, is a prerequisite for present and future sustainability. Unbridled free markets are part of the problem, not part of the solution. Neoliberal capitalism has already significantly failed to deliver either social sustainability or ecological sustainability. From the 1930s' crisis in the US emerged the New Deal, which brought a recognition of the important role of the state in supporting social solidarity and cohesion. The 2007/08 global financial crisis has so far failed to bring about such a necessary rethink, but without this, the future for people and the planet looks problematic, to say the least.

We live in a world where over two thirds of world trade is controlled by multinational corporations that are not democratically accountable to the citizens of the countries in which they operate. The current neoliberal trends towards the privatisation and marketisation of services and production can only increase this divide; therefore, formal political institutions, from the local to the global level, need to play a key role in building a more sustainable world. Democratic systems face significant challenges in delivering on sustainability but other systems of government such as dictatorships and autocracies fare worse.

If we are to build a more sustainable world, we must adopt a more bottom-up approach to policymaking, with democracy and wider political participation at the heart of the agenda. Central to this is the need for a vibrant and inclusive democracy at the local level. We need a local politics where people have a real influence on the key issues that shape and impact upon their lives.

In parallel with this, there is a need for much more active citizen engagement and a well-informed public base. This seems to be more possible in smaller or more devolved countries like Germany, Wales and Scotland, and so may have implications for the size and shape of political entities.

We need to take radical political action. We need to do a different kind of politics and economics if we are to live sustainably within the boundaries of the planet. However, to achieve this, political decision-makers need to be honest with citizens and voters, but citizens and voters also need to be honest with themselves.

Reasons to be cheerful

Despite the many challenges and obstacles in our path, a key theme of this book is that there are real reasons to remain optimistic and positive despite the undoubted major difficulties and challenges that lie ahead. Human ingenuity has helped lead us to the current global crisis. Human ingenuity can also help lead us out of it.

Future scenarios

In 1962, Rachel Carson published the pathfinder environmental text *The silent spring* (Carson, 2003). As an observation of the state of the physical environment of the US, it proved highly controversial and provoked a furious reaction from its critics. As Lear (2003, p x) notes, Carson's thesis that humanity was subjecting itself to a 'slow poisoning' with the misuse of chemicals 'that polluted the atmosphere may seem like common currency now but in 1962 *Silent Spring* contained the kernel of a social revolution'. For Carson, the intensive use of chemicals to boost agricultural production was having disastrous consequences for the flora and fauna of the US. Unchecked, this would literally lead to a silent spring, where the sound of bird song would no longer be heard. As Carson (2003, p 3) observed: 'a grim spectre has crept upon us almost unnoticed, and this imagined tragedy may become a stark reality we shall all know'. Carson (2003, p 187) warned of the 'hazard that lurks in our environment – a hazard we ourselves have introduced into our world as our modern way of life has evolved'. Fast-forward 53 years and Carson's argument seems even more prescient as we grapple with the twin challenges of tackling climate change and creating a more sustainable world. Equally prescient was Carson's observation that 'only within the moment of time of the present [20th] century has one species – man – acquired significant power to change the nature of his world' (2003, p 5). This was a reference, all but in name, to the anthropocene, some 40 years before it became part of the lexicon of sustainability!

However, for Carson, there were still some grounds for optimism, for the power of 'man' could also potentially lead to a more positive outcome for people and the planet. Carson (2003, p 273, emphasis in original) argued that 'We now stand where two roads diverge. The road we have been travelling is deceptively easy, a smooth superhighway on which we progress with great speed but at its end lies disaster', but, for Carson, 'The other fork in the road – *the one less travelled by* – offers our last chance to reach a destination that assures the preservation of our earth'.

Today, as we observe the scene in 2015, we still have an opportunity to take the 'other fork'. Yet, for more than 50 years since the publication of *The silent spring*, we have continued down the 'smooth superhighway' in pursuit of ever-more economic growth and material well-being, with major consequences for people and the planet.

This chapter will now consider two alternative future scenarios. In scenario one, we continue to cruise down the 'smooth superhighway'. In scenario two, we switch on the sustainability satnav and take the 'other fork in the road'.

Scenario one: cruising down the 'smooth superhighway' – a bleak future ahead?

Urry (2011, p 37) asks whether the impact of climate change will herald what he terms a 'new catastrophism', with 'A new and darker epoch' lying 'in the quite near future'. For Guzman (2013, p 1), if we fail to respond to the challenge of climate change, 'we must not lose sight of the very real possibility that it will have a cataclysmic impact on the way we live'. Countless millions could die as a result of climate change. This is a terrifying prospect. Guzman (2013) correctly points out that there is still uncertainty about what the exact impact of climate change might be. However, there are certain things we do know and 'they are not comforting' (Guzman, 2013, p 1). We can see the consequences of climate change in the here and now. Rising sea levels threaten the livelihoods of millions of people, with major implications for poverty and the resultant social and political instability. Delicate ecosystems are being eroded, posing a real and substantive threat to the balance of nature and the health and well-being of humanity.

Future population growth presents major challenges for both people and the planet. The current population of the world stands at some 7 billion people. Estimates from the United Nations (UN) point to a world population of some 9 billion by 2050. Such a large population increase requires a fundamental change in our approach to traditional notions of economic growth, for, as Jackson (2011, p 85) has argued, there is 'no credible, socially just, ecologically sustainable scenario of continually growing incomes for a world of 9 billion people'.

Climate change is resulting in greater political instability as tensions increase amid rising concerns over food shortages and food insecurity. 'Droughts are expected to become more frequent', says Richard Choularton (quoted in Vidal, 2013), a policy officer at the UN World Food Programme. According to Choularton (quoted in Vidal, 2013), 'Studies suggest anything up to 200 million more food-insecure people by 2050 or an additional 24 million malnourished children'.

Animals and plants are coming under increasing threat due to climate change. According to the World Wide Fund for Nature (WWF, 2013), 'Human induced climate change has already sounded the death knell for its first victims', with the disappearance of the Costa Rican golden toad and the harlequin frog as a direct result of global warming. The WWF (2013) goes on to warn that as climate change takes hold, delicate ecosystems could completely disappear or could face irreversible changes, such as those happening to coral reefs. As average temperatures continue to increase, the habitat of many species will come under threat.

Such negative trends will only intensify if we continue to pursue our current course. As we noted earlier, the latest report by the Intergovernmental Panel on Climate Change (IPCC) calculates that global temperature increases might well exceed two degrees centigrade within 20 to 30 years, with all the social and environmental consequences that this implies.

Viewed from the perspective of scenario one, future prospects for both people and the planet look very worrying indeed, but we can still pull off the smooth superhighway, pull over to the side of the road to rest and reflect about where we want our journey to go next. A number of the negative consequences of climate change are already locked in. We will need to adapt to the changes that this will bring for both people and the planet. However, we still have the time to make a difference, to prevent the world from entering into what we described earlier in this section as a 'new catastrophism'. But the clock is ticking. We cannot afford to delay.

Scenario two: the other fork in the road

Taking the other fork in the road, as Carson describes it, will not be easy. The terrain ahead will be bumpy at times and the signs along the road will not always be clear. However, humanity has demonstrated in the past that it has the ability to respond to difficult challenges. So, what do we need to do to build a better world?

Rawles (2012, p 284) has cogently argued that 'we need some new values' and we also need 'to revitalise old ones that are currently smothered in a morass of glitz'. If the global financial crisis of 2007/08 taught us anything, it was that the current way of doing economics based on rampant consumerism and the pursuit of ever-more growth has not worked for the vast majority of the world's population. We need, as Rawles (2012, p 284) again points out, 'to question those most basic of assumptions – that growth is always good, and that our happiness is, above all else, tied up with money and stuff'. Now and in the future, we need to do a new kind of economics, with a focus on equality central to the policy agenda. This is not just a moral imperative; it also makes economic sense. Research shows that high concentrations of wealth are economically dysfunctional (Reich, 2011). Data also suggest that more equal societies prove to be more sustainable, healthy and secure, and with less of an impact on the environment (Wilkinson and Pickett, 2010).

We need what Rawles (2012, p 284) calls a 'new normal', in which we clearly recognise that we as human beings are not somehow separate from nature, but a part of it. We need to recognise that planet earth is the only home we have. The resources of the planet are not limitless and we need to live within planetary boundaries. We would do well to take heed of the old Chinese proverb which states that 'The frog does not drink up the pond in which it lives'.

In taking the other fork in the road, we must, of course, take full advantage of the opportunities that technological advances and renewable energy sources give us in order to mitigate climate change. But such 'ecological modernisation' should not be seen as a magic bullet, as an excuse simply to carry on as we are. Instead, science and technology should be used to facilitate the fundamental change that is needed in the way we do economics and politics. So, we also need to pay attention to indigenous and ancient knowledge and wisdom, which has many insights and much to offer to the sustainability agenda.

With this in mind, we need to move firmly towards what Connelly and Smith have termed 'ecological democratisation'. They argue that 'only through the democratisation of our existing political, social and economic institutions (at all levels) will just and environmentally-sustainable policies emerge' (Connelly and Smith, 2003, p 361). We wholeheartedly agree with this proposition. The solutions that we need to create a more sustainable world will be challenging and will necessitate real material sacrifices by voters, especially those in the 'developed' world. They need to be more involved in the processes that shape those solutions as part of the democratic process. In addition, we need a major psychological shift so that such material sacrifices are viewed not just in negative terms, but as an opportunity to build a more sustainable world, with human happiness and well-being at the heart of the policy agenda. In the words of John Gardener (quoted in Engleman, 2013, p 11), we need to view challenges such as climate change and global warming as 'breathtaking opportunities disguised as insoluble problems'. For too long, many politicians and nearly every world leader has been racing down the superhighway without looking where they were going, constrained by the voice from an outdated neoliberal satnav that is directing them faster and faster towards a dead end.

However, if we are to change direction and make this work, we will all need to play a part. The rich, the poor, the powerful, the weak, world leaders, non-governmental organisations, women's groups, the wider public, the voluntary sector and the business sector; all have a crucial role to play.

The world of education and academia also has an important role to play. We need to get out of our academic and subject silos. This book, with its focus on the analysis by both ESD and political science of the challenges of building a more sustainable world, is one small part in the process of doing this. The challenge of tackling climate change and creating a more sustainable world is multidimensional and multilayered. Academics and educators more broadly need to respond to this. We need interdisciplinary and multidisciplinary approaches across the social sciences and the natural sciences. All disciplines have a part to play in working proactively and cooperatively. A new language of convergence is needed; as is a commitment to framing our specialisms within a coherent whole that tries to address the needs of people and the planet. But academics also need to be more engaged in life outside of the institutions of higher education. They need to embrace what has been termed 'trans-disciplinarity', working with and alongside community groups, pressure groups, politicians and decision-makers to help build more rewarding and sustainable lifestyles.

But we need to be realistic. Change will not occur overnight. The change we require is radical but we will also need to satisfice, to do the best we can, using our skills, commitment and knowledge. Taken together, each individual action can make a difference.

So, let us take the other fork in the road. The journey along this road will not be easy and we will face many challenges in the short and medium term. But let us try to imagine a future of possibilities, with humanity living in harmony with the planet, with sustainable lifestyles that prioritise human well-being and happiness, and with social justice at the centre of the policy agenda. Let us make this future our project. There is simply no other alternative.

References

Carson, R. (2003) *The silent spring*, New York, NY: Mariner Books.

Connelly, J. and Smith, G. (2003) *Politics and the environment: from theory to practice*, London: Routledge.

Engelman, R. (2013) 'Beyond sustainababble', in Worldwatch Institute (ed) *State of the world report 2013; is sustainability still possible?*, Washington, DC: Island Press.

Guzman, A. (2013) *Overheated: the human cost of climate change*, Oxford: Oxford University Press.

Jackson, T. (2011) *Prosperity without growth: economics for a finite planet*, London: Earthscan.

Lear, L. (2003) 'Introduction', in R. Carson (ed) *The silent spring*, New York, NY: Mariner Books.

Rawles, K. (2012) *The carbon cycle: crossing the great divide*, Isle of Lewes: Two Ravens Press.

Reich, R. (2011) *Aftershock: the next economy and America's future*, New York, NY: Vintage Books.

Sterling, S. (2001) *Sustainable education: revisioning learning and change*, Schumacher Briefing No 6, Totnes, Devon: Green Books.

Urry, J. (2011) *Climate change and society*, Cambridge: Polity Press.

Vidal, J. (2013) 'Climate change: how a warming world is a threat to our food supply', *The Guardian*, 13 April.

Wilkinson, R. and Pickett, K. (2010) *The spirit level; why equality is better for everyone?* London: Penguin Books.

WWF (2013) *About our health.* Available at: wwf.panda.org/about_our_earth/aboutcc/problems/impacts/

Afterword

Hugh Atkinson and Ros Wade

In essence, the idea of creating a more sustainable world is clear and simple. However, getting there is quite a different matter. It is all too easy to feel totally daunted by the challenges that lie ahead, but we should not allow ourselves to be ground down by pessimism. There are cautious grounds for optimism. On a political level, tackling climate change and building a more sustainable world are on the global agenda, imperfect and flawed as that agenda may be.

Furthermore, we should not underestimate the ingenuity of the human race and its capacity to adapt to difficult challenges. We need a new anthropocene with human learning and human activity as a positive force for tackling climate change and as a force for sustainability.

Engelman (2013, p 8) has argued that:

> While sustainability advocates may work to enfranchise future generations and other species, we have little choice but to give priority to the needs of human beings alive today while trying to preserve conditions that will allow future generations to meet their needs.

However, Engelman surely misses the point. Seeking to ensure a world fit for future generations and trying to safeguard the well-being and prosperity of the current generation is not a zero-sum game. One depends upon the other. The kind of world that we need to create for the benefit of future generations, including human well-being and environmental sustainability, is surely the kind of world that the current generation needs. This is at the heart of the sustainability agenda. We need to keep our focus on this.

Reference

Engelman, R. (2013) 'Beyond sustainababble', in Worldwatch Institute (ed) *State of the world 2013: is sustainability still possible?*, Washington, DC: Island Press.

Index

Please note:
'ESD' refers to 'education for sustainable development';
'EFA' refers to 'education for all';
'RCE' refers to 'regional centres of expertise'.

C

D